Dec 11

D0699180

HOCKEY
TOWN

HOCKEY TOWN

LIFE BEFORE THE PROS

ED ARNOLD

M&S

Library and Archives Canada Cataloguing in Publication
Arnold, Ed
   Hockey town : life before the pros / Ed Arnold.

Includes index.
ISBN 0-7710-0782-5

1. Hockey – Ontario – Peterborough – History.
2. Peterborough Petes (Hockey team) – History.   I. Title.

GV848.P47A75 2004   796.962'09713'67   C2004-903984-9

We acknowledge the financial support of the Government of Canada through the Book Publishing Industry Development Program and that of the Government of Ontario through the Ontario Media Development Corporation's Ontario Book Initiative. We further acknowledge the support of the Canada Council for the Arts and the Ontario Arts Council for our publishing program.

Typeset in Janson by IBEX GRAPHIC COMMUNICATIONS INC.
Index by Heather Ebbs
Printed and bound in Canada

Unless otherwise credited, all photographs are courtesy the players' family albums.

This book is printed on acid-free paper that is 100% ancient-forest friendly (100% post-consumer recycled).

McClelland & Stewart Ltd.
The Canadian Publishers
481 University Avenue
Toronto, Ontario
M5G 2E9
www.mcclelland.com

1 2 3 4 5   08 07 06 05 04

For Mother

CONTENTS

Introduction

Hockey Towns

When Eric Staal went from his home in Thunder Bay to Peterborough to play junior hockey, he was following the route many National Hockey League players had taken before him. To say that it was no surprise for the people of Peterborough when he became one of the top two junior players in the world in 2003 with his second-overall selection in the NHL draft is not to denigrate Staal. For the people of Peterborough, such success is almost a ho-hum event – it's taken for granted that the local team will have some future NHL boys. So when Staal, at eighteen years of age, was signed by the NHL Carolina Hurricanes and scored his first regular-season goal on October 24, 2003, Peterborough cheered him with the aplomb of people who are accustomed to seeing its young players succeed.

The Peterborough Petes, the second-oldest continuous junior franchise in Canada (the oldest is the Regina Pats) and thus the world, have had more players, coaches, and scouts graduate to the NHL than any other team. The town has put more than 150 players into the NHL. Two dozen coaches, more than thirty captains and assistant captains, more than a dozen scouts, six general managers, and eleven Hall of Famers have been in Peterborough hockey before getting there. Someone who has gone through Peterborough on his way to the big league has touched every NHL team. In the 2004 NHL playoffs, fourteen of the sixteen teams (Boston and Colorado being the exceptions) had a Peterborough connection.

Why Peterborough? Why, of all the cities and towns in Canada, does this central-Ontario city deserve to be called Hockey Town? Why not, for example, one of the cities that is home to a great NHL franchise? Why not Montreal, Toronto, Calgary, Vancouver, Edmonton, or Ottawa? Montreal, Toronto, and Ottawa, especially, have legendary hockey traditions. But they also have distractions – hockey is by no means the only local diversion – and Hockey Town, by my definition, has to be devoted to the sport to the virtual exclusion of others. Sure, these cities have their moments of hockey madness, but they also support major-league football, baseball, and even basketball teams. Their teams are also big business, machines that operate for the big hockey bucks. A passion for the game is not the single overriding force that motivates the people who play, manage, coach, watch, and otherwise participate in the game – as it is in Hockey Town.

What about Detroit, which has not only appropriated for itself the label Hockeytown (their spelling), but also copyrighted the word? Detroit is hockey mad, and sports mad. It is the proud home of an Original Six NHL team. But its stars – Gordie Howe, Ted Lindsay, Sid Abel, Terry Sawchuk – came through Canada before they got to Detroit. They came from towns where hockey is not a business, but a way of life. And a number of Detroit's hockey legends, such as Jack Adams, Bryan "Bugsy" Watson, Scotty Bowman, Larry Murphy, Darren McCarty, and their present-day superstar, Steve Yzerman, practised their trade in Hockey Town, Peterborough, before they found their way to Hockeytown, Detroit. Let's face it: how many hockey greats grew up in Detroit and then went on to play in the NHL?

Of course, there are other hockey towns: Peterborough is not the only one that can claim the name. Arguments might be made for any or all of these other famous hockey cradles, all in the west:

- Regina, the capital of Saskatchewan, home of the legendary junior team the Regina Pats, the oldest continuous junior franchise in the world.
- Medicine Hat, Alberta, where stars such as Lanny McDonald, Chris Osgood, Trevor Linden, Tom Lysiak, Pete Peeters, Kelly

Hrudey, Rob Niedermayer, Barry Melrose, and Ken Holland honed their playing and managing skills. Its junior team, the Tigers, sells an amazing 3,800 season tickets every year, has won two Memorial Cups (the national emblem of junior hockey excellence), and has put more than one hundred players into the NHL.

- Prince Albert, Saskatchewan, where the junior Raiders have won a Memorial Cup, and players such as Mike Modano, Chris Phillips, and Dean McAmmond have played on the community-owned team.
- Saskatoon, Saskatchewan, with a population of 200,000, has been the birthplace of more than forty NHL players.
- Brandon, Manitoba, where the Wheat Kings have nurtured such talents as Wade Redden, Brian Propp, Brad McCrimmon, Jordin Tootoo, Trevor Kidd, Ron Hextall, Bill Derlago, Dave Semenko, and Glen Hanlon.
- Kamloops, British Columbia, where the junior franchise, the Blazers, just more than two decades old, has featured players such as Jarome Iginla, Scott Niedermayer, Darryl Sydor, Darcy Tucker, Mark Recchi, and Rob Brown, and has won five Western Hockey League championships, as well as three Memorial Cups.
- Swift Current, Saskatchewan, where tough guys Dave Schultz and Tiger Williams brought the Broncos fans to their feet and where stars such as Bryan Trottier and Joe Sakic will always be hometown heroes. It, too, is a community-owned team; residents actually bought shares.
- Lethbridge, Alberta, where the Hurricanes, another community-owned team, draws an average of 3,200 people to home games, and where six of the Sutter brothers played with the Broncos, during that franchise's time there, before moving on to the NHL.

There are many other possible aspirants to the appellation Hockey Town: Flin Flon in Manitoba, Viking and Red Deer in Alberta, and New Westminster, Kelowna, and Cranbrook in B.C., to name a few. Their fans pack the rinks and show a degree of support not seen in most Ontario junior towns. Their communities are filled with behind-the-bench volunteers, as well as kids and adults who play the game. They have all experienced the joy of digging skate blades into a new ice surface, the sting of frost on cold cheeks that comes from playing outdoors, and the unutterable freedom that lacing up a pair of skates gives us – freedom from life's harsh realities. As former Philadelphia Flyers coach Fred Shero once said, "Life is the stuff between hockey games."

The province of Quebec has its hockey towns, too, where the arenas are filled even for kids' games, where the controversies of hockey inspire excitement almost as powerful as religion and politics, maybe more. Quebec City's peewee hockey tournament is one of the most prestigious in the world. Other Quebec communities with a claim for recognition include Trois-Rivières, Noranda, Shawinigan, Hull, Rouyn, Sherbrooke, Chicoutimi, and Verdun (birthplace of Scotty Bowman and fifteen others who went to the NHL).

The Maritime provinces are crammed with hockey towns. Even Newfoundland is home to future stars. But the small population base eliminates these provinces from contending as Hockey Town. They simply haven't attained the requisite critical mass.

On this basis, Ontario has to be reckoned the hockey province. Ontario grabs the crown on size alone. Almost 45 per cent of the 505,000 kids playing hockey in Canada each year are lacing up skates in Ontario. That's more than 225,000 kids, compared to the second-biggest province, Quebec, with 88,600, and Alberta, in third place, with 58,700. Ontario is also where 680 of the 3,000 indoor rinks in Canada have been built.

It is in other Ontario communities that Peterborough finds its greatest competition in the world for the title of Hockey Town. And it is one of its most dreaded enemies and closest neighbours, Oshawa, only a forty-five-minute drive away between Peterborough and Toronto, that comes closest to taking the title in sheer numbers. Oshawa's privately owned junior franchise, the Generals, has put almost as many players into the NHL as has the Peterborough Petes, and many of them are legends: Bobby Orr, Eric Lindros, Ted Lindsay, Dave Andreychuk, Rick Middleton, Terry O'Reilly, Dale Tallon, Alex Delvecchio, Jason Arnott, and Keith Primeau, to name only a few. But when the word Oshawa comes from the lips of Canadians, is it more likely to be followed by the word "hockey" or "automobile"? It's the huge General Motors plant that drives Oshawa's economy and community life.

Another two dozen NHL players were born in Oshawa, while more than thirty players learned their hockey in Peterborough's kids' system before getting to the NHL. In the 2004 NHL season the Generals had twelve alumni in the NHL compared to Peterborough's fourteen. But Oshawa is twice the size of Peterborough, a bedroom community, and the team dropped out of the junior loop and didn't rejoin until the 1960s. Consistency over time may be another component of Hockey Town.

There is no town in Ontario that has been in the OHL on a more consistent basis than the Petes. Petes' junior hockey has been in the community since 1956. It has been out of the playoffs just three times and, until 2004, had been in the playoffs twenty-seven straight seasons.

Kitchener, which gave up its junior franchise to Peterborough in the 1950s, is also a legitimate contender. Far bigger in population and size than Peterborough, it has been the birthplace of close to forty kids who went on to the NHL. The Rangers, another community-operated team, is owned by season-ticket holders, run by a forty-person board with a seven-member executive, all local volunteers. The team's attendance figures are so high that other junior teams in Ontario (besides London and Ottawa) can only envy them.

There are other hockey towns that could compete for the crown. Kingston claims to have invented the game (a claim that is still hotly debated). It can also claim the likes of Kirk Muller, Doug Gilmour, and hockey's best-known television personality, Don Cherry. More than forty future NHLers have been born there. But as former *Peterborough Examiner* sports editor Cec Purdue once stated, "If Kingston was the birthplace of hockey, it didn't take long to move it down the road to Peterborough."

Brantford, the birthplace of the game's greatest star, Wayne Gretzky, and close to two dozen others who went on to the NHL, is a notable hockey town. So are Sudbury, Guelph, Thunder Bay, and certainly Sault Ste. Marie, which has a remarkable history and tradition for hockey. But none of them are as hockey-recognizable as Peterborough.

A claim could be made for recognition of any one – or several – of these enthusiastic and historic hockey communities as Hockey Town. And it's true, after all, that the sport is nurtured and enjoyed all over North America to a greater or lesser degree. In a sense – and this is a theme explored in later chapters – Hockey Town is any town where the game is loved and played for the sheer excitement and exhilaration it inspires in all its supporters and participants. But the theme developed and defended in these pages is that Peterborough's claim is the strongest of all.

Peterborough has had many nicknames through its more than 150-year history – it has been known for more than just its passion for hockey. It has been known as Electric City, because it's the home of General Electric of Canada, the place Thomas Edison decided to build his factory in 1898, and Liftlock City, because it's the home of the world's highest hydraulic liftlock. It has also been called Retirement Town, because more than the national or provincial average of its 70,000 citizens are seniors; Lacrosse Capital of the World, because of its junior and senior national titles and its domination of the sport in the 1960s and 1970s; Test Town and Typical Town, because so many products are tested in Peterborough before companies put them on the market. If something works in Peterborough then it will work elsewhere. *Chatelaine* magazine once called it the "ultra-average Canada town."

It has also been recognized, by historian Michael Bliss, as a major player in the renaissance of Toronto as Canada's financial centre. He called Peterborough capitalists George Cox and Sir Joseph Flavelle, who left to expand their vast fortunes in Toronto in the early part of the twentieth century, the "Peterborough Methodist Mafia."

Peterborough has also been home to Canadian writers Robertson Davies, Margaret Laurence, Susanna Moodie, Isabella Valancy Crawford, and Scott Young. Sandford Fleming lived there before he developed standard time for the world. It was also the home of artist

Harold Town and sculptor Katherine Wallis. One of its most famous sons was former prime minister and Nobel Peace Prize–winner Lester B. Pearson, who lived in the town as a boy for four years, starting in 1907, while his father was a church minister. Later, when asked what he remembered about his days in Peterborough, he replied, "The baseball games in the schoolyard and the hockey at the old Brock arena."

This may contribute to one of the strongest arguments in support of Peterborough's claim to be Hockey Town: the fact that many people – especially fans and those who work in the hockey industry – so readily make the connection. Its reputation is huge among professional players, coaches, managers, and scouts, but it reaches well beyond the big leagues. When fans watched on national television as St. Francis Xavier defeated Fredericton for the national university championship game in 2004, they saw defenceman Mike Martone, a native of Sault Ste. Marie, but a former Petes captain, selected an all-star. The year before, the all-star goalie in the championship game was a Peterborough native. Once you've played for the Petes, the town's hockey fans claim ownership; you're from Peterborough. Once a Pete, always a Pete. Even women's hockey could admire the captain of Harvard University's team, Kalen Ingram, who learned her hockey in the Peterborough minor system.

But Hockey Town is much more than a hockey factory for future teams, or what some in professional hockey call the Hockey Mafia. Peterborough, which was the home of the Toronto Maple Leafs' training camp in the Punch Imlach era, is also the birthplace of old-timers hockey: in the 1970s, a few local business people got together and started a tournament strictly for oldtimers. Now almost every city and town in Canada has a similar tournament. Peterborough is also the home of Canadian Hockey Enterprises, one of the largest such organizations in the world, which conducts hockey schools and tournaments all over North America. It is operated by former pro player Paul Crowley, who scouted for the Detroit Red Wings and coached the Peterborough bantam team to the all-Ontario championship. The community was also the runner-up for the site of the Hockey Hall of Fame two decades ago after a massive grassroots

campaign, but the decision was made to keep it in downtown
Toronto. The original curator who had built, organized, and created
the treasures in the Hall of Fame was Maurice "Lefty" Reid, who
once worked in Peterborough and has made it his permanent home
since his retirement.

Peterborough is everywhere in the hockey world. There is not
a national television sports network in Canada that doesn't have a
Peterborough face. Former Petes goalie Greg Millen is an analyst on
Hockey Night in Canada, while other former Petes Dave Reid, Kay
Whitmore, John Garrett, Larry Murphy, John Druce, and Mickey
Redmond do the same job on other networks in Canada and the U.S.
One of TSN's *SportsCentre*'s anchors is Peterborough native Dan
O'Toole. And *The Hockey News*, the bible of hockey statistics and analy-
sis, features Mike Brophy as its senior writer; Brophy covered hockey
and the Petes for more than a decade at *The Peterborough Examiner*.

The city has four rinks with six ice surfaces that feature every type
of hockey, from boys' and girls' to oldtimers', women's, and recreational. The rinks run almost twenty hours every day. The community has twenty outdoor rinks that are built and maintained by
neighbourhood volunteers. When the Trent Canal freezes each
winter, it too is maintained by the city for skaters and hockey players.

Peterborough is the home of the world's largest atom hockey
tournament run solely by volunteers. More than eighty future NHL
players competed in this tournament, which has been running since
1957-58. At its inception, the tournament was a one-day, eight-team
event; it now runs five days with more than one hundred teams. The
tournament has donated more than $200,000 to Peterborough minor
hockey and $85,000 to charities in the last ten years alone. In 2003
it brought in $1 million to the community. Every hotel room was
booked in and around the city with 1,600 children, 400 team officials, and 3,100 family members. Some of the volunteers from the
inaugural year are still with the organizing committee.

Peterborough has been labelled the Participation Capital of
Canada. One in seven people is involved in hockey. The recreational
rinks (not including the home of the Petes) attract more than 700,000
visits each winter for kids' hockey games. Peterborough's economy,

once blue-collar and dominated by factories, now is more white-collar, but General Electric, Quaker Oats, and General Motors in nearby Oshawa still set the tone. The Petes reflect their influence: the community is hard-working, loyal, dependable, and consistent. Petes fans are very conservative. They don't often get off their seats, and they can be stingy with their applause. Their standing ovations are like a critic to a compliment: few and far between. Most of them have supported the team for decades. They are knowledgeable but undemonstrative, critical but protective. The team is family.

Peterborough accepts its place in hockey history as if it was supposed to be that way, and maybe it was – like pie and ice cream, peanut butter and jam. The residents don't ask why they go so well together, they just do. But outsiders always ask why Peterborough has attracted so many hockey people, and there are various answers.

The one cited most frequently is the Montreal Canadiens. Young teens wanted to come to Peterborough, hoping to be picked up by the fabulous Habs. The Montreal Canadiens are hockey's most successful hockey dynasty, famous for being a class organization, with a fan base that extends across Canada, and even North America. Until the Habs came along, Peterborough was just another hockey town. When they established their junior franchise, the Petes, in 1956, it put Peterborough on the hockey map and started what was then a small community of 48,000 on the road to hockey immortality.

As long as the Petes were part of the Habs' system, of course, they benefited from the team's organization. The Canadiens had scouts and bird dogs all over Ontario, they sponsored teams throughout Canada, and they were successful. Success breeds success, so when Montreal jumped into Peterborough, the two hockey cities fell in love, as did the fans who flocked to the games and took ownership of "their" team.

The Habs put in place rules and a structure that helped make Peterborough attractive to young hockey players and their parents. The team demanded that the kids stay in school or have full-time jobs. It enforced curfews and discipline. If a player did not respond positively to discipline, he was gone. The young players were placed with "landparents" (a compound of "landlord" and "parent," indicating that the people who applied to take in a player would take responsibility for looking after his welfare). Landparents were paid a stipend by the team. In the 1950s and early 1960s, they were usually widows looking for extra income. By the 1970s, all landparents were couples, usually with a family, chosen not just to be landlords but also guardians.

Coach Roger Neilson described to a prospective recruit the system the Petes put in place:

> Our players live at homes in Peterborough where the families are interested in hockey. All players live within walking distance of the school. We provide and pay for tutors for boys who are having difficulty with a subject based on the progress reports we receive each month from the principals. The team practices from 4:30 to 6 p.m. each day. The ice is also available from 4 p.m. for extra skating. Your salary would be $60 per week. After spending money and room and board were deducted you would save over $600 by March. Our team visits the YMCA twice weekly. Special instruction is given to build up the individual strength and endurance weaknesses of each player. Weight training, sauna baths, swimming, track and basketball are all included in the program. On November 17 and 18 the team plays in Fredericton and Moncton. On January 6 and 7 we fly to Halifax for two games. Only nine periods of school are missed during the entire season. . . .

Aside from both the mythical and practical appeal of the Habs' organization, the city itself was attractive to hockey parents who were sending their sons away to play junior hockey. Peterborough was a small town with small-town virtues. The community tended to adopt the players as its own: when one of them misbehaved, word soon got back to the Petes. But, as a small town, it was also far from big-city vice. The kids away from home for the first time would not be tempted by big-city distractions. While Peterborough has grown since the Petes' early years, it retains a small-town atmosphere and attitude.

When the Canadiens' organization withdrew from Peterborough in 1966, the Petes were taken over by the community itself, run by a small executive, and supported, as always, by the local fans. As a community team playing in a community rink with no private owner thirsting for profits, there were only two reasons left for hockey: the fans and the players. Ask any of the former players or coaches why Peterborough is so successful and usually the first words out of their mouths are "the fans."

André Lacroix, who starred for the Petes in the 1960s, says, "We hated to lose for them." Danny Grant and Billy Plager, who also played in that era, both support that statement, saying they didn't want to disappoint them. Terry Bovair, who played for the Petes in the 1970s, recalls, "It was a team, a community. The older players took the younger players under their wing and we all became part of the community."

The Petes have been consistently innovative. They had the first team education consultant, they brought in a police officer as an adviser, and they asked the players to become part of the community. They were the first junior team to represent Canada in the inaugural world junior championships, held in Russia in 1974. It helped that they had one of the world's most innovative coaches, Roger Neilson.

Long-time Petes executive Herb Warr said the purpose of the Petes was to win hockey games, but also to represent the community of Peterborough.

Former player and captain Craig Ramsay calls it the "dynasty franchise where parents wanted their kids to go. The team had the history with the Habs, they wanted education for the players, and they cared about them."

Legendary *Hockey Night in Canada* broadcaster Foster Hewitt wrote in a Young Canada hockey day (all-day tournament) program in 1962: "Peterborough has long been one of the keenest hockey centres in all of Canada." He predicted local boys would join the NHL and "it would certainly give me much pleasure to broadcast some night 'that was a great goal by a young lad who learned to play in Peterborough.'"

So, while there may be many other hockey towns besides Peterborough, none has quite the combination of qualities that sets Peterborough apart, like the prime minister within the Cabinet, first among equals.

The things that make all hockey towns special, however, are the same everywhere. Hockey is anything but a solitary sport: it involves a whole community. Most importantly, it cannot function without armies of actively involved parents and committed volunteers. Look at the background of most hockey players and you discover how big a part their families played in their development. Rivalry between siblings has had a lot to do with giving a number of successful players their keen competitive edge. The extraordinary devotion of moms who get their atom-age kids dressed at five in the morning and then drive them for a practice at six has been essential to many hockey careers. So has the endurance of fathers who flood backyard rinks in sub-zero temperatures on long winter nights. It takes more than a family – it takes a neighbourhood or a community – to make and maintain a natural-ice surface in a park through the winter. And it takes the labour of thousands of volunteers to coach, manage, and organize hockey at every level.

Hockey Town is about family, children, teams who wear the colours of their heroes to games, fans who buy season tickets and never fail to show up for home games (traditionally, Thursday night is Hockey Night in Peterborough). It is about victory and defeat and learning to deal with both. It is about kids from other hockey towns who move to Hockey Town as teens and leave as adults. It is about a half-crazy passion for a game. And that's what this book is about.

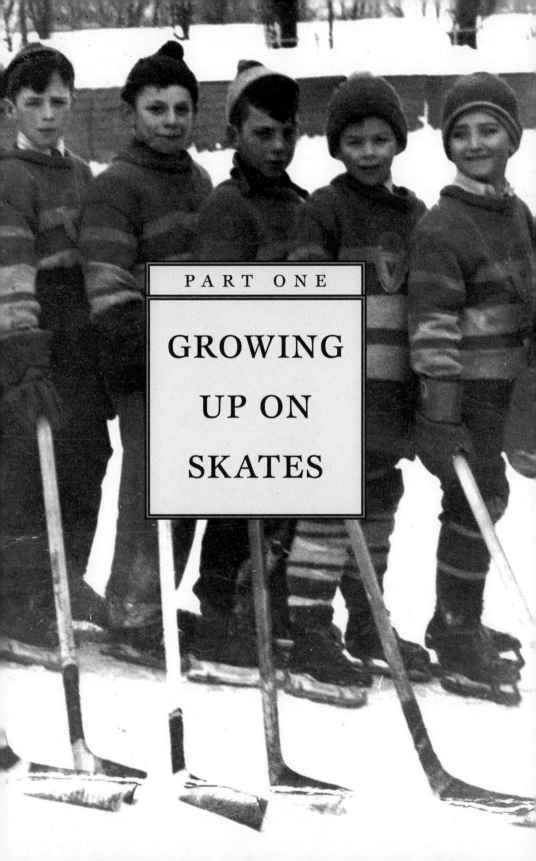

PART ONE

GROWING UP ON SKATES

Hockey Families

$\mathbf{A}$ny boy who has grown up with a passion for hockey has been encouraged and supported first and foremost by his family. Later in his development as a player, coaches and teammates play a role. And so do the people who provide a home for him when he first ventures away from his own family. Even fans can play a role. More than one former player with the Peterborough Petes has said how much he appreciated the support of the fans and how much he wanted to win for them. But the support of the wider community comes later. In the beginning, what's important is the loving encouragement of a mother and father. Or, in some cases, of a grandfather.

Dit Clapper was a twenty-season player and a Hall of Famer who starred with the Boston Bruins of the 1930s and 1940s. He had a long connection with Peterborough and settled there after he retired from the game. He is one of the few players whose grandson – in his case, Greg Theberge – has also enjoyed a stop in the NHL.

Theberge, who played for the Petes and then in the early 1980s for the Washington Capitals, recalls how his grandfather would help him with his shot, setting up a shooting gallery on his verandah, and forbidding him from ever using a curved stick. (The curved stick is now so nearly universally accepted that the objections to its use by oldtimers seem strange. But the curved stick was controversial at one time, and somewhere, no doubt, there are holdouts who still believe that passing and stickhandling require a straight blade.) Theberge also remembers that his grandfather would "never give me advice on the way home from games. Maybe the next day he'd say he wanted me to go to the middle of the ice more often, and he tried to get me to go inside even when I was young. He'd encourage me to use the wrist shot, not the slapshot. And he got me a Bobby Orr Power Puck [a heavier puck that measured speed] to help my shot. He made a big difference in my life."

If grandfather-grandson combinations are rare, fathers and sons turn up with greater frequency. The most famous among them are probably the Howe family and the two Hulls, Bobby and Brett. Like these famous mini-dynasties, Clare Raglan, who moved to Peterborough after his professional career was over, and his son Herb, also had hockey careers that bridged both a generation and different hockey eras.

Clare – or Rags, as he was known – played in the 1940s and 1950s when helmets were for sissies, goalies' faces were for stitches, skates were boots and metal blades, and a hockey player's salary was not enough to support a family. You always had to have a second job. Herb Raglan played at a time when helmets were mandatory, goalies wore fantastically decorated facemasks, skates were custom-made, and the lowest NHL salary was $185,000.

One thing was the same – you did what you had to do to win. Perhaps that kind of desire can be passed on in the genes. Certainly, there are fathers who have passed on their love of the game to their sons.

Ed Murphy, who came from a farming background in Huntingdon, Quebec, fell in love with hockey at an early age, but "was too busy working on the cattle farm for playing." And that's what hockey was when Ed was a kid, strictly for play, something you could do if you had time after chores. He loved hockey so much, on his first date with his future wife, Doris, he took her to her first hockey game – in Quebec City, where a young kid named Jean Béliveau was playing that night. The Montreal Canadiens were Ed's team. Hockey was close to Ed's heart and to his son Larry's too. Larry would become one of the most proficient and consistent blueliners in the NHL.

Harold Watson also loved the game. To say that he was heavily involved in minor hockey in the tiny, picturesque town of Bancroft would be an understatement. Bancroft is a former mining town about 120 kilometres northeast of Peterborough, and in 1952, with a population of just under two thousand, it had fourteen hockey teams. Harold was manager and coach of three teams – the bantam, peewee, and senior teams – and he ran four elementary-school teams and was the trainer for another team. When *The Peterborough Examiner* published a story on Bancroft minor hockey in the early 1950s, Harold's employer, the provincial lands and forests ministry, might not have been well pleased to read that "in his spare time he works."

Bryan Watson's career as a hard-working, often infuriatingly effective defenceman and forward with six NHL teams, including Montreal and Detroit, suggests that his father's extraordinary commitment to hockey had a direct effect on him.

Emotion is one thing, physical attributes, another. The physique, the bone structure, and the DNA of a great athlete all are unarguably in the blood. However, someone has to recognize these elements and develop them for all the pieces to fall in place.

Eddie Redmond was one of those people born to play hockey. The Kirkland Lake native was a former member of the Royal Canadian Air Force and a big bear of a man with a mean streak as long as the highway, but he knew hockey like a great salesman knows his pitch. He played semi-pro for the Quebec Aces with Jean Béliveau and for Canada's Senior A amateur team with the Whitby Dunlops, a team that won the world championship in 1958 in Oslo, Norway. Redmond was not only a defenceman on the team but also its captain and assistant coach. Those who knew him then described him as "one tough son of a bitch."

Eddie gave more than a hockey pedigree to his two boys, Mickey and Dick; he also gave them tactical advice. When the boys played minor hockey, their dad was in the stands for every game. The familiar sound of Eddie, two fingers in his mouth, whistling signals to the boys, either positioning them or tipping them off, would echo through the arena. Both Mickey and Dick inherited their father's toughness and hockey smarts as well. Mickey had a brilliant though injury-shortened career with the Montreal Canadiens and Detroit Red Wings. His brother, Dick, also put in some solid years in the NHL.

Clare Raglan may have been a bit like Eddie Redmond. Clare was old-school. When the supper dishes had been cleared away, he would sit with his son, pencil in hand, and draw plays directly on the kitchen table. When Herb acted up there were no hugs or kisses from Clare, just slaps on the head, and criticism when he didn't do things right. "His bark was worse than his bite," says Herb's old friend Dennie Scott, referring to the elder Raglan, but Herb adds with a laugh that he sure did bark a lot.

George "Red" Sullivan's parents were a different kind of old-school. Red, who would become captain of the New York Rangers, grew up in the Great Depression, a time when many parents were too busy working, just trying to survive, to watch kids play games. Red became a star but his mother never saw him play a game, even as a professional hockey player.

Some dads know the game, others learn it with their kids. Bryan Watson, who toiled for sixteen years in the NHL, remembers his father commenting that he was weak on crossovers. Harold demonstrated how to do it correctly on the outdoor rink. "I watched my dad doing it. He was big on reading how to do things. He'd order books through the mail and then show me how to do it. That day he was coming down the ice trying to do these crossovers and I had to laugh. I remember saying, 'I think you read the instructions wrong.'"

Greg Millen's dad, Ted, wasn't a hockey expert, either. When he died in October 2003 at the age of eighty-three, Greg was in Vancouver getting ready to do his job as a hockey commentator for *Hockey Night in Canada*. Greg didn't tell his fellow workers about the death. He pushed his emotions away and did the show, then took the red-eye flight to Toronto and drove to his home near Peterborough to be with his mother, wife, and four children to mourn. His father's service was private. Many of Greg's friends didn't even know about the death.

As he mourned, Greg couldn't help but think of all the times his parents supported him in everything he did and of those early-morning hockey practices they'd drive him to. Ted didn't know very much about hockey, but he cared plenty about his son. When Greg started playing goal, Ted thought it best that he wear a wire mask, because it was safer than what Greg calls the Plexiglas others were using. Greg wore the wire mask even in his pro career. His father helped develop the first goalie neck-guard for Greg when he was a kid, something that's standard equipment today.

Any hockey parent knows what it really means to support a boy or girl who is playing minor hockey. It means getting up at five o'clock to be at the rink by six. It means standing around in a freezing arena. It means awful coffee and a concession-stand hot dog for dinner. And it means travel to games that are hours away from home. These days, many teams have a policy of always hiring a bus to get the team safely through winter storms to out-of-town games. But this has not always been the case.

Future Philadelphia Flyers star Rick MacLeish was raised in Cannington, a small town outside of Peterborough, in the 1950s and 1960s. His parents tried to get to as many games as possible, but many of the other parents were just not able to take the time off. The kids were usually transported in two or three cars, with a few parents risking snow-covered roads to get to rinks in places like Sunderland, Haliburton, and Little Britain. Al McPhail, a high-school teacher who organized minor hockey locally, remembers that transportation "was an absolute horror. We'd have six or seven kids in the cars going to Haliburton in a snowstorm. Cars didn't have seatbelts and we were taking real risks."

Relatively few parents, however, have gone through what future WHA scoring champion André Lacroix's parents went through in order to get him to games. The Lacroix family lived in Lauzon, Quebec, on the south shore of the St. Lawrence River. After André's father, a former pro wrestler on the junior circuit, had worked an eighteen-hour day, he'd drive to Quebec City to pick André up and bring him home.

"When we got older, the parents used to come to the games. My parents never said I played a good game or a bad game; they just came to the game and enjoyed watching the game. They never forced me to play. Dad would take me to practice. Sometimes we weren't home until one a.m. and he'd have to work in the morning, but he never complained. If he hadn't done that, I wouldn't have been able to play. [To get to] the games I'd have to take two buses and a ferry to get to the Quebec Coliseum and he'd pick me up after every game. We didn't even know if the ferry would cross on some winter nights."

Former Buffalo Sabres star and now Tampa Bay Lightning assistant coach Craig Ramsay's parents, like so many devoted hockey parents, were more than willing to support him, even though they did not really follow hockey. What young Craig learned one day by listening to his teammates was to get his skates sharpened. Once they'd had their first sharpening, Craig quickly discovered it made them work much better – so much better that he skated on to a professional career.

Encouragement comes in different forms. Hard cash can also be effective. Former Oakland Seals captain Joey Johnston's father started rewarding Joey's on-ice triumphs in his first year of hockey. For every goal Joe scored he got a quarter. The first two years weren't especially lucrative for Joey, but by the time he was in this third year, he was claiming more than a bit of loose change. Joey says, "I remember one time I scored ten goals in a game. He paid up, though."

The most effective encouragement may come as a result of rivalry among brothers and sisters. Joey was only nine when he began playing peewee hockey for his church on older brother Tom's team. There was a very pragmatic reason for him to be playing with children a year older: Mr. Johnston didn't want to go to the rink twice. Besides, says Joey now, "having an older brother made me more competitive. We were only one year and one month apart and I wanted to be better than him."

Competition among the bruising Plager brothers, Barclay, Bob, and Billy, who all went on to play in the NHL, was never-ending and, for fans who liked that sort of thing, endlessly entertaining. Their legendary toughness was acquired at an early age. There was a time when Barclay was with the Petes and Bob was with the Guelph Royals and they met one night at Peterborough's Memorial Centre. The fight between them started at centre ice, where they duked it out for a while, but it didn't end there. They kept fighting in the penalty box, and then in the arena's corridor, and then, with sparks flying from their skate blades, as they continued out into the parking lot. On a radio interview right after the game, Barclay, knowing that his parents, Gus and Edith, always listened, crowed, "Mom, Dad, we won, and I beat up Bob!"

The term "hockey parent" has, of course, more than one connotation. The excitement and intensity of the game sometimes are reflected all too vividly in the behaviour of parents in the stands. Canadian hockey parents are some of the most vocal, and sometimes violent, in minor sports. Most of them aren't bad parents, some of them just show bad behaviour in the throes of a hockey game, even if it is just a kids' game. It has become so much a problem that hockey officials have had to institute parent-behaviour codes, even contracts, and promote restraint in national advertising campaigns.

Edith Plager admits she was "a mouthy parent at the rinks. . . . I was a yeller. Gus would go to the other end of the rink during the game. One night a man was yelling at one of the boys. He wouldn't shut up. Finally, I couldn't take any more, and turned around and hit him in the face. He didn't fall, didn't do anything, I think he was in shock." She came from tough stock. Her father had worked in the coal mines of Wales when he was only seven. Billy says his mom "always said Gus got the glory but she took us to the rinks, took us on a sled and dropped us off there."

Craig Ramsay remembers an incident at a game between his Toronto-area minor-league team and another, the Marlies. His coach was a neighbour, Burt Turney, who became, in effect, Craig's hockey mentor. "Mr. Turney had a lot of fight in him but he was even-tempered," says Craig. "There was a scuffle on the ice with pushing and shoving. He pulled two kids apart." Back in the dressing room after the game, Coach Turney was smoking a cigar while the players changed. "Suddenly, the dressing-room door was kicked open and a half-dozen Marlies parents came in accusing him of hitting a player. One of them was the father, who threatened to punch the coach. Mr. Turney said, 'Go right ahead,' and he did. He smashed the cigar into [Mr. Turney's] face. Coach Turney [who was just five-foot-nine] tossed five or six of them around like rag dolls. It was awful to watch as kids."

Craig's coach then went upstairs. Craig continues: "My dad, who was six-foot-five, was there and saw a Marlies parent following him. Mr. Turney grabbed the parent and was going to throw the man over the railing. My dad talked him out of it, but Coach did put the parent headfirst into a garbage can."

Violence off the ice was – and is – relatively rare. But parental politics, as generations of players and their families have discovered, are as much a part of the game as the early-morning practice. In 1975, when Wayne Gretzky was just fourteen but already widely recognized as a hockey phenomenon, the Gretzky family decided to move him to Toronto to get him out of the local environment. The atmosphere in Brantford was not good – some parents had taken to yelling at the boy, jealous of Wayne's growing stardom and the amount of ice time he received.

NHLer and now executive vice-president of the league Colin Campbell's fame obviously was never as great as the Great One's, but he was a talented player, and he worked hard and was focused. As soon as he could, Colin played all-star hockey for Tillsonburg. "I think there were a lot of pushy parents," says his mother, Gwen. "And a lot of politics. Their kids used to win all the hockey awards. Colin never won them, unless it was at an out-of-town tournament. Colin always said he'd let them win all their awards." And then he would add, "I'll get the money."

Al McPhail remembers that having future NHL scoring star Rick MacLeish on the team sometimes provoked a reaction from opposing parents. McPhail recalls, "He'd score six, seven, eight, nine, or ten goals a game. It got so bad that when we pulled into other arenas, [the other] parents were accusing us of cheating, saying we shouldn't be bringing 'that little bugger' with us. They called him a ringer, even though he was younger than the rest of the team."

The parents of future superstar Steve Yzerman and his brother Michael encountered all kinds of difficulties as they negotiated their way through the minor-hockey system in several cities. Ron Yzerman "coached" (Ron couldn't skate) the boys' team when they were just starting out in Cranbrook, British Columbia. In his second year as coach, as the boys got better at the game, Ron gradually came to realize that parents could be a problem.

He was rotating Michael and Steve in goal. The two boys loved to play net. As more games were played, the boys became more proficient, and their team began to win by scores of 5-0 or 6-0. Michael might get a shutout and Steve would get five or six goals, or Steve would get the shutout and Michael would score the goals. But soon Ron was aware of whispers about the fairness of the two brothers playing on the same team. It's true that the Yzerman boys made the one team too strong, but what's a father to do? Should he separate the two kids, have them on two teams at different times?

"I got the message from some others that we were unfair," he recalls.

One Saturday, Ron was asked to go behind the bench for the game following the one he'd just coached, because the coach for the next game hadn't shown up. If he did this, he was told, his kids could play another game. Michael had already left, but Ron asked Steve if he wanted to play in this game. Steve was all for it. They slipped the sweater of the next team on him and he played again.

"I should have known this was a mistake, but had no idea. Stephen still couldn't skate very well, but the little guy always wanted the puck."

The next weekend Ron got his first real indication that the game of hockey was not all fun and games. A parent had complained about the six-year-old Steve playing for two different teams. "I would find out years later this was nothing compared with other things parents did in minor hockey," says Ron, shaking his head at the memories.

The Saturday-morning ritual continued, but in 1973 hockey got a bit more serious when the Yzerman boys were invited to play for a Cranbrook team put together to travel to another community for a weekend of hockey and billeting. Ron drove the boys 170 miles up the road with the other kids.

"We got smoked, hammered, but it was the first time the boys had ever played on a full sheet of ice with twenty-minute running-time periods. They couldn't believe it; it was just like the NHL [for them]." It was also when Ron discovered Steve was as good as some of the better players. Even though the team got smoked, Steve was scoring goals. Ron's coaching career ended that year when he was transferred to Kamloops, a far bigger town of 50,000 people. The family moved during the hockey season in February, but the boys weren't going to let that interrupt their playing. Ron called the minor-hockey association, who told him to take the boys to the local house league. It had never occurred to Ron that there were different levels of play. This was the big time now, real hockey teams playing real games. After the house-league officials had seen the boys play, they told Ron about the Moose Lodge Pups, a travelling team of some of the better town players, and asked to have them attend practices. The practices were at five in the morning. Welcome to minor hockey.

"We had to get up and get the boys up for 4:30 a.m.," remembers the boys' mom, Jean. "They would still be sleeping and we'd dress them, put on their skates, take them to practice, bring them home, feed them, and get them ready for school, which was just a few blocks away, so they could walk. I felt sorry for the kids, and sometimes I'd keep them home. There were a few times they wanted to stay home, but not very often," she adds. The Pups had expected the Yzerman boys to come only to practices, not to play in games. But in that first practice, Steve looked good doing the drills. Even so, says Ron, "I had this feeling some of the adults were very condescending and didn't really want us to be there."

It's understandable that they didn't receive a warm welcome. After all, it was already February; the team had been selected, and along came a new family with new players. And one of the kids was really interested in hockey.

"I don't know why," Ron says. "Stephen was nine years old but he was serious. He was very competitive and just loved hockey. I don't know where that came from. He'd watch CBC's *Hockey Night in Canada* – it was the only station we got – but he seemed to just love the game."

The Moose Pups' practices were causing the coach some mental anguish. Steve was as good as any player they had but he was also a year younger.

"We were outsiders. We weren't being shunned and it wasn't like we were pushing ourselves into the social network. I just sat in the corner. You could see the coach had a dilemma with the parents. Our boys didn't play much in the first or second periods, but by the third you knew the team had a competitive coach who wanted to win. Stephen would play a lot in the third period. I couldn't understand why he wouldn't get a regular shift during the game and didn't realize it until later."

Steve was being recognized as a gifted player. One coach was calling on him, a year younger than his brother Michael, to play some games with a higher age group and on a higher-calibre team. "Stephen was never that thrilled about being called up, but if Michael was playing, he'd usually go." Ron kept his distance from most of the other parents during the games. He was beginning to realize the word "favouritism" was popular among hockey parents. Favouritism in minor hockey usually means one player is getting more ice time and more attention from the coach than others and is being used more often on special teams and at the end of the games. The gifted Steve Yzerman was a favourite of his coaches.

As Ron watched minor hockey through the years (he and Jean had two younger sons in it as well) he understood the precarious position coaches with children on an all-star team put themselves in. The coaches were often accused of showing favouritism toward their own children. Ron didn't, and still doesn't, think parents should be allowed to coach their own children at that level, because they can't separate their emotions from their responsibilities. Meanwhile, once the family moved to Nepean, Ontario, and by the time Steve got to peewee, Jean avoided going to the games. "I couldn't stand hearing what some of the parents would say about Stephen, right while I was standing there."

Parents from their own team were calling him a puck hog or saying he shouldn't be on the power play, or asking why he was on the ice – all the things you hear in the Canadian children's games from jealous, envious, or just plain rude adults.

Once she couldn't hold her tongue and lashed back. "I don't know what I said to this woman but I couldn't take it any longer."

There were no repercussions from the outburst, but that's when she started attending fewer games. "I never sat with the parents," says Ron. "One parent asked me how I could be so calm and I told her, 'Stephen is getting plenty of ice time, he's playing well, the team is doing well. What do I have to yell for?'"

The Yzermans understand the problem when some of the players play more than the other kids. Coaches are trying to win games. Sometimes they cut the bench down to two lines and leave the third line sitting near the end of a close game. But the Yzermans are surely right to say, Don't take it out on the players playing or the parents. It's the coach who's making the decisions.

The team went to a tournament in Boston, and they reached the final. In double overtime, the coach went to two lines, and they won the championship. The team had driven there on a chartered bus, but one of the parents took his son back on a plane because he was so upset that his son and others had not played.

"I thought he'd be disappointed that his child didn't play, but happy that the team had won," says Ron.

When they were in minor peewee, Steve and a teammate, Jeff Brown, who also made it to the NHL, were once asked to take part in a major-peewee tournament in Toronto. The team chartered a bus for the players and their parents. Ron says, "Some of the parents acted as if we were being introduced to royalty. We were used to lousy hotels, the bad hot chocolate at the rinks, McDonald's and Tim Hortons. [On] this bus, the parents had a buffet at the back, serving oysters. We couldn't help but laugh." He continues, "We could feel the resentment of some of the other parents because they knew their kids would be getting less ice time with our kids there. One parent said to me there should be a rule against calling kids up [to another level]."

Steve never really wanted to play up to a different level. He wanted to play with his friends, and sometimes that meant playing other school sports such as basketball, baseball, soccer, and tennis. He even tried lacrosse once. School was something he went to for sports. His marks were average, but there was no pressure on him to improve his marks. Hockey really was everything, say his parents.

For the parents of kids who really take their hockey seriously, the game becomes a way of life. Many parents have coached, or at least assisted the coach, in peewee or minor bantam. Ice time at the rinks is always at a premium in every community where hockey is played, and practice times are rarely convenient. Hockey parents do an awful lot of driving, much of it either before the sun is up or after it has set. And then there are the out-of-town tournaments: the cheap hotels, the time killed in malls between games, and the fast-food diet. The truth of the matter is that the parents make as big a commitment to the game as their children do.

The most common complaint through the years of minor hockey has been ice time for the kids. Peterborough did a survey of its minor-hockey system back in the 1960s and the most common complaints were that their sons weren't playing as much as the star players and they weren't getting to play with the star players.

Adults can do some strange things in pursuit of victory. We were in a public-school championship, I was the team's goalie, and the teacher who coached the team asked if I would agree to sit out because a new kid, an all-star goalie, gave them a better chance of winning. I was only twelve, couldn't understand how we could be in a championship game with me as the goalie all year and then be asked to step aside. Even at that age you know what the coach is telling you. I said no, we played, we lost, I cried. It was my last game of organized hockey. My parents never knew. They weren't at the games. Most of our parents both worked, let us walk off to our games with our green duffel bags thrown over our shoulders, and seldom even asked who won when we got home. That was only for some of us; many others filled the arenas every day to watch the kids and complain about their lack of ice time.

Perhaps it's easier for the parents of the kids who are really talented than for the parents of kids who spend more time on the bench to be philosophical about the ice time that their kids get, and to sympathize with the coach who puts winning ahead of other considerations. It may even be easier for the kids themselves to be philosophical than it is for their parents.

And then there's the little matter of life after hockey – the plight of the hockey parent whose kids have moved on. After the Plager boys all had left home, their mother, Edith, felt their absence keenly. Her husband, Gus, continued to participate in the local hockey scene: "[He] was refereeing and I was alone. I was a hockey widow. I would set the table with Billy's placing every day for a month after he left, hoping he'd come home."

Hockey All the Time, Anywhere

We have all played the game. We have played it on a pond, a backyard rink, a parking lot, a city street, a local arena. We have played it indoors, on a kitchen floor or in a basement rec room, or even on a table-top hockey game. Maybe we have played it mainly in our heads. But at some point in our lives, we have lived for the hours we have spent on real ice or its facsimile. Maybe all that separates those who go on to play professional hockey and those for whom hockey is a much-loved but occasional distraction is the degree to which hockey obsessed us in our youth. (Natural talent, of course, is a factor, but in our dreams, at least, we all can imagine ourselves as hockey stars.)

The kids who have gone on to play in the NHL didn't get there simply by going to their weekly league game or practice. They worked on it without even knowing they were working. There are basement walls still covered in black puck marks (as the foundation blocks and freezer are in Ottawa Senator Mike Fisher's parents' basement). There are dented garage and shed doors, new windows in place of shattered old ones, and countless forests of broken sticks to attest to their zeal. When the kids weren't playing the game, they were watching it on *Hockey Night in Canada*. And in Canada today, thousands of other kids are doing some of the same things. Not because they are made to do it, but because they can't help themselves.

Former Boston Bruin Stan Jonathan grew up in Ohsweken, near Brantford, Ontario, in the 1950s and 1960s. A creek still runs by his family homestead for about two miles, and the kids made good use of it when they were growing up. Stan, the middle child, didn't have skates or sticks or even pucks for much of the time when he was young. But that didn't stop him or others from creating their own version of hockey. They would go out and play on the frozen creek in their boots. They cut hickory limbs from trees for sticks and brought along a tin can. Stan says, "We played under the full moon once a month, all night long, with Carnation cream cans so we could hear it in the dark and find it in the snow. We'd scrape the stream of snow, all the kids, and we'd be outside all the time. We used boots for nets and they'd be filled with ice by the time we were done. Some sticks were just old lacrosse sticks, others were from a tree. It was fun, a good time. It was like field hockey or road hockey but on the ice." As soon as they got skates, which Stan did at the age of eleven, they'd join the others skating the length of the creek. "We'd skate for hours," he says. "We'd skate to see if anyone else was around and then skate back."

Former Petes captain and star of the junior national team, Brent Tully, started skating on Chemong Lake, about ten minutes from Peterborough, when he was four years old. His parents used to take him and his younger sister on weekend visits to see relatives and join other adults and kids to play on the outdoor ice. "We'd shoot the puck down the ice and it would go on forever. I still remember the snowbanks. We'd put people into them and get pushed into them. We'd go there whenever the weekends allowed it," he says. They also made use of the frozen Trent Canal, a haven for both young and old skaters, where he got his first shiner after being hit in the eye by a stick.

When future NHL star Steve Chiasson was about four years old, the family moved from near Barrie to a rural area just outside Peterborough, his mother Betty's hometown. Shortly after they got settled, his father, Joe, bought Steve a pair of bobskates – those skates with two parallel blades strapped to boots or shoes – to try out on a frozen swamp nearby.

Steve's oldest sister, Sue, vividly remembers those days, as she related in an interview after his death in 1999. "I'd be getting off the school bus and he'd be standing at the bus stop waiting for me with his skates on. I'd have to take him right down to that swamp, and he'd stay for as long as he could. I remember the kids at the swamp would be teenagers, but he didn't care, he just wanted to skate. I'd have to pick him up to carry him home, his little skate blades kicking into my legs."

Fredericton-born Danny Grant started skating on a small pond behind his parents' house in Barker's Point, New Brunswick. His parents weren't into sports, so Danny used his mother's skates for a while. A few socks stuffed in the boots made them tight enough for his small feet. Danny knows that in the unstructured environment of pond hockey, you didn't need coaches, you didn't need a schedule, you just went outside and played. "That's how we learned our skills. There were no systems, no dump-and-chase. We loved to rag the puck."

Pond hockey has its perils. Long-time Cannington resident Al McPhail remembers how frustrating it could be. "One time we decided we'd scrape the old millpond and have games there," he says. "So the kids and adults all scraped the snow off the pond, which took a lot of work. We even made some metal nets. There were no boards, but we thought it would be great. We just got everything looking good and sure enough" – and he breaks into a good-natured laugh – "the ice thawed."

In Thistletown, near Toronto, Craig Ramsay says that, in the winter, neighbourhood kids gathered at a creek – an offshoot of the Humber River – that ran along the end of his street. The kids would go there in the early winter, toss rocks onto the ice surface to see if it was hard enough to get on yet. They'd take shovels to the creek when they knew the ice was right, push back the snow, and use the creek as much as they could.

"We knew it wouldn't last and wanted to make the most of it," he says. "We'd take two-by-fours and set them on the ice for posts, which probably lasted until someone slid into them and wiped them out."

If there wasn't a truly natural surface available, of course, a resourceful father could always make one. Garnet MacLeish, father of Rick and Dale, saw the boys' love for skating and knew what had to be done. Dale says, "Dad worked until midnight. He would come home and water the rink. We had no lights, but we'd be out there before our parents got up, before breakfast. We had to be quiet or our parents would have killed us. They didn't know we were out there. It was a little rink, smaller than an in-ground swimming pool, but it was fun.

"We just wanted to skate. We'd be on the ice all day and night. We'd just come in to eat – stand right inside the door where there was a table. We'd gulp the food down and go back out again."

The boys had been on skates since age two, about a year after they could walk. They would skate wherever they could find ice, but because the midgets and juveniles dominated the natural ice surface of the only village rink, the MacLeishes either skated outside on Dad's rink or at the millpond. Occasionally they'd sneak into the curling rink their grandfather managed. "We could go in there and skate anytime we wanted to," remembers Dale.

Herb Raglan started skating at age three in the backyard rink his dad made. "You could buy a kit at Canadian Tire," remembers Herb, "and fold it end over end into the snow. It was just ten by six feet. We all learned to skate by pushing a chair around, but I still can't skate well. Even when I got to the NHL, they sent me to power skating."

Hockey was played wherever you could find the ice. The neighbourhood the Raglans lived in had a park with a rink, boards, and lights. "When I got to be eight I'd hose the park myself," says Herb with some pride. He and neighbour Steve Chiasson used to plug up a creek, damming it so they could freeze the water for about four feet all around to see if they could play on it. More often than not, they'd fall through and run home soaked.

In Bancroft, Ontario, during the 1950s, Bryan Watson and the neighbourhood kids would never forget the backyard rink his dad built every winter. "My brothers and I, along with Dad, skated every day in our yard," Bryan says. "We played hockey every day in the winter, baseball all summer – that's the way it worked."

Former Pete Bill Evo grew up in Michigan, the first American-born player to play with the Petes. From an early age, he was aware of the differences between the two countries. He would have played hockey more often, he says, but "we couldn't get ice time; that was the difference between me and Canadian kids. American boys, we only had two arenas in the whole area." Every winter, to help overcome the ice shortage, his father, a war veteran, created an outdoor rink about one hundred by forty feet, with boards and lights. Bill recalls, "We'd scrape it, hose it, all the neighbourhood kids would play on it. Everything I knew about hockey [came] from there and we went through it all, injuries, broken windows. To this day a fence still stands with curves in the pickets from me shooting pucks every morning and playing hockey with my brothers."

Greg Millen's parents believed in the benefits of kids being outside, so when Greg was only one-and-a-half years old, his father made a skating rink, twenty by sixteen feet, on their outdoor concrete patio. "He loved to be out in the fresh air," his father, Ted, told me. Greg, like many others, learned to skate and keep his balance by pushing a chair around the tiny rink. Every winter for his first few years, that little rink was ready for him, and as Greg got older the other neighbourhood kids would shout through the street, "Millens have ice. Millens have ice!"

It took Steve Larmer, age three, all of twenty minutes to learn to skate when he was let loose on the backyard rink his father built in the winter of 1964. The Peterborough native and future NHL scoring star was sporting a pair of used bobskates. Don Larmer, who didn't play much hockey growing up but did save his first skates from his Haliburton-area farm days, has no idea why he flooded the small backyard to make a twenty-by-twenty-foot rink. He'd be outside late at night and early in the morning, watering the surface in the cold, bitter weather. His wife, Doris, says the rink turned out to be a good babysitter because they could watch their kids through their kitchen window.

The Larmers lived in a brick bungalow in a new part of Peterborough with houses lining both sides of the street. The neighbourhood was full of people just like them – young couples with small babies and young children.

That first skate was the beginning of an almost daily winter ritual for Steve, younger brother Jeff when he turned three, sister Donna, and an assortment of neighbourhood children. "There were some days the rink was just covered in kids. That's where you learned to stickhandle," says Steve.

By the time Steve was five, the Killen family had moved next door. "I met [Steve] when we were outside on our trikes," remembers Brian "Gabby" Killen.

Gabby and Doug McVety, an older boy who lived across the street, would play on the Larmer rink all day. If they weren't on the ice, they were on the road or driveway. The kids on the street learned a lot of their hockey playing outdoors. "Whoever got the puck went with it," says Steve. "You learned a lot about skating, stickhandling. We didn't have summer hockey schools and didn't want any. When hockey was over, we grabbed the next equipment, baseball or lacrosse, and away we went. We did go to Mrs. [Joan] Martin's skating school in the fall a few times, where we couldn't skate with sticks . . . we didn't like that but it did us a world of good."

Jeff, also an NHLer, remembers those days fondly. "I think it's why Steve has the good hands. We'd play morning, noon, and night. We'd play one-on-one, hog, keepaway, and take shots. Mom would lace up our skates and away we'd go."

As in so many other Canadian households, hockey madness reigned. Doris Larmer, the boys' mother, remembers, "I'd put some paper down on the floor and they'd eat their lunch with their skates on and then go right back out."

Steve says, "On school days I'd throw the skates over the shoulder and go to the rink before school. We'd take them off to go into the school, and at noon put them right back on, and again right after school. On Saturdays we'd be gone for eight hours or for as long as we could." When it was dark and time to come home, their parents turned the back porch light off and on to signal them.

Larry Murphy says, "It was outdoors on the rink where we learned the game. The ice surface was small and it had lots of kids, so you had to learn to handle the puck in small areas. There wasn't much room and you held on to the puck, and every game we played was a game of the Stanley Cup finals."

"Ed knew how important skating was," says Doris Murphy, referring to Larry's father. Ed made a deal with Larry that he could play road hockey in the winter as long as he skated backwards around their rink a certain number of times beforehand.

Steve Chiasson's father, Joe, seeing Steve's interest in the sport, built a rink for him behind their house. Joe, who now lives in a retirement home near Peterborough, remembers how short the season was. "Ice didn't hold for very long. When we were kids [growing up in Nova Scotia] it would last all winter, but then [when Steve was a kid in Peterborough] the frost didn't hold. I'd water it when I got home from work at night. A neighbour's kid, Dean Haig, would bring his net over, and Steve also had a net. The rink was good enough to play shinny with six kids on it."

Maybe the Carolina Hurricanes' Eric Staal has the ultimate outdoor rink.

Several miles outside the city limits of Thunder Bay, Ontario, there is a hundred-by-eighty-foot outdoor ice sheet with boards, lines, nets, lights, and a room designed like a hockey dressing room, complete with nameplates above places on the bench where the three boys, who got to enjoy this rink of splendour, pushed on their skates, laced them up, and went out into the freezing air to play the greatest game on earth, ice hockey.

Eric's dad, a farmer, former Lakehead University hockey player, and a hockey fan, built his kids a backyard outdoor rink in the 1990s. This was not just any rink but a regulation-size surface for the boys to use when they were finished their school work and chores. And the three Staal boys – Eric is the oldest – make good use of it.

Petes' general manager Jeff Twohey remembers how the fifteen-year-old's eyes "lit up when he talked about that outdoor rink at his farm. . . . When I went to see the rink it was night, about forty below, and way out in the country. The dad went to the garage and turned on the rink's lights. As soon as he did, the kids came out to play."

For those whose fathers do not provide a private, full-size backyard rink, there comes a point when the backyard rink is no longer enough. Outdoor rinks in schoolyards and neighbourhood parks once provided the only ice surface. Former New York Rangers captain and long-time Peterborough resident Red Sullivan, for example, played in a school league when he was growing up in Peterborough: twelve games and no practices, all on outdoor ice. He never played inside an arena when he was growing up.

Kirkland Lake's Plager brothers had long, cold winters, and every school and mine had a rink. The Plagers had a rink almost in their backyard – the one that belonged to the school just behind their house. Billy Plager, the youngest of the brothers, who started skating at two, says, "Every day we were on them. We played hockey there in grade one. We had to clean off the ice – that was our power skating, pushing the snow around. We had to maintain the ice if we were going to play on it. If we weren't on the hockey rink, we were out playing in the streets from sunrise to sunset. We played shinny; that's where the skills came from and playing all the time."

Former NHLer Doug Evans grew up in Peterborough in the 1970s and usually had an instant team to play with at their outdoor rink in Turner Park. This was a piece of city-owned green land half a block from the Evans household, and one of the more popular outdoor rinks in Peterborough's hockey history.

Dougie was at the park almost every day, even though he was only four or five, and most of the time he played with and against kids much older than he was. His younger brother, Kevin, or four older brothers, Mark, Dave, Brian, and Paul, would be there with other kids from the working-class neighbourhood. They'd want to pick sides and someone would usually yell, "Second captain, first choose." No one really knows how this saying got started, but one kid would usually want to be captain and yell out his intention, so another would yell, "Second captain, first choose," meaning he was willing to be captain of another team but wanted to have the first pick, usually the best kid, for his team.

And Dougie, fair-skinned and blond, the kid with the Dennis the Menace smile, would usually be picked last. "I didn't want to be the last," he says. "I never wanted to be last, and when I was picked last it would make me try harder. I wanted to show them how good I was, and I knew I had to be better than them so that they wouldn't choose me last." But he had another challenge: to be better than his brothers, whom he had admired from an early age.

The Evans boys hit the ice every day it was there, running the fifty or so yards from their house, across the pavement, with their skates on, hoping any snow had already been shovelled so they could just glide onto the sheet of ice. They wouldn't leave until someone, a parent or sister, came to get them. On weekends, it wasn't unusual for them to be on the ice for eight, ten, even twelve hours.

"They wouldn't come home," said their father, Paul, who has died since we talked with him.

"But it was at Turner Park that I learned the most," says Doug. "I attribute my success to playing there all the time, against older kids. I wanted to be better than all of them. I look at the kids playing electronic games now and it has polluted our kids. They are probably better on video hockey than the real thing," he says, shaking his head sadly.

As for future goaltender and broadcaster Greg Millen, he and his friends eventually outgrew his backyard rink and drifted a few blocks away to a nearby park where there was a rink with boards and a shovel left behind to clear the snow-covered ice. For the first few years, the city of Don Mills parks department made the ice, but later it became the volunteer job of Frank and Willie Evans, adults from the neighbourhood. When the kids got older, many of them, including Greg, took midnight shifts flooding the ice.

"That's where we really learned to skate and handle the puck," says Greg. "There was a ton of kids playing on the rink."

Former Petes and NHL coach Gary Green, who is now a television hockey analyst, grew up in Tillsonburg in the 1950s and 1960s. At Harry and Margaret Green's two-hundred-acre farm, the children, two sons and a daughter, skated on anything, from frozen puddles to the creek that ran under a bridge near the farm. They also skated behind the barn, where they would use the "hardest" deposit from the cows for a puck. Gary says, "We even skated on frozen cow piss behind our barn. It was great when it was frozen (don't try it when it's not!). We were only four or five, but it was fun. Dad would take us to some Junior B games in Tillsonburg as a treat. One day he picked us up at school and took us to the rink. He had rented the ice just for my brother, Randy, and me."

André Lacroix of Lauzon, Quebec, remembers, "There was usually so much snow there. We'd go home at 11:45, have a hot lunch, get our skates on, carry our shoes in our hands, go back to school. Every school had an outdoor rink then, and we'd skate until we had to go back into school. On heavy snow days we'd shovel the snow off [the rink]. After school we'd skate until it got dark. Sometimes I'd be alone on the ice. It was great."

By the time future Montreal Canadiens general manager Bob Gainey was five, he was skating in used skates on outdoor rinks in his neighbourhood and on the Trent Canal. Perhaps he'd become intrigued as a child. His mother, Ann, remembers pushing Bob in his carriage to the outdoor rink, where she would skate and he'd sit watching. Whatever the reason, he was drawn to hockey not long after he'd learned to skate.

In the winter, Bob would search out ice to play on after school and on weekends. He says that looking back it seems as if they were skating all the time, but really there was no ice in the park until at least mid-December. The ice would stay until about February. "We'd stay at the rink all day Saturday," says boyhood friend John Swann. "We'd get up early and shovel the snow off the ice at seven or eight in the morning." They'd play for hours, take a break for a hot chocolate at a local store ("crawling on our hands and knees to the counter because we still had our skates on"), and head back to the rink until dark. They even played some shinny above the liftlock because there was always one wall behind them and they wouldn't have to chase the puck.

Of course, even in the colder parts of Canada, the frost can't be depended on much past February. Hockey-mad kids have to find other ways to play their game. And, of course, the biggest game in towns all across Hockey Nation after the ice has melted is road hockey. Who can forget the evenings when parents used to have to call you in off the streets? Who doesn't remember taking off your coat and shirt and going bareback on cool autumn or late-spring days, as the games got longer and more heated?

Maybe there would be three kids, maybe twenty kids, each trying to get the tennis or rubber ball between the two rocks or boots at either end of the street rink. Sometimes we used pucks, but the pavement wasn't as smooth as ice, and besides, there was always the no-raisers rule. We probably got more exercise chasing the ball down the street than we did actually playing the game. And there were always the interruptions, when someone stopped the game by yelling, "Car!" – unless of course you were the kids who played with young Red Sullivan when he was growing up in Peterborough in the 1930s. Cars weren't a problem in those days. Childhood friend Herb Heffernan says, "Hockey would start in September with road hockey. There were no cars, so the games would not have to be stopped and the police would leave us alone. We would use a tennis ball. We all had tennis balls because the ladies at the Quaker Club tennis courts would hit them over the fence at night and wouldn't go get them, so we would find them."

More than thirty years later, Peterborough kids were still hitting the streets. Herb Raglan remembers that "road hockey was non-stop. There were a gazillion kids. Mom and Dad worked, we'd play right after school, then we'd come home for supper, wait for the street lights to come on, then we'd play on the street again."

It wasn't much different in Kirkland Lake, where the winters were colder and the mining companies all had outdoor rinks. Often, parents grabbed sticks and came out to play as well. Billy Plager, who grew up there in the late 1940s and 1950s, puts it this way: "Hockey there was a religion. God, if you didn't play you were an outcast." He goes on: "We were never in the house to watch TV or listen to the radio. We were out on ice or in the streets; even the families played. Our street was a dead end and everyone was out there playing hockey, even Mom and Dad."

The MacLeish boys grew up in the 1950s and 1960s on York Street, in Cannington, a dead end off the main street. That street, which became known as MacLeish Alley, was ideal for playing road hockey, which Dale and Rick loved to do.

Another future NHL player, Doug Jarvis, still has a note stuck in a scrapbook at the Jarvis family home that gives us some insight into his character. He typed it on his mother's old Underwood typewriter, and then left it on the kitchen table. He was only about nine years old, a kid with light reddish hair laboriously punching away at the keys. Here's what he typed:

Dear Mom
Please forgive me for breaking one of your kitchen windows, but the other one is not broke. I feel I should give you the two dollars and I will give you the money I get for shoveling snow until the window is paid for
Your son
Douglas

That in a nutshell is Doug Jarvis. A good kid, a good teen, a good man.

About the time Steve Yzerman's family moved to Nepean, Ontario, the future star player was becoming even more focused on hockey than he had been as a little kid. He and his brother would play road hockey on their street, day and night, or use the nearby empty Loblaws parking lot for games on Sundays. (Ontario grocery stores were not allowed to open on Sunday in the 1970s. The switch to Sunday opening made a lot of street-hockey space suddenly unavailable.) Steve continued to play those road-hockey games every year, including the summer after his first NHL season.

And there was the king of road hockey in Scarborough, maybe even in Canada, Mike Ricci. What other kid, when he was only six and seven, had to spot the other, older team of road-hockey warriors two goals before the game started? The San Jose Sharks' Ricci didn't stop playing in the road after he quit being a kid, but continued as a teen when he was playing for the Petes. Mike was more kid than adult. After school he'd be out on the street in Peterborough playing road hockey with ten-, eleven-, and twelve-year-olds. He and Tie Domi both hit the road in those days, chasing tennis balls, checking kids, carrying them on their backs, having the time of their lives. Ricci also called his parents every day, not because he was homesick, but because family was important. His family attended every home game and many of his away games.

When everyone else has gone home, aspiring hockey players keep playing. They set up targets against a backyard fence or basement wall. They just never quit.

Future NHLer Danny Grant rifled pucks at an old tire outside the house in Barker's Point. Shot after shot after shot, trying to get the puck through the tire. The more he shot, the better he got. Mickey and Dick Redmond shot pucks off plywood in their back-yard or in their garage. They took so many shots they went through three sheets of plywood a year. When he wasn't working, Joey Johnston spent his time in Peterborough's old Memorial Centre parking lot, shooting at the fence, trying to shoot hard enough so the pucks would come back to him and he wouldn't have to walk up and get them.

Future NHL player, coach, and general manager Bob Gainey grew up in Peterborough too. He says, "The dreams and passions to play were with us all at seven or eight." When he was that young his uncle Joe made a net for him out of wood and burlap and Bob and his brothers used it for road hockey or just to take shots in the drive-way. During the 1960s in Scarborough, Larry Murphy's dad, Ed, built Larry a board with a net outside so he could shoot pucks, not so much to make sure he practised his shooting, but to save their garage door. His father wouldn't allow him to take slapshots; he believed the wrist shot should be learned first. Larry didn't practise slapshots until after he was twelve.

Steve Chiasson's dad, Joe, also noticed the after-effects of his son's practice sessions. Steve was in the habit of placing a sheet of plywood on the driveway and taking shots at the garage. Joe says, "One day I came home and saw the doors of the garage and said, 'Jesus, Steve, look at my doors.'" They were covered in puck and ball marks. Not long after this, Steve moved his shooting to the backyard, and the cement foundation of the house took a beating instead of the garage.

Herb Raglan, growing up in Peterborough in the 1960s, remembers that when he wasn't watching hockey or playing outdoors, he would take his stick and pucks to the basement and drive shots against the wall for hours. He drew a net on the wall and set a soup can on a string tied to the ceiling in front of it. He'd shoot to hit the can or the net, but he must have had his share of misses because his dad finally had to board up all the basement windows because Herb was breaking them. "I don't know why I'd be down there. They'd all be up watching TV and I'd be down there for hours taking full slappers."

Former Montreal Canadiens star and now coach of the American Hockey League's Hamilton Bulldogs, Doug Jarvis, grew up in Brantford in the 1950s and 1960s. His mother remembers freckle-faced Doug indulging his passion for the game by playing hockey in the basement. "We had an old tool table about fifteen feet long and [Doug and older brother Howie] used that as the goal. They had goal pads, and at first they'd take shots on each other with pucks, but it was too dangerous, so it was mainly balls they'd use." The light-coloured walls of the basement soon turned black. "He'd spend hours down there, shooting backhand, forehand. If [he] wasn't down there, he was out in the driveway shooting a bucket of pucks at picket fences, knocking out the slats. We'd be trying to replace the slats as quick as could be and he'd knock them out again."

Greg Millen grew up near Toronto in the 1960s and 1970s. When his parents went shopping, Greg would go to stay with his grandfather. The youngster, probably seven or eight, and grandfather would go to the basement with its tile floors and set up goalposts – piles of books – and shoot at each other.

"As he got older," says his mother, "he got some little goalie pads and used them on that floor. He'd be jumping up and down off his knees."

Sometimes Greg played left-handed and other times right-handed, switching hands like a magician with his cane. "Someone told Dad that right-handed shooting would be better, but I still caught baseball with the other hand."

During the same era as Millen, Steve Larmer and his brother Jeff, both NHLers, made the basement their part-time home when it was too late to be outside playing. Don Larmer was a big Leafs fan and usually watched *Hockey Night in Canada* on Saturday nights, but the boys were more interested in the game they were playing themselves. Sometimes they'd be down in the basement wearing their skates and guards and shooting at one another. Other times sister Donna would get called down to be their goalie. The boys would dress her in shin pads, ball glove, catcher's mask, chest protector, and whip shots at her.

"It would take only a few minutes," remembers Donna, "before the puck would be coming at my head. They'd use me for target practice and I'd always end up crying."

Injuries were always a possibility, and roughhousing was pretty much a constant. Larry Murphy's career as a basement hockey player was brief. "We used to play some hockey in the basement of the house," he says, "but my brother chipped his tooth one day and that was the end of that."

When NHL superstar Chris Pronger was growing up in Dryden, Ontario, in the 1970s and 1980s, his father, Jim, remembers, the boys, already bigger for their age than most kids, "would be in the basement with a tennis ball, playing full-body-contact hockey." More than once their parents had to replace the wall panelling. As the boys got older, they were so competitive they frequently fought, going at each other like two bulls. Finally, the parents had to force them to quit the basement game.

Other kids didn't bother moving downstairs with their games as kitchen hockey was also popular across Canada. They played anywhere, anytime. Former Pete Joey Johnston remembers, "Our real entertainment was playing hockey in the hallways of the house. There were kids in every doorway, including sister Mary Ann, who would play net."

Their mother, Kay, remembers those days well. "I used to just shut the doors and let them go. They never did any real damage." She points to the kitchen table-and-chair set as proof: it is the same set the Johnstons brought into their house in 1945.

Joey's friend Dick Meredith also remembers those times. "Every Saturday night we'd be at the Johnstons', except when it was their parents' euchre night. We'd have these mini-tournaments during *Hockey Night in Canada* intermissions. We used this little rubber ball, like the core of a golf ball. The hallway would only be about thirty inches wide. We'd be on our hands and knees, our pants rubbing against the floor and in sock feet. We'd play all night."

Hockey culture has changed over the years. There are fewer kids on our streets playing hockey – if anything, they're likely to be practising their skateboard skills. The game has become more structured. Kids like to play where the adults aren't, and much of the minor hockey now is where adults are.

Hockey schools are big everywhere. There are winter and summer schools in most cities and towns. Organizing kids' sports has become a national pastime.

Greg Millen was in one of the first hockey camps in Ontario, long before it was just exclusively for hockey, before camps became schools. In 1966, when he was nine, he was one of the first kids to register for a week at Haliburton Haven, a brand-new hockey camp run by Jim Gregory and Wren Blair, who are well known in NHL circles. It was a camp for kids wanting to learn hockey in the summer, but they also played baseball and volleyball. The camp was held in August, just before hockey tryouts.

"My first instructor was none other than Johnny Bower," Greg says, smiling warmly at the memory. "That was a big deal. He taught me how to poke-check." One can only imagine his excitement, any kid's excitement, when he met a man he had watched on *Hockey Night in Canada*.

Bernie Parent also taught him. "I had the thrill years later, when he was ending his career, to be playing against his team and told him, 'You're the reason I'm here.'"

"Greg was registered at the camp for only one week," his mother, Barb, says. "We came back to pick him up and he wanted to stay another week, but it was full, so the next year we put him in for two weeks." The camp was one of the first of its kind in the world, and Greg attended it for its first four summers. Greg wrote to his parents from the camp:

> As always I am having a great time. Bernie Parent is not here this week. He supposedly went to get married. He chickened out because he had a throught [*sic*] operation. Like last year there will be a parade and a fair with rides. I am going to be in our float playing golf. Today we had a meet the stars day when all the stars came to the camp. They had a baseball against the counslers [*sic*] and the hockey stars.
> Well, I will try to write again touch wood!
> Bye, Greg
> SOS: I need some bubblegum and some candy.

While at camp he was making an impression on the instructors. One of them wrote on his summer report card, "Skating is the most important part of goaltending and Greg does well. He is a good skater. He moves his feet very well and has exceptional range for a boy his age." Another commented, "He relaxes a bit too much when the puck is in the other end."

Gary Green was a university student from 1971 to 1973. Those were busy years for Gary. He was accepted at the University of Guelph, where he studied psychology. In the summers he continued to take his university courses, but he also worked at a hockey school that Roger Neilson started in Tillsonburg. Then, after graduation and giving up on a pro hockey career, he worked at a hockey school in Belleville and, still later, he started one of his own in Peterborough.

During the summer of 1987, current NHL goalie Zac Bierk went to the Dave Dryden goalie school in nearby Omemee. By 2002 he was offering his own goalie school in Peterborough.

From about the 1970s, power-skating schools were common. Now much of what they taught has been incorporated in the programs offered by hockey schools. Arena hockey is usually the order of the day, with a more structured, disciplined approach to the game, but thankfully many Canadian communities, and U.S. border towns, are still speckled with kids playing on outdoor rinks and in roads. And lone shooters continue to while away the hours in a parking lot with a brick wall to send their shots back to them.

Hockey anywhere, anytime, any way you can. That was, and is, a Canadian tradition.

Another tradition started in 1953 with the first televised NHL hockey game.

He shoots! He scores!

Every Saturday night, across Canada (and in Newfoundland, as Foster Hewitt told radio listeners in the days before the island province joined Confederation), a tradition as invariable as Sunday-morning church service was established: the 8:00 p.m. hockey broadcast. Back in the 1950s and 1960s, the game was joined when it was already in progress. We hated that. We were just kids and couldn't wait for the game to begin. We wouldn't throw a piece of popcorn into our mouths or touch the soda or ice-cream floats until one of the Hewitts, either Foster or Bill, or Danny Gallivan threw out their first words to millions of Canadians.

We started watching *Hockey Night in Canada* on a small black-and-white television, the only tube in the house. We would lie on the floor, elbows propping up our heads, tired from a full day of road hockey, and watch our heroes from the six-team NHL: Howe, Ullman, Delvecchio, Richard, Harvey, Plante, Keon, Bucyk, Hull, Hall, Sawchuk. The CBC was the only station we got: this was long before cable, satellites, and the dreaded craziness of converters. Once the game started, that was the station the family watched. We wouldn't just watch our favourite team or player, but also Ward Cornell as he interviewed our sweaty heroes, and Murray Westgate, the Esso man. We took it all in, and if we didn't fall asleep to awake later to the Indian-chief test pattern ending CBC broadcasting, we went to bed dreaming of our favourite team, wanting to wear what they wore, and have hair cut just like theirs.

The next day we couldn't wait to get out on the road and try their plays, announcing the games as we played: "Keon back to Baun.

Richard picks off the pass. Oh! Bower has kicked it out. Backstrom gets the rebound. He shoots! He scores!"

Life couldn't be better.

And the future NHL stars were just like us.

André Lacroix, grew up watching the CBC's hockey broadcasts in Quebec. "I remember watching *Hockey Night in Canada* on our parents' tiny black-and-white TV," he says. "I'd copy the NHL players. There were only six teams then, and if I heard they ate steaks the day of a game, then that's what I would have to have. But I was raised a Catholic, and we could only eat fish on Fridays. I asked the priest if I could eat meat on Fridays. He tried to convince me I couldn't, but I'd have steak anyway."

Hockey Night in Canada was broadcast just once a week, on Saturday nights, in those far-off days. Craig Ramsay grew up watching Canada's most popular television show near Toronto. He saved NHL players' pictures cut out of the old *Weekend Magazine*, which featured a different player every week. He collected hockey cards and marvelled at the players' statistics. He also collected plastic coins from Shirriff dessert boxes. Saturday-night games of *Hockey Night in Canada* were a fixture as he got older. "The game came on at 8:30 and was joined in progress. I'd pray for a big brawl in the first period or some other disaster so not much of the first period would be over when the game came on," he recalls.

Americans living near Canada's border also watched the program. Future Pete, lawyer, and Detroit Red Wings president Bill Evo says, "Back home every Saturday night they'd watch *Hockey Night in Canada* on the only TV station they got – the CBC."

Greg Millen had no idea, when he was growing up near Toronto, that he would later not only play in front of the cameras but be a regular Saturday-night hockey analyst for the big show. When he was young, his parents would let him watch one period, but as he got older, he graduated to watching two periods and then the whole game.

It was during these Saturday nights that his focus on goalkeeping was sharpened. "I was a forward first, but the more I watched . . . the more I was influenced by Johnny Bower of the Toronto Maple Leafs. I had an attraction to that."

Greg's mother remembers him standing around in the goalie's stance or out on the ice holding his arms out like a goalie. "This is how they do it," he'd tell her.

Peterborough's Doug Evans would also play in the NHL one day. His brother Paul made the Petes when Doug was only six. "I can remember when Paul played for the Petes," says Doug. "I wanted to do the same thing, and when we'd all sit on the floor with our chips and pop for Saturday night's *Hockey Night in Canada*, I'd see those players on the screen and say, 'Someday I'd like to be on there, too.'"

NHL star Chris Pronger watched it growing up in Dryden. "Every kid's dream was to play in the NHL," says Chris. "I was no different. It wasn't life and death when I was eight, but I wanted to play. *Hockey Night in Canada* was on every Saturday night. My brother and I would be in the basement playing ball hockey and watching the game and trying to do what they did on TV."

Former NHLer and Peterborough native Herb Raglan might sum it up best when asked if he dreamed about playing in the NHL in those days of the 1960s.

"Are you kidding me? I dreamed it non-stop. Every Saturday night I had my Hires root beer and ice-cream float and watched the games on TV. It was all we ever did on Saturday nights. All I wanted to do was play in the NHL. Everybody dreamed of it."

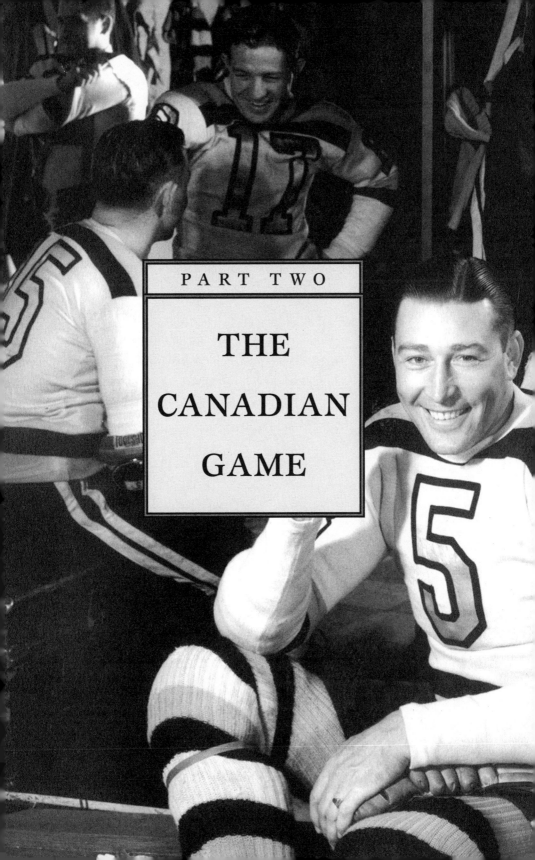

PART TWO

THE CANADIAN GAME

Looking Back

Peterborough was once a big factory town, dominated by General Electric, but most of its citizens now work in health, education, tourism, telemarketing, and white-collar jobs. Although the city has changed over the years, the hockey tradition hasn't.

Hockey was introduced to Peterborough more than a hundred years ago. In 1892, when the Edison Company (which became General Electric) encouraged its employees to play sports, a hockey league of four adult outdoor teams was formed. Two years later, with seven players per team and a wooden puck, Peterborough, under the name the Peterboroughs (the name Petes was first used in 1884 by the town's field-lacrosse team and later adopted by various community sports teams, but most consistently by senior, then junior, hockey teams) captured its first junior-hockey championship defeating a Toronto team.

Other sports, such as curling, cycling, lacrosse, and boating, were played in Peterborough before hockey was introduced, but residents were skating on the frozen Otonabee River and what would later form the Trent Canal, both running through the town, and Little Lake, located in its centre, as early as 1850. By 1863, people of all ages and both sexes were skating on the lake and in the bays, holding carnivals and speed-skating events. The first indoor rink was built in 1870 when the community took over an old flax mill and used it for curling on natural ice. In those days, most "indoor" rinks provided a roof over the ice but minimal protection from the elements for onlookers. The old mill was a distinct improvement on such minimal shelters.

Volunteers with a willingness to go the extra mile have always been strong in Peterborough. (In 2004, there were two thousand volunteers in the local United Way campaign alone.) The community pushed the curling club to allow hockey to be played in the new rink, and by 1891 *The Peterborough Examiner* was declaring that hockey was "an up and coming sport." Early in the following year, on January 4, 1892, the first indoor hockey game, between the Edison Volts (an Edison Electric men's team) and the town team (a group of Peterborough men), was played at the curling club.

By 1893, with the insistence of George Cox, who later became mayor and had also played the key role in getting Thomas Edison to move his company to Peterborough, the Peterboroughs team was formed to play in the Ontario Hockey Association (OHA). The association played only exhibition games. By its rules, teams had seven players and allowed no substitutes. There were no lines painted on the ice, and only posts for goals.

The rules of hockey weren't formalized until 1875 and the first organized game wasn't recorded until 1879. The game started to become popular across Canada as an organized sport in the decade that followed. Peterborough mirrored the rest of the country in this respect. The rules, of course, have changed and evolved over time. Hockey had no lines until blue lines were painted on the ice in 1918. The red line was added in 1943.

The Stanley Cup was donated by Canada's governor general, Lord Stanley, as a prize for which amateur teams could compete. He first presented it to a Montreal team on March 22, 1893. That game was played outdoors using a wooden puck. The "boards" were snowbanks and the teams had nine players on each side.

Peterborough's first superstar came to town when the Whitcroft family arrived from Port Perry in 1891. Son Fred was only eight at the time of the move, and in the next few years he played unorganized hockey on the lake and in city parks. When he was fifteen he began playing for the Colts, one of four teams in a province-wide junior league. It was an important period in the town's hockey development. It was in 1898 that a Peterborough hockey delegation recommended to the young OHA that the junior age be capped at twenty, an age that still holds throughout Canada today. The town's population was only 11,000, but a thousand of them would come out to the Colts' home games. The Colts defeated Stratford 12-0 in a championship game in 1901, a game in which the 156-pound Whitcroft scored eight goals. Whitcroft was known throughout Ontario as one of province's fastest skaters. He played on the Peterborough intermediate hockey team in 1906 that won the provincial title. The competition was clearly not up to the mark: the Colts bowled over Brockville, Uxbridge, Parry Sound, and Goderich, one after the other, winning most games by more than five goals. The team was so good the Brockville newspaper suggested they could compete against senior teams for the Stanley Cup.

The first professional hockey league wasn't formed until 1903, when Pittsburgh, Sault Ste. Marie, Ontario, and its sister in Michigan, as well as Houghton and Alumet got together. The first pro players from Peterborough left the community in 1906 when its stars, Whitcroft and a Peterborough native, Bill Crowley, turned pro in Edmonton. After Edmonton's season ended, Whitcroft was asked to play for the Kenora Thistles in 1907 and became the first Peterborough player to compete for – and win – the Stanley Cup. The next year, as Edmonton's captain, Whitcroft scored an amazing 47 goals in 16 games, again going on to compete for the Stanley Cup, but losing this time.

In 1909 he went to play for the Renfrew Millionaires, a hand-picked team that included Cyclone Taylor, Newsy Lalonde, Lester and Frank Patrick, and Bert Lindsay. They challenged for the Cup twice, but the stacked team lost. Whitcroft retired as a player and went on to manage the Edmonton team before leaving for Vancouver, working in real estate and at the local racetrack. He died in Vancouver in 1931 and in 1962 was inducted into the Hockey Hall of Fame. Peterborough residents had followed his hockey escapades in the local paper, and the more enthusiastic fans, sometimes hundreds of them, would gather around a Teletype machine to get the results of their team's away games.

Whitcroft and Crowley's success strengthened the support for the Colts. However, the biggest hockey hero in town was hometown boy Lionel King, the son of a doctor. Lionel was billed by Toronto newspapers as one of the best hockey players in Ontario between 1894 and 1900. In 1894 his junior Peterborough team won the Ontario title, playing in front of more than seven hundred fans. The following year his intermediate Peterborough team went undefeated and beat Toronto for the Ontario championship in a 7-6 overtime game in which he scored five goals. These were the days of trains and sleighs, and eight hundred Peterborough fans made the trip to Toronto for the game by these and other methods. Peterborough fans had not only fallen for hockey, they were also taking ownership of their teams.

In 1898 the community invited a men's hockey team from Winnipeg to play the Colts in an exhibition game. When the team arrived by train, it was greeted by hundreds of fans who took them in sleighs for a tour around the town. That same year, the Colts joined the senior hockey league, which had ten teams in Ontario. In addition to the four-team adult league, Peterborough now had a junior, intermediate, and senior hockey team. Community people were also getting involved in an organizational capacity. Peterborough native George Horkins became the vice-president of the OHA and in 1899 Lionel King became the vice-president. King had been offered a position on an all-star team to tour the U.S., but declined in order to continue his education at the University of Toronto. Like his father, he became a doctor. Peterborough's association with the OHA continued, and three residents have been president – in 1918, 1932, and 1955.

The early 1900s saw local teams continue their successes, always backed by good sponsors and volunteers who not only got locals to play but imported players from other centres. These imported players would be given jobs in town to play hockey and often ended up staying in Peterborough, and in turn getting involved as volunteers in the local hockey scene.

In 1917 the National Hockey League was formed, and pro teams, looking for indoor facilities and artificial ice, became the better teams, robbing the senior and later even the junior leagues to recruit their players. The Stanley Cup became the NHL's emblem and prize in 1926.

By the early years of the twentieth century, hockey was well established in Peterborough, now a town with a population of about 20,000. In 1917, the Canadian 247th Battalion was stationed in Peterborough and its team played in the town that winter. The star of the team, "Jolly" Jack Adams, was top of the class in the OHA. Like many other top players who would follow him, he went on to bigger and better things in the world of hockey.

Adams went on to play in the NHL. In 1918, he was on the first NHL team – the Toronto Arenas – to win the Stanley Cup. He later led the Ottawa Senators to Cup victory in 1926-27, and then won three Cup championships while he was with the Detroit Red Wings as coach and another four titles while he was general manager, making him the only person to have his name on the Cup as a player, coach, and general manager. He was hired by Detroit on a handshake, without a written contract, and for the thirty-three years he remained with the team, he signed some of its biggest stars, including Gordie Howe, Ted Lindsay, Sid Abel, and Terry Sawchuk. Adams was inducted into the Hockey Hall of Fame in 1959.

Peterborough's senior team won the provincial championship again in 1926. The senior league in Ontario was by then the league that fed the NHL most of its players. Irvine "Ace" Bailey came to Peterborough in 1926 to play a season with its senior team. Although the team lost the championship in the final, Bailey, in a sign of things to come, led the team in scoring. He of course went on to become one of the Toronto Maple Leafs' leading scorers.

Bailey, who grew up in Bracebridge, Ontario, became part of hockey history on December 12, 1933, when the infamous Boston Bruin Eddie Shore, under the mistaken impression that Bailey had hit him, slammed him to the ice. Bailey's head hit the surface, and doctors examining him in the hospital afterward gave him no chance to live. A priest was called in to perform the last rites. Bailey surprised them all by surviving, but his playing career was over.

By the 1920s, a private firm had built a new rink in Peterborough, attracting more than a thousand people every game to watch the local senior team play on the natural ice surface. Blue-collar workers employed in the factories that had sprung up in Peterborough loved their hockey. The season usually didn't start until mid-November and ended in February, and the game was the most popular entertainment for many of the men in the city – for some, it was the only entertainment. (There were women's teams, too: a high-school team and a General Electric–sponsored team.) The local men were mostly spectators, but a few also played on the senior team. Two of them, Biffer Ranger and Bert McLeod, went on to play pro hockey in the East Coast League. McLeod returned to Peterborough to run a pharmacy. Ranger, who was invited to a Montreal Canadiens camp but never attended, returned to work as a tool-and-die maker at General Electric.

Although men's hockey continued to flourish, the Depression of the 1930s killed much of the spectator activity. The local boys still played the game, and in 1938 Ned Vitarelli and Norm Calladine played for the provincial champion Senior B team from Peterborough. That team drove from Peterborough to Niagara Falls for a playoff game, then left immediately after it to go to Goderich for another game, all by taxi. After the championship, the two of them went to the Eastern Amateur Hockey League to help Baltimore win the Walker Cup. Calladine went on to a solid pro career and even played in the NHL. Another Peterborough-born boy was Hank Blade. His family moved to Ottawa in 1928 when he was quite young, but Peterborough claimed him as their own – after all, his other relatives still lived in Peterborough.

The war and new owners led to the demise of the old hockey arena when the floor was covered with boards and the building transformed into a dance hall and wrestling ring. The owners knew hockey attracted crowds but decided that ice on the floor for four months was not financially viable. So the city now had no indoor hockey rink, and for seven years Peterborough teams were forced to play "home games" out of town. But this small setback didn't stop the boys from playing for, and winning, intermediate and Senior B provincial championships in the 1940s. The lake, the river, and the Trent Canal, along with numerous city parks flooded by the municipality, provided venues for hockey and skating. Peterborough's biggest future star, Red Sullivan, learned all his hockey on outdoor rinks, mainly playing unstructured shinny whenever and wherever he could. By the mid-1940s Peterborough's population was more than 30,000, and the community was looking for a new rink, especially for their Senior B team, now commonly known as the Petes.

A committee, once again of city volunteers, raised $100,000 locally, and the city built a small, two-dressing-room rink that opened in 1948. It had natural ice for the first year, and an ice plant was added the next year. The rink meant Peterborough could once again have three major teams and ice two Senior B teams and one Junior B team, all playing indoors. Seating was backless planks and there was no glass or wire around the boards, but that didn't stop more than two thousand people from attending each game.

The two Senior B teams, one sponsored by the local transport company, Toronto Peterborough Transport (TPT), played in the same league, creating a huge rivalry and a split in the community about whom to cheer for. This rivalry got more people out to the games, got more people talking about the games, and became the seed for a growth in men's and children's hockey. Hockey became so popular that the hockey community toyed with the idea of sponsoring a Senior A team or even a team in the now-popular Junior A league in Ontario. They pondered what to apply for, but knew their little wood-and-metal rink was not sufficient to attract a franchise, so just a few years after the small rink had been built, the community once again decided to build a bigger and better one, this time in memory of its war dead.

And once again, the local people came through, pledging more than $100,000 for the new Memorial Centre. Volunteers decided to go after a Junior A franchise. Plans for the 3,927-seat rink with a 1,100 standing-room capacity were approved and the rink was finished below budget at $960,000 in time for the beginning of the 1956 hockey season. (Times and costs change: the same rink was renovated in 2003 for more than $12 million, almost $1 million over budget.)

With the rink in place and with a community in love with hockey and rich in hockey tradition, a nucleus of volunteers already committed to its success, the stage was set for the coming of the Habs and the beginning of Peterborough's glory days as Hockey Town.

The Players (I)

AUBREY VICTOR "DIT" CLAPPER
Born in Newmarket, Ontario, February 9, 1907
Raised in Newmarket, Hastings, and Aurora
Hall of Fame NHL career with Boston

When the Boston Bruins moved from the old Boston Garden to the new FleetCenter, they brought with them a sweater bearing the number 5. A banner bearing the number now hangs between two others, Bobby Orr's number 4 and Phil Esposito's number 7, in the new arena. All three are retired forever.

The owner of that number 5 sweater did things Orr never did and never could have done. He was the first person to play twenty consecutive years in the NHL, all for Boston. He was the only person selected to a first All-Star Team in one year as a winger and in another as a defenceman. He was the first player to come back from a ruptured Achilles tendon to play again and make an All-Star Team. He was the first Bruin to have his sweater retired.

In addition to all this, Aubrey "Dit" Clapper was the only man to be selected to the Hockey Hall of Fame while still an active player – not even Wayne Gretzky can boast that. Here's how it happened.

Clapper quit as a player in the fall of 1946. The day after his last game, he became the Bruins' coach, even though he was still registered as a player. To celebrate his "retirement," the Bruins had

a big night for him on February 12, 1947. When he skated onto the
ice in his uniform, he received his Hockey Hall of Fame scroll from
Hall president Stuart Crawford. After the festivities at centre ice, he
skated off, changed into his civvies, and took up his place behind the
bench as coach.

Clapper had been a tough player. And at six-foot-two and 190
pounds, he was considered large in his playing days. Once, when he
was beating a player badly with his fists, the referee, Clarence
Campbell (who later became NHL president), pulled him off by the
hair – this was in the days before helmets. Clapper smacked him. He
later apologized to both Campbell and his opponent.

Clapper was the first in a long line of NHL players who had
strong connections to Peterborough. He was born in 1907 in
Newmarket, Ontario. His father, Bill, a lacrosse player, had grown
up near Peterborough in the little village of Hastings, and when
Aubrey was still a baby, the family moved back to Hastings for a few
years. Then they moved again, this time south of Newmarket, to
Aurora, where Aubrey started playing minor hockey for his school
and the local church league. By this time he was known as "Dit."
While he was just a toddler, he mispronounced his middle name,
Victor, as "Vitter." People thought he was saying "Ditter" and it went
from there.

When Aubrey was a teenager, father and son both played on an all-Ontario lacrosse championship team. In one game, Aubrey was knocked out by a hit on the head, and in a foreshadowing, perhaps, of the Campbell incident, the father hit the offender, knocking him out. He redeemed himself, however, by helping to revive not only his son but the fallen player, receiving cheers from the crowd.

Clapper played his youth hockey in pickup games on outdoor rinks in 1914 and 1915, joining the Oshawa juniors at age fourteen, just like Orr did almost fifty years later. At seventeen he was playing lacrosse in the summer and hockey in the winter. At eighteen he was playing for the Parkdale Canoe Club in Toronto when Boston scout Eddie Powers saw him and got him signed with the Bruins. Clapper never looked back. He was with the team when it won three Stanley Cup titles playing against the likes of Syl Apps, Busher Jackson, Joe Primeau, and Elmer Lach.

"When I played," Clapper told *The Peterborough Examiner* in 1975, "every team had a great line, and every team was loaded with stars. Now, only a few teams have the real exceptional players and that's because there are too many pro teams around.

"In my career you had to be a real star to make the pros."

Clapper never lost touch with Peterborough. He returned to the town most summers, and in 1946 he bought a business and home there. It's not surprising, then, that when he retired from the NHL in 1949, he returned to Peterborough to live. He opened a plumbing business, then a sporting-goods store. He maintained his connection to hockey as a member of the Peterborough Petes' executive from 1956 to 1960.

Sometimes in hockey the stories are more important than the statistics. It seems appropriate to end with such a story about Dit Clapper. While he was duck hunting one year in the autumn before another NHL season began, he and three other hunters were out in a canoe on the Trent River, which flows near Peterborough. The river was rough, and the canoe was swamped. It tipped and all four men fell into the river.

Soon the men began to weaken in the bitterly cold water and they struggled to cling to the canoe. Clapper removed his heavy clothes, hip waders, and pants, and swam half a mile to shore. He found a boat and rowed it back to save the lives of his three buddies. In towns like Peterborough, stories such as these, stories of bravery and heroic acts, are not overshadowed by the more public life of a skilled hockey player. Their sweaters may be retired, but their feats, both on and off the ice, are remembered.

Dit Clapper died in Peterborough at the age of seventy in 1978.

NORM CALLADINE
Born in Peterborough, July 30, 1916
NHL career with Boston

Norm Calladine was small, five-foot-nine and 155 pounds, a puny kid from Peterborough playing hockey in the Eastern Hockey League for the Baltimore Orioles in 1938. He played big, though, scoring 33 goals and 41 points for 74 points in 61 games that year.

A fluke? The following year he had 53 goals and 41 assists in only 53 games. The next year he was promoted to the American Hockey League. He kept scoring for the Providence Reds and did something in the AHL that no player had ever done there. On February 12, 1942, he scored six goals in a single game. He was finally noticed by the NHL when there was a shortage of regular players during the war years. By the time he was twenty-six in 1942, he had four years of pro experience and was playing for the Boston Bruins. In the 1943-44 season he scored 16 goals and 27 assists for 43 points in 49 games.

Calladine played only one full season for the Bruins. In all, he played 63 NHL games, scoring 19 goals and 29 assists for 48 points. Although he was a spunky lad, he didn't sit in the penalty box very often. In his nine seasons of pro hockey, he had only 41 minutes in penalties.

In 1945 he returned to the AHL and played only five games there. The next year he played 22 games for the EAHL and was gone. Today, few people in Peterborough remember him, but those who watched him found his tenacity and puck-handling skills hard to forget.

HANK BLADE
Born in Peterborough, April 28, 1920
NHL career with Chicago

His isn't a household name in the hockey world, so when Hank Blade died in Peterborough in 2003, his death went almost unnoticed. The family didn't even put an obituary in the newspaper.

However, there had been a time when Blade was a public figure, a star hockey player in Kansas City in the United States Hockey League, and a friend of NHL legend Gordie Howe. He was so popular in Kansas City, fans held an appreciation night, showering him with gifts.

Before turning pro, he was a member of the Allan Cup air force team, the best senior team in Canada in 1942.

Blade was born in the same area of Peterborough that future NHL stars Red Sullivan and Bob Gainey grew up in and where Dit Clapper retired. When he was a young boy, he played on the ice in city parks, but after his parents moved to Ottawa, he played more organized hockey.

As an adult he played hockey in the winter and worked the circuses all summer. While many of his hockey buddies lost weight during the winter hockey season and put it on during the summer months, Blade did the opposite because, he said, circus work was much harder than hockey.

Blade, a big strapping centre, played for teams such as the Ottawa Senators, then in the Quebec Senior League, and in Kansas City, Milwaukee, Pittsburgh, Vancouver, and Calgary, all minor pro cities in the 1940s. But he spent parts of two seasons during his Kansas City stint with its NHL team in Chicago, becoming one of only five Peterborough boys to play in the league before the 1950 era – the others were Sullivan, Clapper, Clare Raglan, and Norm Calladine.

After retiring from the United States circus circuit and hockey, Blade became a private man, living in Florida with his wife and two children. But something happened there that devastated this big strong circus man. A group of youths beat up his sixteen-year-old son, Hank Jr., so badly he would forever be confined to institutionalized nursing care. The father was heartbroken, but he promised to visit his son every day if possible.

He eventually moved his American family to his birthplace of Peterborough so his son could receive care in a nursing home he could afford, thanks mainly to Canada's health-care system.

When the story of the death of the eighty-three-year-old was published in *The Peterborough Examiner* in 2003, most of those who remembered him didn't know he was back home. Only his close family knew, including, of course, his son, who still lives in the nursing home. Today, the son has an urn on a table beside his bed. It contains some of the ashes of his father, the man who kept his promise and visited him every day, sometimes twice a day, for more than twenty years.

GEORGE "RED" SULLIVAN
Born in Peterborough, December 24, 1929
NHL career with Boston Bruins, Chicago Blackhawks,
  and New York Rangers

George "Red" Sullivan ("Red" because of his flaming hair) was born into the Great Depression of the 1930s. Its effect was as dev-astating on the Sullivan family as it was on many thousands of fam-ilies across the country. George's father, John Sullivan, a big strapping man, was one of the 1.5 million Canadians without a job. George's five sisters slept in one room while George, the youngest in the family, shared a room with his older twin brothers. George has no memory of the Depression, but his older sister, Mary, remem-bers her dad joining the corps of relief workers who together cut more than four thousand cords of wood to get fuel for their own and other families. He also swept city streets as part of the government-organized relief campaign.

Little George was oblivious to it all. He began to play sports as soon as he could walk and soon became a regular at the ball diamonds and the rinks, where older boys picked him for their teams – he was that good. When he was eight, he got his first pair of skates, a used

pair given to him by a neighbour. Although they were too big, he looked after them as if they were his best shoes, proudly keeping them by the family wood stove. He almost wore them out playing on the five neighbourhood outdoor rinks.

"I thought I had died and gone to heaven," he says of those days. All day he'd play shinny on free outdoor rinks with the neighbourhood boys and older teens. He also played outdoors for his elementary school's hockey team against other city schools. If he wasn't playing hockey, he was collecting hockey cards or Bee Hive honey caps with hockey players' pictures inside them.

Every Sunday morning the family headed to church, along with everyone else on his street. George was an altar boy for two years, but his sister Mary remembers how sports consumed her youngest brother's life. "I bought him a little baseball uniform through Quaker Oats one time. It came from Chicago. He put it on and would never take it off, except when we went to church, and then he would put it right back on. He wore it until it became rags.

"We were warm, had lots to eat, but we didn't have money for extras," she adds. Sullivan himself recalls, "We always had three square meals. It wasn't bacon and eggs in the morning like nowadays. Maybe some milk and bread or porridge, but whatever we had was good."

Fresh vegetables grew in their back garden, and eggs were gathered from chickens in the yard. Their mother baked bread. Everyone in the family knew how to play the piano, and even the sports fanatic George had learned to chord. Sometimes a dozen of those fresh eggs would be traded for piano lessons. Mrs. Ellis, the piano teacher, told their mother George was a natural if he would work at it, but sports got in the way. Mary says, "It was twelve eggs or thirty-five cents a lesson. Sometimes the whole family would gather around in the parlour singing and playing. Other times we'd sit around the radio listening to *Amos and Andy*.

"George was a real good boy. He was the baby so he usually got what he wanted," says Mary. As far as school went, his friend Mark O'Donoghue says, "Red never did homework. He never had time." Sullivan likes to say that the only thing that kept him from college was "not going to high school."

John Sullivan died at the age of fifty-two in 1940. Life remained hard for the family: the effects of the Depression were overtaken by the privations of war. Not least among these privations was the trans-formation of the only indoor rink in town into a dance and bingo hall and wrestling ring.

The sports equipment George used was mostly either hand-me-down or improvised. "We wore catalogues for shin pads and cut up old [inner] tubes for rubber bands to put around the catalogues. We'd pull up our socks and put our regular pants over them. We always used borrowed or found equipment. We didn't wear shoulder pads or helmets and the gloves we wore were whatever we had." He would get a new stick for Christmas. It would have to last him the year, and usually it did.

George would skip school to play hockey. He'd play anywhere, with anyone, at any time. When the guys he hung around with were getting part-time jobs, Red was down at the rink playing hockey. From these early days to his days in the NHL, he was always the first to arrive at the rink and usually the last to leave.

When he was fifteen, Sullivan and a friend hitchhiked to Windsor, Ontario, to try to talk the Red Wings into giving them a tryout. General manager Jack Adams, who had played senior hockey in Peterborough for a year in the 1920s, let them stay for five days before handing them each $25 and sending them home.

Sullivan's desire to play hockey remained undiminished. He quit school in grade nine and at sixteen was playing Junior B hockey and working in a factory making clocks. He knew he wasn't going to be there long, though. That winter a scout, Harold "Baldy" Cotton, walked into the Varsity Arena dressing room in Toronto where Sullivan was playing for Peterborough in an out-of-town game. Cotton gave him $50 to sign a form, making him the property of the Bruins, and sent him to St. Catharines.

That year – 1947 – was the beginning of the Sullivan legend. He came home that summer wearing a St. Catharines Junior A Teepees jacket and with about fifty kids hanging off him. A year later, in 1949, he was called up by Boston to play in the NHL. He signed for $2,500.

George's memories of that time are crystal clear. He remembers the team just told him to go to Toronto and take a train to New York – they would be playing the Rangers at Madison Square Garden that night. "Holy jeez, I got there and I had never been to any city like it. I was shaking and shivering when I hit the ice."

He wasn't ready for the NHL, however, and the Bruins sent him to the Bears in Hershey, Pennsylvania, in the American Hockey League. In the 1953-54 season, he set a record for most points in the AHL in one season (a record not broken until 1983 by Ross Yates). His record 89 assists remained unbroken until 2003.

By 1954, Sullivan was ready for the NHL, so ready that he even saw his portrait in a Bee Hive cap. Boston traded him to Chicago for cash that year and he played there for two years before being traded to New York, where he became captain in 1957-58. It was in New York that he really established his reputation as both a tough-checking forward and consistent point-scorer. He was an in-your-face player who would do anything to win.

Sullivan played eleven seasons in the NHL, accumulating totals of 107 goals and 239 assists in 557 regular-season games. He kept his ties to Peterborough throughout his playing career, coming home some summers to work in Dit Clapper's sporting-goods store. He was the first Peterborough native to become captain of an NHL team, and the first bona fide star – he appeared in five All-Star Games.

His career almost ended with the kind of tough encounter that characterized his style of play. Montreal defenceman Doug Harvey speared him in a game in 1961, rupturing Sullivan's spleen so severely that he was sent to hospital in a cab, and a priest was called to give him his last rites. He would come back to play the following year. Because of radio broadcasts and wider media coverage, he became better known than past hockey stars of the community, more of the hockey hero kids dreamed of being when they played on the rinks and roads of Peterborough.

After his playing days were over, Sullivan coached for the Rangers, the Pittsburgh Penguins, and the Washington Capitals, and also became a scout.

George Sullivan spends his retirement with his wife along the Indian River just outside Peterborough.

CLARE "RAGS" RAGLAN
Born in Pembroke, Ontario, September 4, 1927
Raised in Toronto
NHL career with Detroit Red Wings and Chicago Blackhawks

Clare Raglan was born in Pembroke, but grew up in Toronto during the 1930s. Young Clare started skating on the frozen Humber River. By the age of fifteen he had graduated from the rough and tumble of river hockey and was playing organized hockey in the Metro Toronto league. Future Maple Leafs owner Harold Ballard saw him in action and asked him to play for his Marlboroughs junior team in 1944. When Rags learned the team practised in the afternoon – his current team's practice started at 6:30 a.m. – he jumped at the chance.

Somehow, the Toronto Maple Leafs overlooked Raglan, and the Detroit Red Wings snatched him out of their backyard when he was twenty. Raglan didn't think he was ready for professional hockey, though, and instead chose to play in the senior league for the Quebec Aces in 1947, where future Leafs coach George "Punch" Imlach was behind the bench. That year, Clare helped lead the team to upset the

heavily favoured, and much-loved, Montreal Royals in the league finals. The Red Wings still wanted the big (in those days anyone six feet and over was big) six-foot, 197-pound defenceman to sign after that year, but he stayed on as the Aces' captain to win the Quebec championship the next year. Raglan became the toast of the province, quite an accomplishment for an anglophone, even then.

In 1949, he turned pro playing for the Detroit affiliate in Indianapolis. This was the first team to sweep all playoff rounds and win the American Hockey League's Calder Cup. Their goalie was twenty-year-old Terry Sawchuk.

In 1950, Raglan made his NHL debut with the Red Wings, replacing a young Marcel Pronovost. The year before, Pronovost had been named the United States Hockey League's rookie of the year and had been called up by the Wings, but now he was being sent down.

Raglan didn't stay with the Red Wings, though. In 1951 he was traded to Chicago in a deal that made sports-page headlines across the country. Detroit owner Jim Norris sent six players to Chicago for $75,000 and one player. In fact, the deal didn't cost the owners much because the "owners" were the same family: the Norrises. In effect, the money went from one family pocket to another. Detroit alumni made up 90 per cent of the Chicago team.

Although Raglan played with injuries – all players did for fear of losing their jobs – they hampered him sufficiently that he didn't get to play in the big league very much. Over the next few years, he moved from Chicago down to the minors in St. Louis, then to Edmonton, back to Quebec, to Buffalo, and finally to Vancouver, where he fractured his leg eighteen games into the season. This injury ended his pro career. In 100 NHL games, Clare Raglan scored 4 goals, assisted on 9 goals, and had 52 penalty minutes. He did play later in 1959 for Belleville, who won the world championship in Prague, and after some stints with Kingston and the Washington Presidents, he joined the Eastern Hockey League's Windsor team in 1960-61, but the leg was never the same and neither was Rags. In those days, players had nothing to fall back on, and once a pro career was over, they were left to find their own way. By 1964 Raglan's hockey involvement was limited to coaching a Lindsay Junior C team that won the Ontario championships.

Clare Raglan found work in Peterborough in the early 1960s and finally settled his family in the town in 1966. He started his own renovating business and then took a job at the General Electric factory. The family would grow to include five daughters and a son, Herb, the only one of the six to be born in Peterborough.

Clare Raglan died in Peterborough at the age of seventy-four in April 2002 after a battle with cancer.

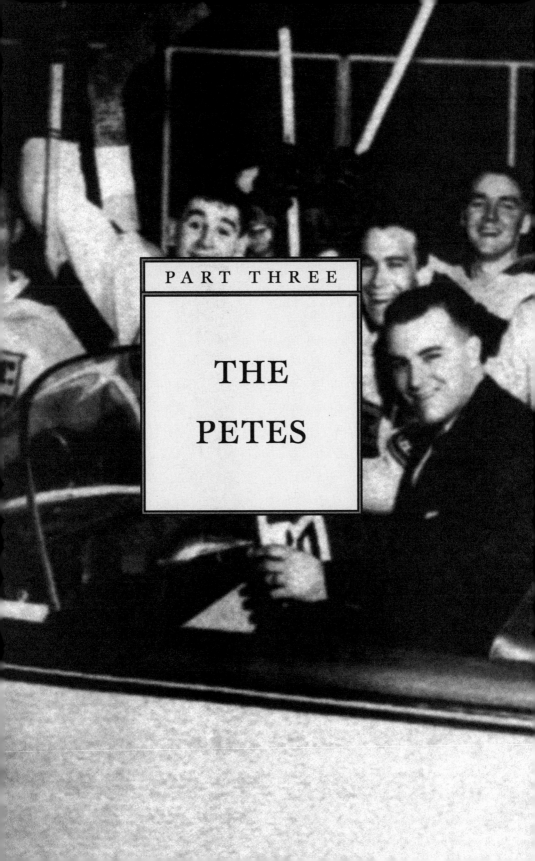

PART THREE

THE

PETES

The Coming of the Habs

In 1956, the Montreal Canadiens moved its Junior A franchise to Peterborough from Kitchener after the new Peterborough rink, the Memorial Centre, was built. Peterborough Petes fans have been thanking Kitchener and the Montreal Canadiens ever since.

The president of Canada Packers, Lionel Browne, and one of his managers, George Batley, and Ray Tanner, general manager of Toronto Peterborough Transport (TPT), whose father also owned the company, were behind it. Most importantly, Peterborough's Frank Buckland, a General Electric employee who was also president of the OHA and a former senior and junior hockey coach, was among the community leaders who formed the idea that the town would benefit by persuading the fabled Canadiens to place a Junior A team in the city. Economic considerations were a key part of their thinking. It was thought that a Junior A team could result in a small economic boom, as well as give Peterborough a higher profile outside the area because of the media coverage the games would get.

This group had the foresight to realize there would be no new rink in Peterborough without a major attraction, so in 1954, two years before the rink was to be completed, they approached Sam Pollock.

The Senior B team, sponsored by TPT and already called the TPT Petes, played in the Civic Arena, the small shell the community had built to allow their boys to play home games after years of playing all their games out of town. The community referred to the players then, and still do, as "their boys," but there was a mix of local and imported players. Eddie Redmond was imported from Kirkland Lake to coach (at $15 per game) and play. He also was given a job at TPT worth $1,000. He kept working at TPT, becoming manager of the company, the position he held when he retired.

A real-estate agent, Ed O'Toole, was president of the Peterborough hockey club, and former NHL great Dit Clapper was a director. The team played only thirty-six regular season games, its season starting on November 13 and ending February 26. They played against Kingston, Oshawa, Orillia, and Belleville. The club imported players from Noranda, Kirkland Lake, Iroquois Falls, Toronto, Sault Ste. Marie, Perth, and Owen Sound, all with the promise of a job.

The team program was sponsored by almost every business in town. So many people came to the games, the fire chief had to limit the crowd to 2,000 for their own safety.

The Petes' management held its meetings in the old Canada Packers office, and it was during these meetings that the push began to get a junior franchise in Peterborough. Frank Buckland was the major mover behind this scheme. Buckland saw the future in junior hockey. Peterborough had a proud history at both levels, but he also saw the city as perfect for the junior circuit. It helped that Buckland knew both Sam Pollock and Frank Selke of the Canadiens. He also knew the NHL club was looking at the possibility of folding the Kitchener Green Shirts because the senior team there, the Dutchmen, was so successful, the juniors didn't get much attention.

Selke was the Montreal general manager, but Sam Pollock was the hockey genius in the Habs' organization. Pollock and Selke both knew that Senior B hockey was already attracting more than two thousand people to the small Peterborough rink, and they were promised that the new rink would have a seating capacity of 3,200. For their part, local business leaders knew Montreal supplied the players, paid for the scouting, and gave the team a $10,000 start-up fee. Other income would come from attendance, advertising, and team sponsorship. Like the other teams in the NHL, Montreal would dictate hockey policy and supply the coach.

Before long, an agreement was reached, and Peterborough joined Rochester, Ottawa, Montreal, Shawinigan, Fort William, Regina, Winnipeg, and St. Boniface as part of the Canadiens' system of teams used exclusively to train players in order to improve its roster. In those days, NHL teams could, and did, sign kids age fifteen and up to what they called C forms. The team usually gave the kid $50 to $100 and in return the player gave the club all future rights to his playing. The player became the club's property. Montreal had an extensive system of hockey people who acted as scouts and bird dogs who scoured the country for up-and-coming stars. Many bird dogs were former players living back in their communities or coaches of minor teams loyal to the Habs. The team, and other NHL teams, actually subsidized youth teams and leagues all over Canada in the hopes of getting kids' names on C forms. This deviant form of servitude was abolished in the 1960s, but all NHL teams profited by it for as long as it lasted.

The minutes from those early meetings with the Habs reveal other terms of the deal between the Peterborough club and the NHL club. Montreal agreed to subsidize the club up to $5,000 annually, to supply all players, the coach, and the trainer, and sponsor an exhibition game with the NHL club. For its part, the local club paid staff salaries, took all program revenue, and also gave minor hockey in Peterborough an annual subsidy. TPT undertook to sponsor the team for $2,000.

The board of directors was an unwieldy ten people, including a doctor and various local businessmen. Through the years, the executive has not been the wealthy of the town, but hockey people, including factory workers, many of whom once played the game. The mix of backgrounds has remained a common theme. Today, one of the first Petes, Pat Casey, is a member of the board.

Selke, Pollock, and their staff looked for players who hated to lose, even in scrimmages, players driven by the fear of being cut, players who would threaten the Habs' current players so they, too, would fear for their jobs. Earlier, Selke had engineered the Leafs to three Stanley Cup wins and he would later get the Habs to six championships. He laid a solid base for this success by making sure the

farm-system players were well coached in the Habs' style of play –
plenty of speed and plenty of movement.

The OHA included players – virtual unknowns at the time – such
as Eddie Shack, Howie Young, Murray Oliver, Stan Mikita, Bruce
Gamble, Harry Neale, Claude Ruel, Carl Brewer, Gerry Cheevers,
Frank Mahovlich, and Bob Nevin. Pollock predicted Peterborough
would be in the Memorial Cup finals within three years. The first
year would be a growing one, with the team made up mostly of
rookies – twenty of its twenty-two players – but Pollock knew most
of them would be back for the second and third years.

Baldy MacKay, a former pro player, earned $4,500 a year as the
Petes' first coach, while trainer Gunner Lynch made $25 per week.
There were two team doctors, volunteers who were given a pair of
season tickets, as was the team lawyer.

The Petes kept a tight financial ship, and that reputation would
stay with them into the next century. The board of directors worried
about every penny, even chasing down any equipment players tried
to keep.

While the Habs had "sole authority to sign, purchase, trade, sell
or in anyway engage or dispose of players, trainer or coach or
manager," the local club had the burden of the financial pressure.
There was no guarantee that if the team lost money Montreal would
help. The directors feared this and brought it up several times with
Selke and Pollock, but the issue was not resolved.

The Petes didn't make the playoffs in their first year. They made
a small profit, but less than they had expected. Their revenue fore-
cast was too high. While they had a sellout on opening night, the fans
began to dwindle as the team lost games. Some nights there were fewer
than 2,000 people in the rink to see the last-place Petes. It may have
been one of the reasons the board wrote in its minutes that coach
MacKay "would not be back under any circumstances." They may
have forgotten that the Habs had sole authority in the choice of coach.

The following year, the board sent Dit Clapper and a committee to look for a coach and they hired former Leafs great Ted
Kennedy, who had recently retired. The Habs must have fumed over
that selection and the salary of just over $5,000 which set a

dangerously (from the Habs' point of view) generous precedent. The next year the executive voted to reduce the coach's salary to $5,000 and pay the trainer $800 for the season.

One significant move the directors made – agreeing to a proposal made by Buckland – was to establish Thursday as home-game night. Not only was this payday in Peterborough, but most of the teams in other cities played weekends, so Petes' players wouldn't miss too much school. Petes' home night is still Thursday. The players in 2003-04 missed only five school days, a big selling point for parents entrusting their sons to the organization.

The players ranged in age from sixteen to twenty and were from anywhere Montreal Canadiens sent them by car, train, or bus, but mainly from Ontario, Quebec, and the Maritimes. In the 1970s the Petes were the first OHA team to offer players education packages, and today they give players who don't go on to the pros $3,000 toward higher education for every year they play for the Petes. There was no university or college in Peterborough in the 1950s (Trent University was established in the late 1960s), so it made it difficult for the older players who were too old for high school, but the Petes got them full-time jobs. Most of them weren't there for education. Hockey was the thread that brought them together. The kids that arrived had spent most of their free time playing sports; it was their main interest. You would never mistake them for being worldly or having skills in other areas.

Scotty Bowman would take over the players' paycheques when he came in in 1958. They'd get $60 a week (today they get only fifteen more) for a twenty-week schedule. However, because the players stayed for the whole school year, they needed money for forty weeks. Bowman knew these young players would have to stretch their money, so he took back $30 to pay for weekly room and board and $10 went into a savings account in the player's name. They would each get $20 a week for their own use. "If they wanted any money they'd have to get me to co-sign for any withdrawal at the local Bank of Montreal," says Bowman.

The Habs insisted their players stay in town after the season ended. They wanted them to become part of the community, to be seen at public functions, and to participate in other ways. Today, many of the players go home right after hockey season, finishing their schooling in their hometowns.

The coach was the man who checked on discipline and enforced the punishment, usually fines or less ice time or the ultimate penalty: being sent home.

The Habs implemented strict curfews, sometimes 9:00 p.m., usually no later than 11:00 p.m., with strict bed checks by management, usually the coach. The drinking age was twenty-one in those days, so none of the players were old enough to be in bars, which can be a problem with junior teams now. Today, the Petes still enforce a strict curfew and do bed checks. Roger Neilson didn't want any of his players drinking and traded away many who did. The rules are a bit looser today, now that the drinking age has dropped to nineteen in Ontario, but, remarkably, most of the system put in place by the early Petes is still there.

Player curfews were an important part of the Bowman regime. Pat Casey once missed a curfew by five minutes, getting in at 11:05. His landlady told him Bowman had called at eleven. Casey called Bowman back right away. Nevertheless, the next day he was fined $10. Bowman knew all the tricks. Sometimes he'd call the house at eleven, and even if the player answered, he'd call back half an hour later, knowing the players sometimes waited for the curfew call, then sneaked out. One curfew story involves Barclay Plager, who was out with some of the guys one night, a few minutes past curfew. Whenever they saw a car coming, they ducked into an alley, afraid it might be the coach. When they saw an old truck coming down the street, they didn't hide – and sure enough it was Bowman. He told them angrily to get home, pack their bags, and be at the train station at eight the next morning. This was the worst threat he could make – they were scared to death of being sent home. At the train station the next morning, Bowman met them and relented, telling them he would give them one more chance. They didn't miss curfew again.

The Habs didn't recruit all their players from out of town. Local boys were looked at as well, and did quite well financially because they would get the room-and-board money that they didn't need. Mike

Fryia, a Peterborough boy, played for the Petes in the 1970s during the Neilson years. He says he was paid $70 a week, even though he lived at home, and in the summer would collect unemployment for $48 a week. "Car payments were only $40 a month – what a great life," he says with a laugh.

When the Montreal Canadiens brought the Peterborough Petes into their system, the town experienced a huge expansion in the popularity of minor hockey. Peterborough's first youth hockey league was formed in 1898 when there was a four-team outdoor league consisting mainly of boys under fifteen. From 1939 until 1955 it had a league of more than a dozen teams playing on various outdoor rinks and commonly called the church league. Hockey officials called all denominations for a meeting held at the local YMCA and the Peterborough Community Church Hockey League, with priests and ministers, agreed to start it for the 1956 season with twenty-six teams ranging from ages eight to eighteen.

It was the year the Peterborough Petes entered the picture, the NHL was getting popular on black-and-white television, the city was experiencing major growth in industry and population, but most importantly, says local resident Ken Self, it was the year the local church-league peewee team went to Goderich, Ontario, and Canada's most prestigious tournament during the Easter break. They reached the finals and the local media (at that time meaning the local radio and television station, the daily and weekly newspapers) took notice.

Self was born and raised in Peterborough. The former factory employee volunteered with the church-league hockey system for more than fifty years, almost as long as he was married. His sons played in the system, two of them eventually playing for the Petes, and one of them, Steve (now an assistant coach with the Petes) even getting a short stint with the NHL's Washington Capitals and a longer career in semi-pro hockey. Two of Ken's grandsons played in the OHL: Brad for the hometown Petes and Mike with the Windsor Spitfires. Hockey is in the Selfs' blood.

Self remembers the outdoor rinks, outdoor leagues, factory leagues, senior-team successes, and the building of the new rinks, but most of all he remembers "that explosion in minor hockey" that followed the Goderich tournament. He says, "The media in Peterborough blew it up big. They treated it like it was the biggest thing that had ever happened." That tournament (Peterborough lost in the final game to a Toronto team) was the turning point in youth hockey, says Self. The next year the church league was swamped with kids who wanted to play. Soon after, another association, called the City League (or Peterborough Minor Hockey Association), was formed. Here was a city of 48,000 people with two youth leagues, a major junior franchise, and only two indoor rinks.

The two leagues didn't get along with each other. The church league was much stronger and had bigger numbers. Every year an all-star team was picked from each age division in each league to play against the other to decide who would represent Peterborough in Ontario Minor Hockey Association (OMHA) playdowns, against teams from other cities. In those days the kids were also allowed to play house league, where kids of all capabilities played. Today the all-stars can't play in house leagues, and various calibres of all-stars are selected, with A being the lowest all-star level in large communities and AAA being the highest. There are even D and C centres in rural leagues. The smaller the community, the lower the calibre you compete in. It makes for plenty of confusion for hockey parents and fans.

But in the 1950s in Peterborough, the big youth action was the annual playoffs between the church- and city-league all-stars. The old Civic Arena would be packed for the games between the two leagues from juvenile to tadpole, creating quite a rivalry. The church league won nineteen of twenty city-wide championships, and from 1956 to 1971 it won eight provincial championships and was a finalist in four others. Their league had also grown from twenty-six teams to one hundred during that time and had more than 1,800 kids in 1971, while the city league had a healthy 900 kids.

To make matters even more confusing, in 1970 the OMHA (which rules most of Ontario's minor hockey) came in and named the city league, not the far older, stronger, and bigger church league, to represent Peterborough in provincial playdowns, and decreed that the all-stars could play only on one team. No more city rivalry. An all-star system that would later become known as the Minor Petes was formed. Those kids today represent AAA hockey in Peterborough from the ages of eight to eighteen. They play teams from other centres, wear the Peterborough Petes' colours and emblems, but have no other connection with the junior team.

Clearly a number of factors came together to help build up minor hockey in Peterborough, but the coming of the Habs was among the more significant.

Herb Warr was involved in Peterborough minor hockey for more than a decade before being selected to the Peterborough Petes' executive, where he stayed for more than thirty years. He was once asked the goal of the Petes. "As a hockey club our goal every year is to put the best team we can on the ice, but more importantly, we try to be a top ambassador for the city." Even today, the kids wear maroon-and-white jackets, with shirts and ties, slacks, no ball caps, and are told they represent the city.

The number of volunteers involved in hockey in Peterborough remains enormous – one in seven people plays a role. There are now four city rinks with six ice surfaces, and even that is not enough, so kids' teams often find themselves on rinks in one of the surrounding communities. Girls' and women's hockey has also had an explosion in registration in the last ten years, as has oldtimers hockey.

In 1969 OMHA executive member Charles Wilson cited four major factors affecting a boy's future: home life, education, religious instruction, and recreation. "Most parents give a good deal of thought to the first three and within the scope of their financial and moral capabilities do the best job possible. But, all too often, little attention is paid to how their boy can best profit from the game which he plays. If the boy is encouraged to have fun in sport, be happy to participate with friends, be modest in victory, and able to smile in defeat, then he will have assumed an attitude to sports that will be reflected in his attitude to life."

The Montreal Canadiens could go along with that attitude and in the 1950s had every reason to believe a good, healthy minor-hockey system in Peterborough would help their club in the future. It would also help attendance if they had more hometown players on the ice, who had the comfort of home and family. Putting up players became part of a system that developed into more than just a matter of room and board: it became an important part of the life of the city.

Landparents

When out-of-town hockey teens arrived in Peterborough to play for the Petes in the 1950s and early 1960s, they would usually arrive alone by train or bus, be met at the station or the rink by a team official, and, once they made the team, be put up in a permanent boarding home.

The players, just kids between sixteen and twenty, were treated like most boarders, no different from any other single working person with a need for a place to stay. The kids got room and board, the homeowner got $25 a week, nothing more, nothing less. No season tickets for the landlord, no family environment for the boarder. The Petes in those days liked to have their players live near the rink so they could walk to school, home, and hockey practice.

The landlords were usually widows who needed to supplement their small incomes. It was the same practice for junior hockey teams across Canada. Over time, the Montreal Canadiens introduced some changes. Under Scotty Bowman, they made sure they found landlords who would make decent meals and watch the boys' curfews. When coach and general manager Roger Neilson arrived in 1966 he refined the system. He kept Scotty Bowman's practice of encouraging the boys to stay in school and, if they dropped out, making sure they had a full-time job. He also would check on all the landlords before the players arrived and keep tabs on them during the season. He also made sure that schools reported to him on the boys' progress.

In Neilson's time, the nomenclature changed: landlords became landparents. The landparents were required not only to provide food and shelter for the hockey players, but also to provide a family environment. They weren't supposed to replace the boys' parents, but they were made aware that the boys were in their care, which meant good meals, clean clothes, good study habits, observance of the curfews, and a good, solid lifestyle.

Gradually the pay to landparents rose, to $55 per week in the 1980s and 1990s (still no season tickets), to about $75 today, never enough even to feed these growing athletes. But few landparents now are in it for the money. Most do it because they support the local team, have sons who like going to the games, or just think it would be good for the family to add a hockey player. Some simply take pride in being a Petes landparent. (And nowadays they *do* get season tickets.)

Some players can't wait to leave home. They have been billeted before at tournaments, aren't shy, and feel comfortable wherever their suitcase falls. For others it's not so easy. They feel homesick, uneasy, or uncomfortable when they leave the nest. The team relies on the landparents to deal with these settling-in issues. While there have been some problems, maybe the wrong fit for the player or the landparents, generally the system has worked well and most of the players remember their landparents with the fondness normally reserved for relatives.

Kids in their mid-teens who have a passion for hockey and have enjoyed the minor celebrity that is sometimes accorded high-school athletes are vulnerable in a number of ways. If they're really good, the fame can go to their head. If they're really not as good as they thought they were, the shock can be hard to deal with. Just going away from home can be tough both for the player and for his parents. And then there are the temptations of freedom: the wrong crowd, nightlife and alcohol, and girls.

The Petes have from the start been more or less aware of their responsibility to the boys who come into their organization. The Montreal Canadiens established the rules that were meant to keep the boys out of trouble, and they insisted later that the team be operated by a non-profit community executive that is sensitive to problems.

When Sheldon Kennedy bravely went public in 1996 with his revelation that he had been sexually abused by his coach, Graham James, it caused – as it should have done – an enormous public outcry. The *Globe and Mail* went so far as to call for the abolition of the junior hockey draft. That step was never seriously considered, but the revelation and its aftermath made all hockey organizations aware of their responsibilities to their young players. Many of the reforms put in place by other teams had already been made by the Petes. They had, for example, in landparent and policeman Walter DiClemente an unofficial (because unpaid) liaison with the police department. After the Kennedy case, DiClemente says, "I started going to landparents' homes with Jeff Twohey, the assistant manager, for interviews with the parents, making sure the people were competent. Don't forget, hockey players' parents were dropping off their fifteen-, sixteen-, and seventeen-year-olds to virtual strangers. The Petes have always been conscientious about what Petes players did off and on the ice so it was a perfect fit."

All the kids who have played with the Petes and lived with landparents have been shaped by the experience – most in ways that are positive and memorable. The majority look back on that part of their lives with fondness.

Soon after the young Mike Ricci arrived in Peterborough, he got in the habit of going to the Walter DiClemente home with other Petes for meals and to watch TV. DiClemente, a big friendly man, already had one Petes player staying at his comfortable home in a quiet subdivision. He recalls, "One day he asked if he could stay here, move from the house he was staying at." DiClemente talked with the coach and the move was approved.

"Mike was Italian. I don't think his mom and dad knew much about the OHL and they were apprehensive about him moving from home at fifteen years old. If Sault Ste. Marie had drafted him, he wouldn't have gone. Even though it was a great Italian community [there], it would have been too far away. I don't think when he came here that they thought he would even make the team and he'd be back home. His father was a big Habs fan and was thrilled when he made the Petes because he knew they used to be owned by the Habs.

"[His parents] were excellent people. They made sure Mike was brought up well. He gets his character from his parents. When he walked into my house, it was like he'd been there from day one. He was so polite, and great with all the neighbourhood kids." But Ricci had a good role model in the constable, who also taught the Petes about the bad side of town, the bars, the girls, the other temptations that every junior hockey player faces, and how to avoid them.

While the majority of landparents work out well, the ideal situation for any player coming to the Petes was to find relatives who could provide a suitable home and were willing to take the boy in. Doug Jarvis's parents were happy to send him to Peterborough, not only because their son would have a good hockey coach and Christian man in Roger Neilson, but also because Doug could board with his uncle and aunt, the Reverend Arthur and Ferne Wilkin.

"He was such a fine boy, quiet, so well mannered," says his aunt. "I had known him since he was a little boy. He came here at seventeen and was lonesome at first. He was a good student, though, and [soon] met some friends." Living with the Wilkins made the transition and focus on hockey easier for Doug and his Brantford family.

In the 1950s and 1960s, players were sometimes assigned to unsuitable homes. A few people obviously volunteered to take part in the program because they wanted the small amount of cash that was part of the deal. Stan Jonathan remembers that his first Peterborough landparent was "always bitching about costs," and he wasn't enjoying where he lived. Different – and much happier – arrangements were soon made. André Lacroix, the gifted playmaker from Lauzon, had a similarly unhappy initial experience. He describes his first landlady as "miserable. She was a lady [living] by herself who locked her fridge door. If you weren't there for meals between five and six, you didn't get any. I had come from this family-oriented home.

This woman obviously just wanted to make some money." Bill Evo's first landparent was totally unsuitable. He remembers being "frustrated at first, but I wouldn't call it being homesick. My landparent, when I first arrived, was a smoker and drinker. He'd come home some nights after bowling and be so drunk he'd be puking, so I moved."

Anyone who took on the job of landparent for a growing hockey player thinking that it would be a money-making proposition really wasn't thinking clearly. A recurring theme in the recollections of landparents is the astonishing appetite of teenage hockey players. The families who opened their doors to the out-of-town boys also opened their fridges, and frequently their hearts.

Landparent Bonnie Coombes remembers the young Colin Campbell for his practical jokes, teasing, and happy-go-lucky personality. Many of the Petes would gather in her home almost weekly. Her oldest daughter, Cheryl, was only three when Campbell started staying there. She says, "Colin would tease Cheryl all the time. He'd torment her. The poor child still suffers from it." But she laughs at the memory. Bonnie also remembers Colin for his dining habits. Bonnie says, "These were the days before the big pasta kick so it was usually meat and potatoes. Colin had this strange habit of eating with three plates, meat on one, potatoes on another, and the rest on another.

"We had liver once, and Colin told Cheryl it was from the inside of the cow with lots of blood inside it. She's never eaten liver again. He also had a weird habit of having mustard on his fish and chips, mixing cookies and cake in his milk, and saying, 'What's the difference – it all goes down the same place.'

"We had an Italian neighbour who invited him over for spaghetti one afternoon before a game. And of course there was wine. When he came home, I knew he had had too much, but he said he had to play that night. I drove him to the rink and he played the best game he had ever played."

One day she came home to find that a big batch of cookies she'd baked had been eaten by Colin, Bob Neely, and Bob Gainey. She made them come back on a Saturday morning to bake more. She remembers, "We had a Dodge Swinger, a four-speed with a black vinyl roof, that Colin really liked. We were buying a new car so he bought that one. On the way to Toronto to pick up our new car, we smashed up the one Colin had just bought. He cried when we told him. Later [when] he signed with Vancouver, [he] came back to see us in his brand-new Monte Carlo.

"Playing hockey was fun for them. Hockey and fun was first. Now it's career first, then hockey, and then fun. Those kids would have played for nothing and would have done anything for Roger [Neilson]."

Some, though not all, players suffered from homesickness. When Danny Grant arrived in Peterborough from New Brunswick, the Habs' organization set him up with his landlady, a widow, Alice Crocker, just a block from the rink. He was so homesick that he almost left. Everything was different – the city, province, people, school, and world. There was so much to get used to. The turning point came when team trainer Rock Batley, a Peterborough man, befriended him. He talked with the young boy, drove him around the city, showed him the sites such as the liftlock, the lakes with their plentiful fish, introduced him to other people outside of hockey, and took him to the homes of some of the other players. The kind attention worked. When Danny went home to Barker's Point at Christmas, he was supposed to stay for ten days, but after five days he wanted to get back to his hockey home, so he cut the trip short.

The young Craig Ramsay was desperately homesick when the Petes assigned him, too, to live with Alice Crocker. Craig says, "She babysat me. . . . She was fantastic. She was so nice. I didn't know anybody on the team. She cooked meals. Some of the other players were getting grilled cheese sandwiches and tomato soup while I was getting roast beef meals for game day." Those meals might account for Ramsay gaining five pounds every year he was with the Petes. By the time he left, he was around 175 pounds and five-foot-eleven.

Larry Murphy was another victim of homesickness when, at age seventeen, he was billeted with the Fitzpatrick family, who lived in the city's west end. Jim Fitzpatrick was a senior lawyer in Peterborough. The Petes had come a long way from the 1950s and 1960s, when widows who lived around the rink were the usual billets. "It was almost like the landparents were adopting him," remembers Doris Murphy. "We had to stand back and let it happen. We didn't phone there very often, and when we'd drop him off after a Peterborough home game, we'd never go in."

Teammate Terry Bovair remembers Larry's arrival. "I used to babysit him. I was the first guy to take him out for a beer. He was shy, never much to socialize. He had a tough adjustment socializing, but because of the way another Pete, Keith Acton, had treated me when I arrived, I treated him the same way. We became good friends."

The Petes have been lucky enough to find a number of landparents over the years who have been exceptional in every way: generous, understanding, and wise. Some have been providing homes for Petes players for decades.

One couple that became famous among Petes alumni was Vince and Lottie Garvey. The Garveys answered a newspaper advertisement placed by the Petes. They had some experience as landlords – they had recently asked a student boarder to leave after he got in some kind of trouble – and because they lived directly behind the Memorial Centre, where the Petes played their home games, it seemed boarding a player might be a better option than boarding a student. Vince called Roger Neilson, talked to him, and some time later got a call. Lottie remembers, "They said there was a boy. They said he was an Indian boy. I had nothing against Indians and Roger said, 'I'll send him down.' He came to the door all dressed up with a white jacket, shirt and tie. We sat down and talked. He was a really nice lad. I showed him a room. He said it was better than what he had at home. He went and got the rest of his clothes and that was that." Stan Jonathan, after his first bad experience, had found a home.

"The Garveys were the best," says Stan. "They didn't care if you were white, Indian, Chicano, they treated everyone on the same level. I had never been catered to before and wasn't used to it."

Lottie says, "Stan did everything he could to help. He was used to helping with that big family of his. He was easy to feed; you could cook him anything. He'd load the dishwasher, clean around the house, and help with anything.

"He even helped shop for the groceries, although I think he did that because he'd like to throw in certain things." Lottie laughs at the memory – she quickly figured out why the players liked to go grocery shopping with her. It didn't take her long to realize that $25 per week wasn't going to feed a player. But the Garveys weren't in it for the money. They virtually adopted the players who stayed with them.

"I was shocked once to hear a player say his landparent 'caught' the player helping himself to a pop in the fridge and she told him he'd have to pay for it. I never heard of that – even if there were a half-dozen kids in the house they could help themselves. They were like my own kids, free to go to the fridge when they wanted and get what they wanted. The only one that made money off those kids was Loblaw's," Lottie jokes.

"Stan was family. There was nothing bad about him. He kept his room clean, he met curfews. I told all the players who stayed there I'd never lie for them and never did." The Garveys' hospitality extended to Stan's parents, who would visit, have supper, and even stay the night.

The friendship lasted long beyond Stan's time as a Pete. Lottie fondly remembers, "[When] Vince was in the hospital with cancer years later . . . Stan came back for a while and stayed. He wouldn't let me do anything. He got the meals ready, cleaned up the table, tidied the house, and wouldn't let me raise a hand, just told me I had enough on my mind already." Vince has since died. Lottie lives in a seniors' home where Stan still visits her and telephones regularly.

The Garveys helped to persuade the Yzerman family that Steve should make the move to Peterborough. "They were incredible, they became like his grandparents," says Steve's dad, Ron. "No, his parents," says Jean, who admits she was taken aback by just how generous a home the Garveys provided. She reports that Steve was always "bragging about [Lottie's] cooking. What? Now my cooking isn't good enough? I was hurt."

Lottie Garvey, who, by the time the Yzermans came along, had been taking in Petes for more than a decade, remembers her introduction to Steve. "The Petes called me to say they had a young boy coming over from Nepean. When they arrived, his mother told me he was very shy. He was so quiet that first day I thought he'd be going home the next day on a bus, but he phoned his parents and said he loved it.

"Vince was always joking about how shy he was, so he took Steve out and showed him the city. He was quiet, but things were better after that. One night he overheard Vince talking about his relatives in Cranbrook and Steve spoke up to say he was from there." It turned out that Vince's family lived only a few doors down from where the Yzermans had lived.

Lottie remembers Steve as a fussy eater. "He didn't eat carrots at home, but I did some special ones and he loved them. He told his mom, 'You should learn how to make these carrots.' [They were glazed in butter and sugar.] The next time his mother called, the whole family was eating those carrots," Lottie says with a laugh.

"Around the house, Steve was just like one of our own. I loved him," she says. And Steve loved the Garveys. Lottie adds that the local girls were crazy about him. How couldn't they be? He had long brown hair, great looks, and super talent. He had also grown to five-foot-eleven and 175 pounds.

Steve and Stan will never forget the Garveys. Vince and Lottie dispensed more than food – though it's amazing how often the subject comes up – they also gave hockey advice. Vince was known for passing on his thoughts about how the boys played. While Greg Theberge was playing for the Petes he, too, boarded with the Garveys. "He called me a chicken one night," remembers Theberge. "He said I was shy in the corners and needed to get tougher."

Theberge was later drafted by the Washington Capitals and went on to play for them. When he came back to Peterborough a few years later with a new car, he went to the Garvey place to show Vince. The car was a metallic silver New Yorker with blue velour interior. After

Vince took a good look at it, he turned to Theberge and said, "See what you get when you go into the corners?"

The landparents usually made sure the players kept their rooms clean and made their own beds, something most of the players didn't have to be told. Hockey advice, clean clothes, and, most importantly to the player, food, were the key ingredients. More food stories are told by another landparent, Debbie Ralph, who helped to nourish Tie Domi. The future popular enforcer for the Leafs moved in with the Ralphs after his first year as a Pete. The move brought him closer to other Petes like Mike Ricci and Jamie Hicks, in a newer Peterborough subdivision. Tie and the others often could be found playing road hockey on the streets with the neighbourhood kids.

The Ralphs had two small boys, and Tie treated them like little brothers. "It wasn't uncommon for the boys to be wrestling with the toughest guy in junior hockey," laughs Debbie. Tie would hold out his arms, flex his biceps, and shout out his favourite line: "You look tired. You tired? Then jump on these bunk beds."

Debbie, a nurse, says it was the first time they had had anyone else living in their home. They converted a downstairs room near the family room into a bedroom for the new guest. "These boys need tender loving care when they're here, and guidance. They are only teenagers, and . . . when you take them in you're taking in some-one's teenage boy and the responsibilities that go with it," says Debbie. "It's a family affair. They eat with you. Tie went to our family functions, he went to our kids' communions and confirma-tions. He became a son."

The son must have wondered about his new parents when he first arrived. Debbie remembers her first pre-game meal for Tie. Tie came home from school and sat down to a bowl of chili. "He just looked at me," says Debbie, "and said he couldn't eat that before a game." Tie went to a nearby restaurant with a buffet for his meal that night. "I didn't know," Debbie continues. The Petes didn't supply the landparents with food guides or nutritional information, so Debbie went to some of the other landparents for advice and found that, although most were serving filling and nutritional meals of meat and potatoes or pasta, some of them were feeding the kids Kraft Dinner. "He was a fussy eater though," says Debbie. "He wasn't your roast beef type of guy."

Debbie also recalls how important his appearance was to Tie. He was always very neat, she says, and "his wardrobe was impeccable. . . . He was wearing Hugo Boss clothes before anyone even knew what they were. He even gave me a lesson in how to do his laundry; what to hand wash, what to put in the washer." She'd iron his shirts: "His neck was as wide as his arms were long." He always cleaned up after himself and was "never a problem. Not a drinker or a smoker. He loved the kids, always playing with them. He didn't like to stay alone in his room. He'd always come out and be with us."

Moving in takes an adjustment for both landparent and player. Many times, a player stays with another player at a landparents' home. The process sometimes involves an adjustment on the part of the new family members, some of whom were not accustomed to getting along with siblings. Greg Millen's introduction to his new family was abrupt. "My biggest adjustment was that I was spoiled," he says now. "I was an only child and spoiled, used to getting my way. I never liked being an only child."

He and teammate Glen Wagner boarded with a farm family, sharing a small bedroom. "We could touch each other, the beds were so close together. When I got to Peterborough I was selfish, cocky, and used to being looked after. I was acting like an only child one night and Glen drilled me right in the face. It's the best thing he could have done."

Adjustment is part of the process for both sides when they are new to landparenting. Chris Pronger also had an adjustment to make when he moved in with the Whites. Roger White, a local business-man, had a family of four children, which included two teenage boys, one around the same age as Chris. The family had renovated a loft above the double-door garage attached to their home for their first Pete.

Roger and his wife, Debbie, remember the skinny six-foot-six kid walking into the house and needing to duck to get past the doorway.

They also remember one of his first nights with them. "He came in, sat on the chesterfield, and started eating [a chocolate bar] in front of the kids," says Roger. "Debbie says, 'I hope you have one for all the kids,' who were staring at him. We had to teach him to share and not eat that stuff before supper." Roger laughs at the memory.

During Chris's time in Peterborough, he spent a lot of time on the phone with his parents who, being 1,200 miles away in Dryden, Ontario, weren't going to get to many games. The Whites recall how he was "really focused on hockey. He would read anything about it – books, papers, and magazines. We didn't know how good he was at the time but it didn't take long to find out."

The Petes were paying landparents $55 a week at the time, but, in a pattern familiar to landparents over the years, the Whites dished out $200 a week in groceries for the family. Chris "ate more and more and anything he wanted. We got kidded all the time about this because he was actually losing weight for a while," says Debbie, who would later see him put some beef on his bony frame. "On game day he'd come home and take a nap, then he'd come down with his white robe on and sit at the table waiting for his supper. He never ate with us on game day, and he'd leave for the rink long before the scheduled game." He always wanted to be at the rink hours before the game, and he kept that routine throughout the two years he was there.

"He really became part of the family and we treated him just like all the kids. He certainly had an air about him, but he always knew what he wanted and, obviously now, that was a professional hockey career. He'd do anything he could to avoid work around the house, and he wasn't much for school, but he was a good kid," says Debbie.

Another player from far away – in this case from the northern United States – who found a home with the Whites was Jamie Langenbrunner: When the Langenbrunners arrived in Peterborough, they met the Whites. "We were so relieved, so some of the tenseness and worry was gone," says Patrice Langenbrunner, Jamie's mother. "They made me feel comfortable. We stayed there in his loft apartment."

Debbie White remembers, "Jeff Twohey called and told us they had a kid they wanted, but the mother didn't want him to come to Canada. I called her in Minnesota and we spent three hours on the phone. She asked every question possible. She wanted him in church, he had [had] a good Catholic upbringing and [she] wanted to make sure of that [continuing]."

Mrs. Langenbrunner left her oldest son in Peterborough: "There were plenty of tears on the way home." Debbie White recalls that Jamie was "shy, quiet, and kept to himself for a long time." He was homesick, but as time went on he started to move right in. "He would heat up food – he was used to doing that at home – and got along with all our kids. While Chris [Pronger] had been neat and tidy with his clothes, Jamie wore running shoes, usually untied, his tie was usually untied when he left for the games, and he always ate his pre-game meal with us." He was also unlike Pronger in that Jamie took his time getting to the rink.

Junior hockey teams such as the Petes know there is more to life than hockey. Scotty Bowman knew it; that's why he wanted the players in school or working full-time and started a system that remains with the Petes today. Roger Neilson knew it; that's why he expanded on the system. He wanted to make sure the players got a well-rounded life, knew there were other opportunities, and that they not only had the opportunity to succeed in hockey, but outside hockey. The landparent system, when it worked well, provided a second family for boys who would have been lost without it and whose parents probably wouldn't have survived the winter months worrying about their child.

Scotty and Sam

The first coach of the newly formed Peterborough Petes was Baldy MacKay, who had played pro hockey for five years until he injured his knee in an AHL training camp. When MacKay arrived, the team was wearing Montreal colours and was sponsored by the Toronto Peterborough Transport Company, or TPT. The team became the TPT Petes. (The maroon and white now worn by the team wasn't introduced until 1974, although the Habs colours and TPT sponsorship were gone in 1966, and the name Petes was on the sweaters by 1970.) Under MacKay's supervision, the Petes got ready for their first game, on Sunday November 4, 1956; it was played in Toronto against the Marlboroughs before 5,200 fans and the Petes lost 4-1. Four days later, on Thursday, November 8, they played their first home game, against the St. Catharines Teepees led by Bobby Hull.

Frank Selke and Sam Pollock (who had predicted the team would be a contender for the Memorial Cup in three years) were in the stands for the home opener, as was NHL president Clarence Campbell, who dropped the puck for the ceremonial faceoff. More than 3,200 cheering fans, a sellout, were on hand; 1,200 of the fans were season-ticket holders. The Petes won in sudden-death overtime.

The team won only eleven of its fifty-two games that season, and crowds varied from 1,200 to 3,000 during the season, a sure sign that Peterborough fans were going to support only winners.

In the Petes' second year, Toronto Maple Leafs legend and former captain Ted "Teeder" Kennedy was hired to coach, replacing MacKay. His philosophy was to play all the players, giving them all a role, and his practices were hard and disciplined. In fact, he had the players go harder in practice than they ever would in games.

Former player Pat Casey, who came by train to Peterborough from Kirkland Lake to camp in 1956 ("and would have walked there to play for Montreal"), remembers Habs scout Lou Pasador as "tough – tough-looking and tough-talking. We were all afraid of him. If we had three bad games in a row, Sam [Pollock] and Lou would start coming to the games. We'd see them in the stands and play better. We all feared being sent home." Casey also remembers Baldy MacKay, who had just finished playing pro in the Montreal system, as a "yeller who was so loud by the end of the first period he'd lose his voice. He was too emotional and it was too early for him to be coaching right after playing." Casey remembers Ted Kennedy as a good practice coach. "He was tough at practice, but the games – every game was fun because in practice we worked so hard we would love playing the games." Kennedy, too, had just left the game as a player and, in Casey's words, "was still playing the game" as he coached. "We played once in St. Catharines, where all his friends and family had come down to watch the game. We lost 5-2, and he came in punching the walls, crying."

Gary Darling, raised in a small village just outside Peterborough, played for the Petes that year and says being picked for the team was a defining moment in his life. MacKay had cut Darling the previous year for being too small – Darling's growth had stalled at five-foot-six and 128 pounds – but Kennedy saw a spark in him that he thought could help his team. "Kennedy was a stern coach, he knew what he wanted, and if you didn't do it you sat on the bench," says Darling. "I remember one time in Hamilton he told me he wanted me to shoot the puck in every time we crossed centre ice. I didn't, once, and ended up sitting on the bench for the rest of the game."

Kennedy got the Petes to the playoffs that year, 1958, but at the end of the season he was replaced by one of the Canadiens' own, the legendary Scotty Bowman. Of course, at that time he wasn't a legend, just a young man from Montreal with high expectations, and the support of the Montreal organization, plus a $5,000 salary ($500 less than Kennedy's) with the possibility of a $500 bonus after each successful playoff round.

Pollock's prediction was about to be fulfilled. The Petes went into the playoffs in 1959 with big gunners, including the seventeen-year-old Wayne Connelly, and Bill Mahoney, a Peterborough native who would eventually coach Minnesota in the NHL. Mahoney played for McMaster University after leaving the Petes; the university team was the first to win the national CIAU hockey title in 1963 and Mahoney was selected MVP of the tournament. He coached that team from 1964 until 1979, being named CIAU coach of the year in 1979. He left McMaster to join the NHL as a coach, first in Minnesota, then as assistant coach with Washington. He was in the NHL for five years, before leaving to open a chain of doughnut shops in London, Ontario.

The Petes' goalie, Jacques Caron, was another player who would make it to the NHL. The little guy from Quebec went on to become the goaltending coach for the New Jersey Devils, coaching Martin Brodeur, one of the best in the world.

But the player from this period who became best known for his later exploits was the tough guy and top defenceman, Barclay Plager, who was captain and later coach of the St. Louis Blues. Also in this era, Darling, Claude Larose, and Port Hope's Jimmy Roberts were great defensive forwards – the shadows who stay glued to the other team's top scoring forwards. Larose and Roberts later starred in the same role for both Montreal and St. Louis. Roberts also coached in St. Louis.

These stars were the first of many who would come to Peterborough to try to get to the NHL and to work with a young coach who was about to lay the groundwork for the Petes' future success.

When Ed Rowe, a former Petes executive, attended a dinner held in 2002 to honour coach Roger Neilson, he saw another former Petes coach, Scotty Bowman. Bowman had coached the Petes almost forty years earlier, and Rowe had not seen him in decades. He was impressed when Bowman, walking by his table that night, said, "Hello, Ed."

Rowe was amazed that Bowman remembered his name. He promptly described Bowman's remarkable feat of memory to his wife.

"It might have something to do with the name tag on your jacket, Ed," she said.

Rowe laughs at the tale, but chances are the most successful coach in NHL history *did* remember him. He can remember many things from Peterborough: the address he lived at, the person who sold him his first car, the merchant who donated the first prizes, and the clothier who hired players to work part-time in his store. He remembers their telephone numbers and names as if it were yesterday.

Bowman arrived in Peterborough in 1958, two years after the Petes began playing there. He had just spent a year as an assistant coach (not on the bench – assistants were used mainly for practice then) in Ottawa for the Montreal Canadiens' junior team. Now, in Peterborough, Bowman was the only coach either at practice or behind the bench – there were no other coaches and no assistants. At the age of only twenty-five, he was succeeding the legendary Leafs captain, Teeder Kennedy.

"Kennedy had found it too much for him," remembers Bowman. "He was commuting to Toronto." It was close to a two-hour drive then, but about seventy-five minutes now. "He was in the transportation business in Toronto, and his son required medical care [there]."

Bowman, the son of Scottish immigrants, was born in Verdun, Quebec, in 1933, and dreamed about playing in the NHL while he was growing up in a rough area of Montreal. Some of his road-hockey chums turned to other professions: safecracking and thievery. Bowman, with a talent for playing hockey, aided by a good Catholic upbringing and a sharp mind, decided to stay with hockey. Because he was a Quebecer, the Montreal Canadiens owned his hockey rights, as they did that of all the kids in that province. It didn't matter that he had grown up cheering for the Boston Bruins!

After playing minor hockey for three more years, he started playing for the Montreal Junior Canadiens and was a regular by

1951-52. That season the team was playing Trois-Rivières Reds in the playoffs when the stick of Jean-Guy Talbot (a player Bowman later signed when he was coach and GM of the St. Louis Blues) hit him on the head, cutting his skull. For the rest of his career, that incident was overblown. The story reported repeatedly is that he had a skull fracture and a plate was inserted in his head. The truth is that the wound was a five-inch gash that required fourteen stitches and Bowman missed only one game with the Junior Canadiens as a result. He competed in the rest of the playoffs, but he wasn't the same player. He had headaches and blurred vision and had lost his confidence. He played two more years for the Montreal Royals but, as the realization sank in that he would progress no further, he took a job as a paint-store clerk. More importantly, he started coaching kids on area teams that the Montreal Canadiens sponsored.

By 1955 he was coaching a Junior B team that was not associated with the Habs. On his lunch breaks he would go to the Montreal Forum for tips and to pick the brains of any Canadiens he could corner during practices. The Canadiens' officials were impressed.

In 1956 the Junior Canadiens were moving to Ottawa, and Bowman accepted a job offer from Sam Pollock as assistant coach and assistant manager. Two years later, in 1958, the team won the Memorial Cup.

Pollock liked the kid, his enthusiasm, work ethic, and, most of all, his hockey intelligence. When he asked Bowman if he wanted the coaching position in Peterborough, Bowman was ready for the challenge and promotion. "I was single at the time, and it was hard moving and living there," he remembers. "I lived at a home with a widow [in her late sixties], Mrs. Turner [her son Phil later became the city's mayor]. It was really a boarding house and the same place Ted Kennedy stayed at whenever he stayed overnight."

Bowman's life was hockey. He walked, talked, ate, breathed, slept, and loved it. He was as passionate as the players. Winning was everything. His job was to develop players for the Montreal Canadiens and their farm teams, but the only way to make them like Habs was to be sure they were winners.

The Peterborough Examiner

Scotty Bowman in the new boat the Petes bought him for getting the team
to the Memorial Cup final.

Pat Casey was a player on the first Petes teams. He remembers the
fresh approach that Bowman brought to the game. "His practices
were fun. We'd shoot, skate, pass. He knew what it took to win. He
would cut back to whoever his best eight or nine players that night
were. You never knew who they would be, so everyone would be
working hard to make sure they got ice time.

"He had us all have scribblers and take notes on every player in
the league so we would be prepared and know how to beat them.

"When playoffs came, we would have all the information in our
scribblers. We even took them to school and studied them. We knew
who scored, how, and why. We knew how to score on the goalies. He
taught us what to expect. He was always thinking of how to beat the
other guy." Bowman still has some of those scribblers.

Bowman also experienced a problem with ice time. "We always
had a tough time with the figure skaters at the rink. They wouldn't
move their schedule, and I always wanted to change mine. Instead
of [practising] right after school at four p.m., I wanted to try six p.m.
I'd have to go to the executive and they'd usually come through," says
Bowman, telling a story that's still familiar with the Petes today.

Sam Pollock and Scotty Bowman worked together like syrup
and pancakes, coffee and doughnuts. Pollock gave Bowman the

players, and Bowman moulded them into a winning team. Their partnership established the Petes tradition that endures to this day.

Pollock long has been recognized as one of the cagiest NHL general managers ever, planning trades and drafts years in advance to get the first pick, as he did one year to nab Guy Lafleur. Petes executive Doug Cochrane remembers a board meeting of the executives of the junior teams, when Toronto Marlies manager Stafford Smythe was waiting for Pollock to arrive. "I've got that bastard now," he told the others. "We [the Leafs] have signed the best player in northern Ontario – I'm just waiting for the phone call. I can't wait to tell Pollock."

Pollock arrived late and Smythe was on him, teasing him about the big signing. The phone finally rang but it was for Pollock. When Pollock returned to the board meeting after taking the call, he asked Smythe what he was so excited about. "We've got this great kid we've signed – Ralph Backstrom," Smythe said. Pollock just looked at him, and said, "Oh, him. We just moved him to Quebec and put him in school there so he could qualify and play for us. We just signed him."

Not every player came to the Petes by way of structured hockey. One of the great players came to the team not from intense scouting, or a trade, or Montreal networking, but as the result of a telephone call from a priest.

Pollock, born to squint, and in those days with a nasty habit of constantly working a handkerchief in and out of his mouth, kept getting telephone calls from a priest in Hearst, a small town in northern Ontario. The priest told him about a good kid who should be at their training camp. Pollock listened but didn't want to make an offer. The Petes already had eighty-five kids in camp and had never heard of this one. Finally, Pollock relented. He told the priest to bring the kid to Peterborough. Bowman asked the priest, Monsignor Melanson, head of the diocese in the Hearst area, where the kid, Claude Larose, had played. "He's just a river player. We have no rinks," was the reply.

Larose made the team and two teams that Bowman coached, Peterborough and Montreal. He was one of the strongest checkers, best skaters, and all-round players Bowman would coach. Larose had a sixteen-year NHL career from 1962 to 1978, scoring 483 points and taking more than 800 penalty minutes, most of those served with someone from the other team.

Larose and the other players would learn that the Petes and other out-of-town teams historically had a difficult time winning against St. Michael's, but the Petes learned the secret of their success. Pat Casey recalls how former coach Ted Kennedy taught the players to "keep our rear ends against the boards and don't work off the boards. That way when you throw the puck around the boards you're not coming back to get it. You didn't have to do any extra skating."

Bowman also remembers Kennedy coming back from Toronto to help his centres take faceoffs. "After ten minutes of watching, he said he knew what was wrong: 'They aren't cheating enough.'"

Bowman also started shadowing players. "That was his idea," remembers Gary Darling. "He'd have me shadow the other team's top player, like [Stan] Mikita. 'Just stay with him everywhere,' he'd tell me. Mikita only scored one goal in a playoff round when I was shadowing him," says Darling proudly, "and I wasn't on the ice for it."

Bowman also brought with him a Montreal philosophy that would stick for years: Don't dump the puck in. You work too hard to get it, why give it away?

Darling, who had been benched by Kennedy for *not* dumping the puck, was one of those players who would do anything to score. Once – and people swear this happened – he couldn't go through or around a defenceman, so he dived through the only opening he had: between the player's legs. Many people report seeing this, but Darling says, "Don't believe everything you hear."

The players say Bowman made players uneasy when he used the same seven or eight players in the crucial times in a particular game. The others might not play at all that night, except to give the others a rest. "They'd wonder if they'd get any ice time, and he'd never really tell them if they would play regularly," remembers Darling, who was one of the people Bowman played.

George Montague was one of those who was often left sitting. Darling says, "Scotty said something and George just got up and threw his stick and gloves on the ice during the game. He went to the dressing room, then left the rink. By the next game everything was patched up." (Bowman had ordered him to serve a bench penalty.)

Bowman, only five years older than many of the fellows on the team, didn't socialize with the players, and some of them considered him self-centred. Although he asked the players for their views, he only occasionally took their advice. Casey recalls one of the exceptional instances. Casey used to play with and against Toronto's star Dave Keon in northern Ontario. He told Bowman he could handle Keon in the playoffs, so Bowman matched the lines, putting future NHL coach Bill Mahoney and future NHL scout Gary Darling on with future Petes executive Casey. That line not only kept Keon off the scoresheet, it also scored all the Petes' goals.

It was during this Toronto-Peterborough playoff series that Gord Campbell, a sports reporter with the *Toronto Star*, wrote the following: "In six playoff games, the Petes have played to 22,280 fans, an average of higher than 3,716 per game. It is their most successful season to date and has caused enthusiasts to call Peterborough, Hockey Town, Canada." Only two weeks later, *Peterborough Examiner* columnist Ted Galambos wrote, after the team won the Ontario championship: "Hockey Town, Canada opened up with everything they could lay their hands on early Thursday morning in welcoming the newly crowned Jr. OHA Champs home."

Darling remembers the series Campbell was writing about. "It was our toughest series against St. Mike's. We were losing three games to one but we went on to win the series."

Some of the stories from that era are still told today, like the Jacques Caron story: In the eastern Canadian finals against Montreal in 1959, goalie Caron went into hospital for surgery because of an injury and was replaced by one of the league's best goalies, Denis DeJordy. DeJordy played for St. Catharines, but the Petes were allowed to take him because their starting goalie had been sidelined. The Montreal Juniors accused Caron of faking the injury.

Bowman picks up the tale. "Jacques had been complaining about an arm injury and we had lost two [games] in a row. We asked the doctor: if he was a hockey player what would he do? And the doctor said he'd drain the elbow. We asked Jacques what he would do, and he said it hurt too much to play so we had to drain it.

"The OHA president was Frank Buckland, from Peterborough [and the man behind getting the Petes to locate there]. Montreal had asked for a neutral doctor to examine Caron. Frank was a real taskmaster but had a soft spot for Peterborough. A neutral doctor was called in from Lindsay. Little did Montreal know that he was the family doctor for one of our players from Lindsay. It was just rubber-stamped; the doctor didn't even come to Peterborough."

The Petes won the eastern Canadian championship that year and, after winning four playoff series, travelled to the Memorial Cup in Winnipeg. The team was making their first cup appearance in only their third year in the league, just as Pollock had predicted.

It was a weekend Peterborough hockey fans would not soon forget.

John Tanner was only thirteen when he and his father, Ray, a Petes executive whose family owned TPT, went to Winnipeg by plane.

"It was my first plane trip," remembers Ray. "We were so excited when the plane stopped we got right off, and had to get back on when we realized it had stopped in Thunder Bay."

What he also remembers is the great Bowman wallet incident in the final game.

Bowman was so upset with the refereeing during the Memorial Cup that, with six minutes left in the game, he pulled out his wallet and offered it to the game officials, who tossed him, forcing Pollock to come out of the stands and coach the remainder of the game.

Others, especially the players at the time, may well remember Bowman's words, quoted by John Robertson of the Winnipeg newspaper during the tournament:

> The suave coacher had to do two laps up and down the darkened arena halls before he cooled out enough to put his feelings into rational words for the prying press types.
>
> His tigers had just blown another one to the Braves, and the Scot was understandably not in a baby kissing mood.

As he wheeled to face his inquisitors, he managed a tight, teeth gritting smile before the words started flowing low and slow like a smouldering tire.

He then threw verbal abuse at his players seldom heard today. He not only complained about them, but he singled them out: "My playoff guys like Connelly, Babcock and Montague are shooting the puck into the left field every time they get in close. . . . I'm also disappointed in the defensive work of Boddy and Clarke. Boddy gave them the winner. . . . We haven't had the goaltending edge I expected."

And he demanded a change in the on-ice officials. "Everytime there's a flare up we've always wound up with an extra two minutes," he said, questioning whether the referee was afraid of the hometown fans. "The guy's so inconsistent it's a joke. We want a change and that's that."

There was no change. They lost, but they had placed Peterborough on the map. When the Petes returned home after that first Memorial Cup appearance, their fans greeted them at midnight with an impromptu parade of eighteen trucks, two ambulances, five fire engines, and two motorcycles. Bowman had never seen anything like it.

The mould had been formed that created top-scoring forwards, great defensive forwards, big, tough defenceman, top goalies, and strong team play. The team's success also brought the cash into the team, which made a walloping profit of $22,000 and earned Bowman a raise of "up to $6,000 maximum including bonuses." Some raise. Oh well, the team did get him a motorboat for getting to the finals.

In his Peterborough days, Bowman was an enigmatic figure. Doug Cochrane, a former Peterborough resident who now lives in Nova Scotia, was a bank manager during the day, but when he wasn't working at the bank, he was the Petes' radio announcer and the man Pollock selected as the team's president, an unpaid position.

Several times a week Bowman would visit Cochrane's home, where the two men would sit drinking tea or coffee and nibbling on some toast until one or two in the morning. "We'd sit around and talk about hockey. Everything was hockey with Scotty, that's all he usually talked about, all he thought about. He'd pace my floor with his hand in his pocket, jiggling, rubbing two silver dollars that he always had in his pocket. He'd think about line changes, who was starting the next game. By two a.m., I was dead tired, and he'd tell me who was going to be the lines. I learned never to tell anyone though, because by game time none of those lines ever made it." Cochrane, who still sees Bowman today, laughs at the memory.

"I didn't have much of a social life," Bowman remembers. "It was pretty well hockey twenty-four hours a day. At night I used to ride with the police in their cruisers. The police were big Petes fans and we'd drive around looking for players, but it was really just something to do."

A Peterborough woman remembers dating him at the same time she was dating Petes star Barclay Plager – neither of the men knew she was seeing the other. She recalls, "Scotty was a great guy, truly great. He was older than I was and always a perfect gentleman. Hockey was all he'd talk about. I can remember him saying, after I told him I didn't think he had much of a future in hockey, 'You watch, you'll see me on television some day.'"

Bowman says, "After many of the games I'd go to the Legion with Ed Redmond. I didn't go to the bars or pubs. I wasn't a boozer. I'd have a couple of beers and that would be it. The odd night I'd go watch minor-hockey games at the Civic Arena. A local businessman would take me out to dinners, but that was about it for my social life," he says.

Redmond was the great senior hockey player from Kirkland Lake who had moved to Peterborough with his family to coach a senior team and manage the TPT company. His two sons, Mickey and Dick, were local minor-hockey stars. "I hung around a lot with Ed," says Bowman. "His son, Mickey, was a talent even then. I'd let him practise with the Petes when he was only thirteen. We almost lost him to the Oshawa team, but his mother, Mae, wouldn't let him go."

In his second year, Bowman moved into a small apartment with Petes season-ticket holder and local businessman Ted Doughty, who says Bowman was "99 per cent hockey, not a big drinker, and went on two dates that I remember. He wasn't tight with his money, but he looked after it well."

"He was a man who could focus. He could watch a game on television while listening to two other games on transistor radios and know what was going on in all three games. He'd come home from road trips and call Sam Pollock and detail the entire game talking from 1:30 a.m. until 4:00 a.m."

Another player from that time was Bob Rivard, who grew up in Chicoutimi, Quebec, and had signed with the Montreal Juniors. But Montreal had too many players, so he was sent to Peterborough in the 1950s. Although he spoke no English, he settled right in, so comfortably, in fact, that he married a Peterborough girl. Rivard came from a large family – he had five brothers and three sisters – and learned to skate, at the relatively late age of ten, on his brother's "crooked blades when minor hockey was all outside." He says, "Why parents spend thousand of dollars on equipment today, I don't know. If you're good enough, they'll find you. You have to be a natural and you have to love the game."

When he arrived in Peterborough, he knew Bowman liked him. "That was good; you got more ice time," he says. "He was a good coach. He kept our heads in the game."

"Scotty's contract was always for one year, and he'd make less in the year than he'd make per day in the NHL," says Cochrane. "We used to offer the coach an outboard motor if the team made the play-offs, a boat if it made the semifinals, and golf clubs if it made the finals."

It was clear that more than pay motivated Bowman. Local businessman Marlow Banks remembers Bowman coming in to Banks's bicycle shop to sell program ads. Although he spent time talking hockey, he never left the store without selling an ad. Banks remembers his stubbornness – or dedication – in another story. The team was on its way to Guelph for a game. They ran into a major ice storm. Bowman stopped the bus so he could telephone Guelph to say they were still coming. Then he had the bus driver go off the main highway and take a back road. Banks, who was on the bus with the team, recalls, "We got there [about ten hours after leaving] and the game started at 10:30 p.m." – two-and-a-half hours after the scheduled start.

Cochrane's memory of Bowman was of someone "very distant if you didn't get to know him." But Cochrane was one of the people who did get to know him well. "One night," says Cochrane. "Hap Emms, who was with the Barrie Flyers, told me before a game their goalie was no good, [so we should] shoot high and on the stick side. I instantly went and told Scotty, who didn't believe it but told me he might use it. He didn't until the third period, when we were losing, and then we were [suddenly] shooting high and we won the game."

If the team didn't win, the trip home would be a long one. "You never talked to Scotty if we lost. He got downright surly and wouldn't talk to anyone."

Bowman was a bit of an authoritarian – it was the way things were done in those days. Casey says, "There was no talking back then, no asking questions. I remember one game in Toronto [that] Montreal scout Lou Pasador was coaching because Scotty was suspended. I didn't get much ice time; my best seat was on the bench at centre ice. I didn't know what to say – you were never to ask questions. When the game was over, I approached him and Scotty in the hallway and asked about my ice time. Pasador said he would talk to me about it tomorrow.

"The next day was the next game, and during the game Lou, who even looked mean, was pacing up and down the bench yelling at me. In the dressing room he was screaming while everyone watched. 'Don't you ever talk to me about that again. Remember who you work for,' he screamed."

Bowman was a hot-tempered, fiery coach known for throwing sticks on the ice; he even scuffled once with an opposing player. In another game he was ejected with twenty-one seconds left for coming on the ice – he claimed a linesman was choking one of his players. Police had to escort him out of the rink, and Habs vice-president Ken Reardon coached the team for the six games Bowman was suspended.

Cochrane says the Canadiens treated the Petes' volunteer executive well. The Canadiens brought members of the executive to Montreal – either flying them in or bringing them in by train – for afternoon football games, dinners, and evening hockey games. "We had a great time, all because of Sam Pollock," Cochrane recalls.

Peterborough lawyer Sandy Fleming was a Petes president and director who remembers Bowman as a nice man, while Pollock was "always tough." Pollock's eye for the dollar is legendary. He had a bookkeeper's background before joining hockey, and finances were usually on his mind. "One thing about Sam, though, if he gave you his word, you didn't need it in writing – his word was gold," says Fleming.

Pollock kept his eye on everything, including the team stationery. It was cheap management for the Canadiens and would turn out to be excellent management in the years ahead.

Pollock met with Fleming every month, arriving from Montreal on the train. "One time we went to the Memorial Centre and Sam saw a [hockey] stick in a pail of water, and another stick with its blade in a vice. He went crazy. 'How the hell can they take a pass with curved sticks? They need to take passes from both sides of the blade,' he yelled, and then took the stick and snapped it over his thighs, throwing it [away] in disgust." "You teach them how to skate, we'll teach them to play hockey," Pollock would remind anyone within earshot.

Bowman stayed in Peterborough for three years, taking the team to two winning seasons that saw great profits of $22,000, then $12,000, followed by a dismal third season marred by injuries to key players and a loss of $8,344, before taking a job as the Habs' Ontario scout. "I still wanted to coach, but the scouting job was more money and it was a promotion," he says. However, he found there was too much travelling involved with scouting and he missed coaching.

In 1964 he took a coaching job with the Montreal Junior Canadiens. When the NHL expanded in 1967 from six to twelve teams, he became assistant coach and then head coach of the St. Louis Blues. Bowman took his team to three Stanley Cup finals, two against Montreal, one against Boston, all without success, but with some familiar faces on the team: Jimmy Roberts, Jacques Caron, and a man who would stay in St. Louis forever, Barclay Plager. When Bowman became St. Louis general manager in 1968, he remembered the Petes' organization as well. He hired Frank Mario, who had succeeded him as the Petes' coach, as personnel director, and Gary Darling was named Ontario scout.

Bowman's story is well known to any hockey fan: he was the NHL's most successful coach, winning the Stanley Cup five times with Montreal, once with Pittsburgh, and three times with Detroit, and he had more wins than any coach in NHL history. He retired from hockey in 2002, after his Red Wings won another Stanley Cup title. Bowman had come a long way from the tough streets of Montreal, doing things his way, earning some enemies and friends along the way.

Looking back to the days in Peterborough, he says, "I had a good time in Peterborough. I wish I had gone back more and kept in touch and seen these people before they passed away. It was great being there."

After Bowman left the Petes, Pollock hired several coaches from 1962 to 1966: Neil Burke, Frank Mario, and Roger Bedard.

The season of 1961-62 was the year the community almost lost the Peterborough Petes, who found themselves in desperate financial circumstances but managed to keep it away from the media . . . until now. The situation was so bad the Bank of Montreal threatened to foreclose on them and stop paying the weekly overdraught for team expenses. Attendance had dropped from just more than 100,000 the year before to close to 30,000. What was worse was that the entire OHA was seeing drops in attendance and several teams had worse attendance than Peterborough's. The directors were told in one of their meetings that "the Habs were deeply concerned with fan interest in amateur minor pro hockey throughout Canada and particularly in Peterborough," report the minutes from that era.

The team had an overdraught of $9,000 and the bank ordered the club to stop issuing cheques. It was so serious by January 1962 that a weekend road trip was in doubt. But the directors proved to be wise, and had a trust fund they had saved for just such a rainy day. The fund had actually exceeded $50,000 and was used to pay the debt, dissolve the present club, and form a new Peterborough Petes Hockey Club with a smaller executive of local people (a lawyer, a banker, a farmer, and two businessmen) hand-picked by Pollock.

Attendance started to climb again with aggressive advertising and the help of some new stars. During that Habs ownership, Pollock's network found players like André Lacroix, who would go on to play in the World Hockey Association and win the scoring championship with 124 points in 1972-73 and again in 1974-75 with 147 points, Garry Monahan, Montreal's first pick and first overall in the 1963 amateur draft, and two of the greatest scoring stars in Petes history, who both went on to 50-goal seasons in the NHL: Danny Grant and Mickey Redmond.

After fourteen seasons as general manager of the Habs, from 1964 to 1978, Sam Pollock left the Montreal Canadiens and hockey, joining the Labatt company and Blue Jays baseball, where he was a major stockholder and executive. No other NHL general manager has won as many Stanley Cup titles as Sam Pollock, the most successful GM in the game's history.

From 1956 until 1967, the Pollock era put more than thirty players into the NHL through Peterborough, a phenomenal number when you consider the NHL had only six teams until the 1967-68 season. After the expansion, the NHL ruled teams could no longer own junior franchises, so the Petes' great tradition had to continue without the Habs' ownership. They left the franchise in good hands with the Peterborough community and a man who was scouting for them, Roger Neilson.

The Innovator

When Roger Neilson came to Peterborough in 1966 at the age of thirty-three, nobody could have known he would become one of the most innovative hockey coaches of all time. What they did know was that he was obsessed with hockey, so obsessed he spent most of his waking hours watching it or thinking about it. And he had plenty of waking hours, because he slept for only a few hours out of each twenty-four, and it wasn't always at night that he caught those few hours of sleep.

Neilson, a Toronto native, had a *Globe and Mail* paper route while he was in his early twenties, originally to help him get through McMaster University in Hamilton, where he was studying education, but the route was so profitable he kept it going after he graduated, even after he began teaching in Toronto. At the time, he was one of the oldest "paper boys" in Canada. The route made him thousands of dollars every year. In the early 1960s he delivered more than six hundred papers, many in the wealthy Forest Hill area of Toronto, where he sometimes got Christmas tips totalling $2,000.

He and his helpers, usually teenagers from the various ball teams he coached in Toronto, delivered the newspapers every morning. He would drive the van, and his helpers would walk beside it, as he tossed the papers to them through the open van windows. Even when he was hired to coach the Peterborough Petes, he didn't want to give up the lucrative route, so his long-time friend Dick Todd kept

Coach Neilson in plaid pants. Greg Millen in front row, far right.

it going for him until Roger, who also worked as a high-school teacher in Peterborough, was confident he would be keeping the coaching job.

Neilson's parents were evangelists, and he lived his life as a committed Christian from the age of twelve. His strong Christian beliefs were unusual in Canadian sports circles, where he began coaching youth baseball and hockey teams when he was only seventeen. Neilson had played hockey when he was growing up. As a goalie, he made a Junior B team, but realized he was going nowhere playing the game, so he turned exclusively to coaching and scouting. After graduating from McMaster, he continued his involvement in young people's sports. He'd drive players around in his beat-up old van, its doors tied shut with string. He took groups of teenage players to World Series games in New York in that van, without booking accommodations or game tickets. One season he coached six ball teams. In ten years of coaching minor baseball, his teams won nine pennants.

He did not find his social life in bars – he was never a drinker. His social life was his teams. A confirmed bachelor, he told close friends that athletes lost their focus when they started dating.

In the early 1960s, Neilson was not only coaching hockey but was also the supervisor of the entire minor system, from peewee to midget, for the New York Rangers' Toronto organization. He joined the Montreal Canadiens in 1964 and was one of their twelve scouts, but he kept teaching in Toronto and coaching kids. After his first year as a scout, he became the Canadiens' head Ontario scout under their director of personnel, Sam Pollock. In this capacity, he made sure the Habs' Peterborough organization was fed top-quality players, including, for example, future NHLer Garry Monahan. He ignored his friend Dick Todd's advice, however, when Dick argued vehemently that the Petes should take another kid by the name of Pete Mahovlich.

When the Habs and the other NHL teams were ordered to give up their ownership of junior teams in 1966 because of the upcoming 1967 NHL expansion, the Petes, coached by Roger Bedard, were looking for someone to take charge of their player personnel. Pollock suggested Neilson, who readily accepted the invitation. In his first season, 1966-67, he had to get behind the bench when Bedard was suspended for a wild punch-up with Ted O'Connor, coach of the Oshawa Generals.

It didn't take Neilson long to establish his unorthodox approach to the game. In his first game as coach, Neilson switched his goalies every five minutes and kept doing it in subsequent games. He thought it would upset the other team and also serve as a useful delaying tactic. In his third game as coach, one of his defencemen got a ten-minute misconduct, but Neilson, wanting the team to become more disciplined on the ice, implemented a new team rule, and he sat the player the next game. In his six games as interim coach, the team had four ties, one win, and a loss, not a great record but enough to impress the Peterborough executive that he was their man when Bedard resigned after returning from the suspension. (Only a year later, Bedard would coach the Montreal Juniors to the Memorial Cup, a feat never accomplished by Neilson.)

Pollock had told Herb Warr, a member of the Petes executive at the time, to "keep your eyes on Roger Neilson – he has no idea of the value of a dollar." This was a rare misjudgement on Pollock's part. Neilson soon became known as a penny-pincher, but those who knew him best say he just didn't care about money. He spent little on either the team or himself. He never owned a new car, seldom bought new clothes (unless it was a tie), and generally ignored the dollar's power to purchase new things. About five years after Roger became coach, says Warr, "I kept seeing the players' equipment was bad, shin pads were damaged and coming through the socks. I asked Roger to get new equipment, and finally I went to a local sporting-goods store and bought every player, twenty-one of them, some new equipment. I thought the executive would eat me alive [for spending the club's money without their permission]. That cost $1,600, a lot of money out of the team's meagre budget at the time – you couldn't outfit one player today for that amount." (The executive had no choice later but to approve of the purchase. In fairness to Neilson, past coaches had kept around old equipment for years, and the executive used to chase down players who did not return equipment after the season.)

Mike Fryia, who started playing for Neilson in 1972, was born and raised in Peterborough and dreamed about being a Pete. He remembers the old equipment, too. "As kids we'd go to watch Danny Grant and Mickey Redmond. We looked up to them and someday wanted to wear that Petes sweater. The first time I played for the Petes, I came into the dressing room and there was a big pile of equipment. I was putting on my helmet and saw Mickey Redmond's name and number in it. Our gloves didn't match, we'd have to torch our blades, and then go play the Marlies, who had all the best equipment."

Neilson made the Peterborough area his permanent home, buying a cottage on a nearby lake. In the summers he coached a Peterborough senior baseball team. Another legend was born with a game believed to have been played in the summer of 1974 between the Peterborough team and Kingston. The other team was at bat and had a player on third, itching to get to home plate. Neilson had his pitcher throw the ball wildly over the third baseman's head and the runner darted home. Unfortunately for the runner, what the pitcher had thrown was not the ball, but a peeled apple, and when he came to the plate the catcher tagged him with the game ball. The rules have since been changed to disallow this type of subterfuge.

Working around the rules was one habit that Neilson became known for. Others included his use of videos and letting his dog on the ice for practice. Sometimes – not often – he would have his big dog, Jacques, stand in front of the net to show his players that even dogs know enough not to chase the man behind the net. Arena officials were worried the dog would leave behind a bit more than a lesson, and one day he did. That was the end of the dog's ice time, but he was usually in the arena, and retrieved pucks from time to time. He also rode on the team bus.

Hockey changed its rules when Neilson tried another creative move. When the opposition was awarded a penalty shot, he sent Petes defenceman Ron Stackhouse into the net to replace the goalie. Stackhouse would skate out and check the forward. In six attempts, he beat the shooter every time.

He also had someone keep track of individual ice times of players, something that is routine today.

Yet another innovative move that no other coach had tried was pulling the goalie in the first period during power plays to add an extra attacker. He also started sending another player on the ice if his team was a man short near the end of the game. As the rules then stood, the extra man could be given a penalty, but the penalty would not be served until the other penalty had expired. So, Neilson figured, why not do this? If the extra man wasn't noticed, they had another man on the ice; if he was noticed, they would not be short another man. Hockey soon changed that rule.

Neilson discovered that the home penalty box in Maple Leaf Gardens was closer to the net than the visitors', and knew that the rules decreed that the box closest to the net was supposed to be for the visitors. When a penalty was called against the Petes at a game at the Gardens, Neilson sent the offending player to the home penalty box, causing quite a stir, but he was ready for the officials. He had the rule book open and the measuring tape out for the referee to measure the distance.

Dick Todd also points out that Neilson was responsible for getting rid of the rule that allowed junior teams to protect eight players from their own city. Although this rule had helped the Petes keep players like Bob Gainey and other Peterborough boys, it had given a huge advantage to the Toronto Marlies, who were situated in the biggest metropolitan area in the country. The Marlies could choose from hundreds of local teams, while cities like Peterborough had only a few teams to choose their eight players from. The league changed the rule to what is today a draft that includes on the list all players in Ontario.

Roger coached with strategy, discipline, passion – he was known to throw sticks and water bottles – and had a willingness to do any-thing to win. If a fight was necessary, a tough guy was sent out. If he wanted penalties killed, he had a system.

Dale MacLeish, former Petes player and brother of NHLer Rick, remembers the contrast between playing for the Petes' previous coach, Roger Bedard, and Roger Neilson: "Bedard played to win at all costs. Roger [Neilson] was hard to adapt to. He was more of a teacher and into systems. We had never heard of systems until [we played for] Peterborough. It used to be the best players were on the ice most of the time and the others got to skate between periods!"

Neilson's Petes also got to represent Canada in the first World Junior Championship, held in the Soviet Union in 1974. It was a far cry from today's international affair, where the best players from all across Canada compete as a team. As a result of going to the cham-pionships and watching the European teams and coaches, Roger introduced his players to a regimen of running every weekday morning and began measuring their fitness levels. Former Petes goalie Greg Millen gives credit to Neilson for the emphasis he placed on getting in shape. "He got me into fitness for the first time ever and had us all going on runs, many of us for the first time."

Before the advent of the World Junior Championship, junior teams would always warm up with a few pucks in the corners to pass to a player coming in from the blue line. In the USSR, they were amazed to see that the Russians were using about sixty pucks in their warm-up. Mike Fryia says, "The first thing Roger did when he got back was do that, then the whole league was doing it." More players got to touch the puck in warm-up and it was common sense. Another time, when his team failed to score, Neilson got two thousand pucks – nobody seems to know where they came from – set up four empty nets, and had his players shoot pucks into the nets. He told the media that maybe if they saw they could score goals here, they'd get one or two in a game.

He was the first coach to let his players watch video replays of their mistakes or other teams' weaknesses. He took the idea with him to the NHL, where he became known as Captain Video. (Ironically, he was the Leafs' coach then, and in the early 1950s they had used film to dissect every player in the six-team league, but this creative use of film was only for the management. The players never saw the replays.) He also changed the Petes' team colours to maroon and white, helping to design the new logo along the front of the jerseys.

Neilson cared for his players and their education. Just as the Habs had, Roger wanted all the Petes' players not only in school but doing well. Even if the players got back from a game at five in the morning, they had to be up for school the next day. What some saw as discipline and control, Roger saw as being organized, and most Petes players appreciated the training it gave them for life in the years after they left the Petes. Neilson wanted them to be well rounded and not depend on hockey for their future.

Former Pete and later Leaf Bob Neely once told the *Examiner* Neilson was the first coach that actually showed him how to be a good all-round player and also got him to control his temper. Neely had played for the Hamilton junior team before being traded to the Petes and found a world of difference. "Nobody had helped me before."

Neilson would get the players from out of town, arriving for training camp and not yet part of the team, registered in high school and set up with landparents as soon as they arrived. He was questioned about it, because it appeared he had already determined who was going to make the team.

"Keeping them in hotels is costly and school is vital," he replied.

He also tried different motivation tactics, offering twenty-five cents for any player with six or more contacts in a game, or charging them $10 if they didn't do their defensive job in the game's first ten minutes. Neilson once even put a $5 bounty on Red Laurence, who after being traded from the Petes made some uncomplimentary remarks about the coach. Mike Fryia remembers that "Laurence found out and went by the bench asking if anyone had collected." Neilson also fined players $5 if they were overweight.

"He always made sure practice was fun," remembers player J.J. Johnston, now a scout for the Dallas Stars. "We never knew what we were going to do at the next practice. It was never the same practice twice, although we'd be practising the same thing. We just didn't know it. He'd work on the basics and fundamentals. Sometimes he'd take an hour to just [work on passing] the pucks. If you did that today the parents would think it was a waste of money, but passing the puck is important and Roger knew it.

"He was just like a kid. He'd play ball hockey with us and get involved playing table tennis. He was always playing games and was so competitive."

Fryia says Neilson had special rules for the older players. For example, they could go in some bars when the age was lowered to nineteen only because the law allowed it, but certain unsavoury ones were prohibited, and he'd "have people who would tell him if we were there.

"The whole team would get behind Roger," Fryia continues. "He thought hockey all day and night. There was no talk about going to the NHL. We couldn't even sign with agents until we were twenty. We were all friends doing things together and Roger was usually involved."

Former player Dallas Eakins, who later became a close friend of the coach, says, "He was somebody you always wanted to be around. He made your life better." (Eakins played for Dick Todd's Petes but Neilson got to know many of those players.)

While the vast majority of players who were coached by Neilson appreciated his interest in their welfare and the systems he put in place, there were occasional exceptions. Stan Jonathan, who later emerged as one of the tougher enforcers during his years in the NHL, was not a Neilson fan. Neilson had given Stan a chance to play, improve his skills, and develop as a player, but when Stan Jonathan left Peterborough, he was glad to be leaving. It was his landparents he remembered fondly. "If not for the Garveys and people like [fellow player] Paul Evans, I wouldn't have stayed," says Jonathan. "I owe the Garveys, they were the best. I had had enough of Neilson; he didn't treat people equally. He had his favourites. I had asked him to trade me a few times but he wouldn't."

Neilson wasn't stupid. How could he trade Stan away, knowing his players would then have to face him?

The problems between Neilson and Jonathan can be traced back to life outside the rink. In his job as coach of the Petes, Neilson dealt mainly with immature teens. Stan was the same age as his teammates, but he had had a different kind of upbringing. "I had worked all summers, all my life. He didn't understand that. I put 8,500 miles on my vehicle that last year. It was 156 miles from the rink to my door [on the Six Nations reserve near Brantford]. I'd drive home at three a.m. the night after a game and be back that day for a four p.m. practice. [Neilson] would never know about it."

The end of the relationship with Neilson came near the end of that last year. "Roger accused some of us of playing for ourselves," says Stan. "I couldn't believe it. I'd go in the corners and get cut, bruised, do whatever it took, and he'd say that. I know he's passed away, but I lost all my respect for the man after that. I never spoke to him after leaving the Petes. Never."

Greg Millen's impression of Neilson may be more typical of other players' experiences. "The transition to Peterborough wasn't difficult. Roger really helped, although I wondered about him, because he would walk right past you at the rink. You'd think he was mad at you, but later you learned that he had eight things on his mind. He was a space cadet. He used to scare you to death with his silence. Roger was a father figure to us, though."

Neilson was not only the Petes' coach, he was also the team's general manager, promoter, and scout. Over his nine seasons coaching them, he brought the team fame with his innovations. He created promotions such as kids' nights and program bingos that many hockey teams have adopted in the years since. (He even managed to bring in three Montreal Canadiens – Peter Mahovlich and former Petes' players Bob Gainey and Doug Jarvis – for a shootout during one home game that attracted the biggest crowd of the season.)

But the players were his greatest concern.

Craig Ramsay was on the receiving end of a lot of attention from Neilson when Neilson was trying to recruit him for the team. His recollections give some insight into the way Neilson worked.

Craig was sixteen, and playing Junior B for the Etobicoke Indians, when the Ramsays became aware of Neilson's interest. He had tried out earlier in the year for the Petes but lasted only a week in training camp when Neilson offered him a position on the local Junior B team. "It was a funny thing," says Barb Ramsay. "Every time we went to the games and looked in the stands, Roger Neilson would be there." He would stop and talk with the family at each game, mainly about Craig joining the Petes, but Craig wasn't convinced that it was the right course for him. He decided to play for the Junior B Indians. Then he got a letter from Neilson. "As you know," Neilson wrote, "we have decided to make several major changes in our hockey club. Most of these changes involve using younger players. I must admit that since I talked to your father two weeks ago at the Centennial Arena we were counting heavily on you to centre one of our lines. You can be sure that we were very disappointed by your decision to stay in Toronto."

Neilson went on to say that he would be making changes to the Petes' lineup that weekend and he wondered if Craig had made the right decision. He listed the following questions for Ramsay to consider:

1. You appear to have a promising future in hockey. Where will you develop the necessary skills (e.g., skating) most this season?
2. You were with our club for training camp and several exhibition games. Do you feel that you have the ability to play on our team?
3. Could you maintain a good standing at school by changing schools after two months?
4. Will it be any less difficult to leave home next September?
5. Would you, as a 16-year-old hockey player, be happy in Peterborough?

Neilson then outlined some information about the Peterborough Petes:

Craig, if you are honest in answering the above questions, I think you should consider very strongly playing for the

Petes this season. Henri Lehvanon, Rick MacLeish, and Ron Plumb are other players with three years to play in junior hockey. By next Monday, two or three more players your age will be added to our team. These boys will be established Junior A hockey players by the end of this season.

Our plan to go with a younger team includes you, Craig. We play at home on Sunday evening. If I haven't heard from you by then, I will contact you by phone after the game.

You can be sure, Craig, that I wouldn't be pressing you like this if I didn't think it was in your best interest. I know that your parents are also most anxious to do what is best for you. Your decision should certainly be a family one rather than a personal one.

Not surprisingly, perhaps, Craig Ramsay was persuaded to become a Peterborough Pete.

Neilson saw to it that he got a copy of the boys' report cards, as well as reports from the schools on the players' educational development. He brought in defensive hockey systems, a strong work ethic, and team play. He was a workaholic, always busy coaching, watching videos, and travelling to scout out prospects. While he was in Peterborough, hockey agents and lawyers had not yet arrived on the scene, so he usually had to deal only with players' parents. He had only a trainer as another paid team employee, so many responsibilities fell on his shoulders and he willingly took them all on. It was difficult to figure out when he slept, but it was clear he did, even if at inappropriate times.

Ramsay remembers going to Neilson for advice when he was overwhelmed by homesickness in his first weeks in Peterborough. He was a reserved youth and reluctant to come forward, but finally he got up enough courage to approach Neilson in his Memorial Centre office, a cramped little room. "I was homesick. I wasn't that good a hockey player and I knew it. The team wasn't good. I had had a dose of reality. What's the sense? I thought. Surely he could find someone better than me?" With his head down, the shy Ramsay expressed all his doubts and misgivings, his feelings of futility and sadness. When he was finished at last, he looked at Neilson. "There was silence," says Craig. "Roger was sound asleep. I just sat there. He had his head against the wall and he was sleeping and slept for a few minutes until he finally fell forward and said we could talk about it the next day." Ramsay never did return for the talk.

Herb Warr remembers another instance of Neilson's erratic nap-taking. "One night we were coming home from scouting in Lindsay [with Roger at the wheel] and I looked at him. He was sleeping and the car was going into the rail guard." Warr pulled the car back into the lane. The story is similar to one told by former player Greg Millen, who went scouting with Roger one night. They were driving along Highway 401, heading for Toronto, when Millen noticed that the coach was asleep. "We were going into the other lane, and I had to punch him to wake him up." He made the coach pull over and took over the driving.

The Petes had two Ontario scouts. Soon after their reports arrived, Neilson would go to watch the prospects. It helped that he had an executive that didn't interfere with hockey. The purpose of the community executive was to make sure the team didn't go into debt, kept winning, and represented itself well in the community. The members were not always hockey wise and left the coaching up to the people they hired. In this respect, the team was unlike privately owned ones – owners are known to interfere with their coaches' and general managers' work. Neilson's Petes teams during his tenure failed to make the playoffs only once, and more than thirty of his Petes' graduates, including such players as Bob Gainey, Craig Ramsay, Colin Campbell, John Garrett, Greg Millen, and Keith Acton, went on to the NHL. He brought more national attention to Peterborough when the media featured this innovative coach in print articles and television programs. He also continued the team's success and improved upon the Petes' systems for scouting, education, land-parenting, and other features that would draw more players. Many of those systems are still in place today. When he left the Petes to become head coach of the Dallas AHL team in 1976, he continued his innovative ways. He started using a new statistic, scoring chances, that is now in everyday use.

He was in Dallas for only a year when the Toronto Maple Leafs offered him a job at $40,000 per annum. The offer was made – and accepted – over the telephone in 1977 while Neilson was vacationing in South Africa (not bungee jumping this time, as he did in 1999 in Africa at the age of sixty-three). Leafs owner Harold Ballard announced the deal before a contract was signed. Neilson, now forty-three, turned down a Vancouver coaching job to become the Leafs' twelfth head coach. It wasn't until then that he quit coaching baseball in the summers to focus full-time on hockey.

The Leafs job led to a string of accomplishments: Neilson coached exactly 1,000 NHL games as a head coach for eight different teams, a league record (Jacques Martin stepped aside as head coach for two games in the 2002-03 season in Ottawa to allow Neilson to reach that mark). He was head coach or an assistant for ten NHL teams – Toronto, Buffalo, Vancouver, Los Angeles, Chicago, the New York Rangers, Florida, St. Louis, Philadelphia, and Ottawa – more than anyone else in league history. In spite of this impressive record, Neilson never coached any of his teams to a Stanley Cup victory, making it to the final only once.

His career as a coach was not always an easy one. After he was fired in Toronto in the 1978-79 season, he was rehired a few days later by misfit owner Harold Ballard, but he left the next season to join Buffalo, where he was hired as co-coach with ex-Pete and fellow legend Scotty Bowman in Buffalo. The plan was for Neilson to take over the head-coaching job and Bowman would move to general manager, but it didn't work out that way because the Buffalo owners decided they wanted Bowman to stay on as the coach.

Neilson took the Vancouver Canucks to the Stanley Cup finals in 1982, a series that is remembered for the night he waved a white towel to signal his surrender to the referees. At the next game in Vancouver, all the fans were waving white towels, a gesture that has become a bit of a tradition. At the dinner before Neilson's induction into the Hockey Hall of Fame in 2002, the guests all stood and waved white towels.

He was fired the year after his big Vancouver season. He sued when the team didn't pay his $173,000 buyout and won the case. A

lawsuit like that might have ended another coach's career, but Neilson
was so well liked and respected in the NHL, it didn't have that effect.
He signed with the L.A. Kings in 1983, replacing Bob Berry, a Petes
player from the 1963-64 season and a former star for the Kings. He
next went to Chicago as a co-coach, and then on to the head-coaching job with the New York Rangers, who hired him in 1989. Rangers
captain Mark Messier didn't like Neilson's defensive system and
Neilson was let go in 1993. He was then head coach in Florida until
1995, and an assistant in St. Louis. In March 1998 Philadelphia
Flyers general manager Bob Clarke reached for Neilson to take his
team to the Stanley Cup, but in February 2000 Neilson came down
with bone-marrow cancer. His sister, his only living relative, had
earlier died of cancer. Even while he endured the disease and the radi-
ation treatments, Neilson still wanted to continue coaching, but
Clarke didn't think he should and the two had a very public dispute.
In 2001, Clarke replaced Neilson with Craig Ramsay, the former
Petes captain who had played for Neilson in Peterborough.

Ottawa Senators coach Jacques Martin, another former Petes
assistant coach and a friend of Neilson's, hired him as an assistant in
2001. Neilson was able to keep coaching while fighting his disease.
He also was inducted into the Hockey Hall of Fame as a Builder and
received the Order of Canada.

Roger Neilson was never married. There was no time, he said, and
it wouldn't be fair to his spouse. He was married to hockey, and it
dominated his life in countless ways. In addition to being immersed
in his coaching career, he ran a summer hockey camp every year in
Lindsay, near Peterborough, and for a few years did the same in Israel.
He also helped run a Christian hockey camp in western Canada. He
subsidized some of the kids' schools, paid for kids' equipment, and
set up a non-profit Tier II team in Lindsay. Although people know
him for his coaching exploits, he is not as well known for his benev-
olent activities, making sure his hockey schools got money back to
children and ensuring scholarships were available for needy kids. It
is estimated he had coached more than five thousand youngsters over
his lifetime.

Just before Roger's death on June 21, 2003, only six days after his sixty-ninth birthday, Peterborough named a street after him. Roger Neilson Way runs beside the Memorial Centre where the Petes have played all their home games for almost fifty years. Weeks after his death the local public board of education also named a new school after him.

The Controversialist

In 1976 Roger Neilson moved on to the pros, and Garry Young, a former NHL coach, came to Peterborough as the new coach. Gary Green remained as assistant coach and assistant general manager, now with a salary of $9,000 a year. After Young left after only one season, the Petes executive decided to hire Gary Green. He was twenty-three – the executive thought he was twenty-six, but didn't ask his age – and full of energy. Green was now making $25,000 a year.

"I think his success was because of his public speaking. It helped him forever," says his mother, Margaret, who used to come with her husband, Harry, to the Petes' games to watch her son coach, just like other parents came to watch their kids play.

In his first year, 1977-78, he took the team to the Memorial Cup final, only to lose. Former Pete Terry Bovair, who played for Green then, says he was a special guy. "I would have done anything for him, and I think all the players would agree. He made you feel if you didn't make a commitment you disappointed him. You felt good about yourself – even if he was telling you about mistakes, you walked away feeling good." However, Bovair remembers a bitter moment that first year in the final game to get into the Memorial Cup. "He took me down to the restaurant of the hotel and face to face said he wasn't going to play me in the eighth game of the series at home. We had too many players we [had] picked up on the trading deadline and I was the odd man out. I was shocked. I will always remember how devastated I was. I was so pissed off at him, but later I learned coaches pick guys they want. I had a lot of respect for him the way he did it face to face. I knew from his face how tough it was and later he told me that. . . .

"[He] didn't belittle people," says Bovair. "A lot of coaches are threatening. He didn't [tell you] if you weren't playing well, but you always knew. He never created a mountain out of a molehill. . . . He was fair and, if guys earned their ice, they were rewarded."

While they lost the cup final that year, the next season would be different. The final game for the Memorial Cup in spring 1979 was to be held in the Montreal Forum. Green wanted the players away from all distractions, including fans, media, and parents. He phoned Scotty Bowman to ask where the Habs stayed for their finals and was told they rented a lodge in the Laurentians. Arrangements were made to rent the same lodge and the players moved in the night before the final game. They had a relaxing time there, sitting around the fireplace and exchanging hockey stories.

The next morning at 6:30, Bowman called Green to tell him American television was planning coverage of the Habs game, and the Memorial Cup final was being moved down the road to Verdun, Quebec. The next morning, the day of the game, Gary recalls, "We got up for breakfast, walked to the bus, with each linemate and each defence pair getting on the bus together. We thought about all those six a.m. skates. Nobody was in better shape than we were. We didn't need any rah-rah stuff. It was quiet when we got inside that dressing room.

"Dick [Todd, the trainer and assistant manager] thought it was too quiet. You could hear a pin drop in that dressing room. Dick came in and took me out of the dressing room. 'What have you done to them? They are as dead as can be,' he tells me (with a few obscenities thrown in). Only Dick could say that, and I said, 'Don't worry, they're ready. Trust me.'"

It was a great game. The Petes were playing the Brandon Wheat Kings, with Brandon stars Brian Propp, Laurie Boschman, and Brad McCrimmon "hardly ever off the ice." The game was tied 1-1 at the end of regulation time.

As they went into the overtime intermission, Petes star Keith Crowder entered the dressing room upset. "He thought we had come all this way and now we could lose on a fluke goal in overtime. 'All this work and we'd lose,' he said. I went ballistic," admits Green. Once again, he reminded them of the year they had gone through.

Just a little over two minutes into overtime, the Petes' Larry Murphy took a pass from Terry Bovair. Murphy took a point shot, which was tipped in by Bobby Attwell. The Petes had won their first and, so far, only Memorial Cup. The celebration was wild, the noise in the dressing room deafening, and in a time-honoured tradition the players threw Green and Todd into the showers.

While the celebrations continued, Green quietly left the dressing room. "I went to the bus, curled up in my seat, and went to sleep. I was mentally and physically exhausted and completely satisfied. When I woke up, the bus was moving. For the next three days I didn't sleep. There was a parade in Peterborough and the city went crazy.

"It is a great city. They love their team. . . . The fans cared about the Petes. They cared about all of them, and we didn't want to disappoint them."

Gary Green was named coach of the year, and nine members of that team were drafted to the NHL.

In 1979, Green left Peterborough to become coach of the AHL Hershey Bears. He was replaced by Mike Keenan, who became coach and manager.

The Petes had considered two coaching prospects – Keenan and another young man, Bryan Murray, who would get a job as head coach of the Regina Pats that year (and who later coached and managed in the NHL with Washington, Detroit, Florida, and Anaheim). Keenan, with his slick black hair and squinting, narrowed eyes, took the Petes to the Memorial Cup final in his first year. It was the third consecutive year the Petes made it to the final. This 1980 game became the most controversial in Peterborough's hockey history.

Keenan, the strategist and self-made psychologist, had played minor hockey in Oshawa and Whitby, two of Peterborough's most hated opponents in both hockey and lacrosse. He had also played junior hockey in Whitby and had been in a few games for the OHA Oshawa Generals. He attended St. Lawrence College in New York State from 1969 until 1972 on a hockey scholarship, getting his B.Sc. in Physical Health and Education while playing on the university's hockey team. He then went to the University of Toronto, completing his education degree and again playing for the university team, which was coached by future NHL coach Tom Watt.

In 1973 Keenan joined the Roanoke Valley Rebels of the Southern Hockey League in the United States, but it was clear he wasn't going to make it any further in professional hockey as a player. The passion for and knowledge of the game were there but the skills weren't. He returned to Whitby, where he coached and managed a senior team that had been rejuvenated; he also played on the team, finding time to score twenty goals in each of his last two years and to teach school.

He coached the Oshawa Junior B team for two seasons, 1977-78 and 1978-79, winning provincial championships both years. He was also a phys. ed. teacher at Forest Hill High School in Toronto, coaching hockey, lacrosse, football, basketball, and even swimming. In the summer, he ran hockey schools in Pickering, near Oshawa.

At the age of thirty, he was coming to Peterborough with two things on his mind: winning, and moving on to professional hockey. The team he inherited from Green had most of the players who had won the Memorial Cup the year before but were used to the very personable Gary Green, a young coach (the youngest ever in the OHL) who was close to and honest with his players. Mike Keenan, a deep-thinking, introverted disciplinarian, was like a bitter green apple coming into a basket of sweet red McIntoshes.

"He was the most unpredictable person I've ever seen," says Terry Bovair. "He took great satisfaction out of making you wonder what would come next. If things were going good, he'd really find a way to find chaos. He was successful, yes, but fun? Definitely, no.

Mike Keenan in 2002.

"We would go through the wall for Gary the year before and did go through the wall. Gary earned our respect, but Mike didn't give you the opportunity to get respectful. Mike made life tough."

Bovair, now a successful Peterborough businessman, remembers leaving a practice once because Keenan had three veterans, including him, skating back and forth across the ice for forty-five minutes.

"I left the ice, right through the door into the dressing room. I had one skate off and my shoulder pads off when Dick [Todd] came into the room. I told him I had enough and wasn't putting up with it any more. Dick got me settled down. I went back on the ice and the other two were still skating. I don't even think Mike knew I had left."

Bovair also remembers an incident when Keenan fined veteran players for being a few minutes late for curfew the night before. "He knew we were out at a bar and left at 10:50 to get home for the 11:00 p.m. curfew, so he called and then fined us all.

"The next Friday we were ready to leave the bar, this time at 10:40, when he came in and ordered beers for us and we stayed until midnight. Nothing was said. I never understood that. He was so unpredictable."

Former Petes president Ed Rowe, who had attended Clarkson College, a key opponent of Keenan's old alma mater St. Lawrence College, says Keenan was "a taskmaster. I didn't like him at first because he went to St. Lawrence," says Rowe, laughing. "He wouldn't fool around. It was always business and discipline. Socially, when you got to know him, he let loose." He also knew how to win hockey games

– the Petes set a team record with 47 wins and only 20 losses in the 1979-80 season. Keenan's antics – throwing tantrums, assigning fines, pulling goalies, yelling – and his moodiness became well known, but it was the 1980 Memorial Cup where he came to national attention while playing in Regina and Brandon, both Cup hosts that year.

The question still most often asked about that championship of 1980 is: Did the Petes throw a game?

The Petes had won fourteen consecutive playoff games before they assured themselves a spot in the final by defeating the Regina Pats 4-3. The Petes had to wait to see who they would face in the Memorial Cup: it would be either Regina – the team now coached by Bryan Murray, the man Keenan beat out for the Petes coaching job – or the Cornwall Royals. Peterborough would play Cornwall the following day in a meaningless game for the Petes but a decisive game for Cornwall. If Cornwall won, they were in the final against the Petes and Regina was out. Cornwall, having been trounced by Regina 11-2 earlier in the tournament, were believed to be a weaker team, and thus it was expected that the Petes would defeat them easily, making for a Peterborough-Regina final.

Some of the Petes players were afraid the referees would favour a western team and thought it might be preferable if Regina didn't make it into the final; this could be accomplished only if the Petes lost the game. Some observers accuse some of the Petes of letting up in the third period. One Petes player even shot six feet wide on a breakaway.

Did Mike Keenan throw the game?

The players say no, but it's a qualified no. He didn't direct them to lose, but he didn't do much to help them win. "The format was bad," says Larry Murphy, who was the Petes' all-star defenceman. "We were in the finals, and didn't care [about the Cornwall game]. Mike wasn't going to play the better players as much as he normally would. What would he gain by playing them? It was like a pre-season game."

Regina Post columnist Bob Hughes agreed with the format criticism. He wrote at the time, "It was a blow so low, so foul, so distasteful, so disgraceful, that Canadian Junior Hockey might need a long recovery time before it will be able to stand tall again to lift itself from the doubled over position it woke up in this morning."

Bovair, a forward in those games, remembers, "The western fans were already pelting us with eggs and yelling before the game even began. It was hard to play. We really felt threatened. . . . The fans never gave us a chance to compete.

"Mike at one point was saying 'Whoever wants to go out, go.' It was that bad. We were so concerned with the threats."

Cornwall defeated the Petes 5-4, scoring three unanswered goals in the third period. This third-period comeback aroused suspicion, but the result stood: Regina was out of the Memorial Cup.

The next day, I was sitting at home in Peterborough, having a day off from my job as editor of *The Peterborough Examiner*, when the phone rang. It was Petes president Jack Shrubb, calling from Brandon to tell me how ugly the situation was there. Media, fans, and coach Murray were accusing the Petes of throwing the game.

Keenan felt threatened, actually fearing for his life, and had refused to talk to the media in that biased and angry atmosphere. Shrubb had Keenan in his room and put him on the phone to talk to me and explain the situation. "The media acted like fans. They didn't ask me if we blew it, but only why we blew it. I thought the question was ridiculous so I didn't answer," he said. He assured me the game had not been thrown, but blamed the tournament format for the problems. (The tournament format has since been changed.) Why would Peterborough play their best players when the next day they had a game for the Memorial Cup? he asked. What coach in his right mind would do it? The team had absolutely nothing to gain.

"I'm glad everyone thought we can win at will. Listen, if Cornwall wasn't good enough they wouldn't be here. I'm sick and tired of any suggestion we blew that game," he said.

The Petes still had to play Cornwall the next day, in Brandon. Once again, they were pelted with eggs and debris as they came on the ice. At the end of regulation time, the final game for the Memorial Cup was tied 2-2, the second consecutive year the Petes had gone into a Memorial Cup final overtime. Overtime lasted less than two minutes – the Royals' Robert Savard scored, and the fans, most of them from western Canada, gave the Royals a standing ovation.

After only one season, Keenan left the Petes, signing with the Buffalo Sabres of the NHL to coach their AHL Rochester team. He had had a good year in Peterborough, coaching the Petes to its best regular season ever and taking them to the Memorial Cup final. But it was one of the most controversial years in the Petes' history.

Keenan coached in Rochester for three seasons, leaving in 1983 to take a coaching job with the University of Toronto, then returning to the NHL to coach Philadelphia in 1984 and take them to two Stanley Cup finals. He earned a reputation as something of a tyrant, giving rise to his new nickname, "Iron Mike." But many of his players liked his ways, especially if it put extra money from winning in their pockets. He didn't practise power plays and allowed the better ones to use their instinct and creativity.

He went on to coach the New York Rangers to a Stanley Cup victory in 1994. In his NHL career, he has been the head coach of eight teams, the same as Roger Neilson, and continued his controversial ways. He became known as Captain Hook for his constant pulling of goalies. He once sat former Petes goalie Greg Millen in Chicago for all but fifty-eight minutes of an entire season. In November 2003 he was fired as coach of the Florida Panthers and the following year hired as its general manager.

The Players (II)

WAYNE CONNELLY
Born in Rouyn, Quebec, December 16, 1939
Peterborough Petes 1956-60
NHL career with Montreal, Boston, Minnesota, Detroit, St. Louis,
  Vancouver
WHA career in Minnesota, Cleveland, Edmonton

In 1956, the brand-new Peterborough Petes were helped to a good start when a sixteen-year-old scoring sensation from northern Ontario by the name of Wayne Connelly was added to the team's roster.

Connelly came by his hockey skills honestly: his father, Bert, had played in the NHL for New York and Chicago in the 1930s. Wayne Connelly left the mining town of Kirkland Lake after signing with the Montreal Canadiens in 1955. He was only fifteen when he went to play Junior B in New Hamburg, Ontario, a team affiliated with Montreal's Junior team in Kitchener. When the team was transferred to Peterborough, he went with it. Connelly, a prolific goal scorer, was so popular in Peterborough that the Petes had a night just for him when he left. Montreal gave him a three-day trial in 1960-61, and then traded him to Boston, where he went up and down in the minor pros.

He played in the NHL for the Minnesota North Stars in 1967-68 and was named the league's top player in the west division, scoring 35 goals with 21 assists in 74 games. In 1972 he was the first NHL player to sign with the new World Hockey Association, playing for the Minnesota Flying Saints. He led the team with 40 goals and 30 assists and the next year got 42 goals and 53 assists. The Saints folded in 1976, and that same year he went to the Cleveland Crusaders, which folded, and then he split the last part of the season between Calgary and Edmonton before retiring. He now lives in Kirkland Lake, where he is a successful businessman.

BARCLAY PLAGER
Born in Kirkland Lake, Ontario, March 26, 1941
Peterborough Petes 1957-61
NHL career with St. Louis

BOB PLAGER
Born in Kirkland Lake, Ontario, March 11, 1943
NHL career with New York Rangers, St. Louis Blues

BILLY PLAGER
Born in Kirkland Lake, Ontario, July 6, 1945
Peterborough Petes 1962-66
NHL career with Minnesota, St. Louis, Atlanta

If you didn't play hockey as a boy in Kirkland Lake in the 1940s and 1950s, you were either a sissy or a girl. That's the way the Plager family felt, and in this they were no different from many other northern Ontario mining-town families.

"Dad" in the Plager household was Gus, who had been a military cop during the Second World War. When he returned to Kirkland Lake, he went to work in the gold mines. It was a hard way to earn a living, but he had a family to feed and very few employment options. Gus, his wife, Edith, and their three sons lived in their three-bedroom home with Edith's brother and father. The boys – Barclay, Bob, and Billy – shared a bedroom that had holes in the walls, testament to their many scraps.

Gus Plager and Eddie Redmond had played senior hockey together, but Gus's playing days ended with an injury that occurred

Barc, Bob, and Bill in Kirkland Lake.

when Redmond tried to jump over him and his skate cut Gus's head. However, even if you couldn't play, you could be a referee, and that's what Gus did whenever he could.

The boys skated on Kirkland Lake's outdoor rinks. The town's single indoor rink wasn't for kids; only the older boys and men's teams could play there.

"I'd take Barc [the eldest] in a carriage to the indoor rink to watch his dad play," remembers Edith Plager, now in her eighties. "Gus was a good hockey player before I met him. He had been offered a junior contract but his father wouldn't let him leave home to go play. You obeyed your father then. So he worked on the railway and ended up in the mine."

Barclay

Barclay was the first Plager brother to leave home to play hockey. At just fourteen in 1957, he went to play junior hockey in Quebec. "Barc was obsessed with hockey," says his mother. "He always said he was going to play in the NHL. When he left home . . . I didn't want him to go. Gus said we had to let him go, but Barclay called every night crying. Gus wanted him to stay where he was. I said if he wasn't happy to come home." Barclay had made up his mind that he wasn't cut out for hockey, or at least for the life change it required, and he came home to Kirkland Lake.

If he was going to stay in Kirkland Lake, his only option was to go to work, so Gus took him to the mines, put him in the hoist with the other miners, jammed in like too many potatoes in a quart basket, and took him 2,700 feet down in the darkness. Barclay urinated in his pants. "Now, do you still want to quit hockey?" asked his dad. The answer was obvious.

As his mother says, "The boys had to be tough. You were expected to be; you were miners' sons." Barclay obviously survived the early trauma and developed the disposition expected of a miner's boy. "Barc was the rough one," says Edith. "He was a poor loser, but dedicated, always dedicated."

The Montreal Canadiens sent Barc to Peterborough's training camp, where it became quite obvious his skills and ruggedness was what the team needed on defence.

Barclay Plager was the Petes' team leader, says former Pete and later NHL scout Gary Darling. Toronto's junior coach, Turk Broda, a former Maple Leafs star goalie, had other words for him: "The dirtiest player in the league." (It should be noted that Broda's team led the league in penalties.) Barc once set the record for penalty minutes in the OHA, in 1959, but two years later brother Bob broke that record while playing for Guelph. *The Peterborough Examiner* described Barclay this way: "He was a crushing defenceman who used to come across the ice and catch you blindsided. Barclay Plager's hit would put people out of the game, he hit one so hard the sound could be heard all through the rink."

After graduating from the Petes, Barclay joined the minor pros and got his first big break when the NHL expanded in 1967 and he was picked up by Scotty Bowman's St. Louis Blues.

Barclay Plager came a long way from the day his father frightened him by taking him down in the Kirkland Lake gold mine. He had become a rugged 200-pound NHL defenceman, a fan favourite in St. Louis who was appointed captain. He played in the All-Star Game in 1970, 1971, 1973, and 1974. He also had his nose broken fifteen times in the pros and had hundreds of stitches. He was the team's top shot blocker and hitter. In 614 NHL games he had 1,115 minutes in the penalty box. After retiring in 1978 he was a scout for the Blues, then assistant coach, later head coach, then joining team management until in the 1980s, when he fought cancer, a disease too big for even him to conquer.

Greg Millen, a former Pete and NHLer who played for Barc Plager in St. Louis, says, "He was the smartest man I ever met in hockey. He was like a father to us in St. Louis. He had the ability to give you hell, and you'd walk away feeling good about yourself, because he was always right. He had a brilliant hockey mind. He was so tough but he cared. He had that gentle way – you can't teach that stuff."

Bob

Bob Plager was arguably a better all-around athlete than his older brother, Barc, but like his brother he had a mean disposition and hot temper when it came to playing hockey. Bob was being looked at for future football scholarships, but left home, at age fifteen, a year older than Barc had been, to play junior hockey in Guelph and to continue his high-school education, unlike Barc, who had quit school after grade eight when he moved.

Bob, another rugged defencemen who hit and fought his way to stay in the NHL, played in the minors for most of the 1960s, although he did get in a few games with the New York Rangers. In 1967, with NHL expansion, he joined brother Barc in St. Louis, where they

became known as the Bruise Brothers, hitting and fighting their way to be two of the most popular players in team history. Bob worked most of his career with St. Louis, retiring as a player in 1978, and was an executive for the team in 2003.

Billy

Life for a kid who played hockey in the 1940s and 1950s was much different from today, according to Billy Plager. "We'd just go to the games ourselves. It didn't matter if one of our hockey socks was red and the other green. We weren't there to look pretty.

"At Christmas we either got a pair of used shin pads, elbow pads, or socks, one or the other. The odd time we got new shoulder pads – we never wore arm pads." Mrs. Plager agrees. "We were poor, but we didn't know it."

Billy was a goalie when he was twelve because he was the only one with pads. "We didn't have belly pads, just used catalogues tied around our belly. There were no masks. For arm pads we'd maybe tie some cardboard around the arms. Our skates were made of hardly nothing."

Edith has many happy memories of her boys growing up. She recalls watching one outdoor game in particular. "We were all freezing. We looked at our net and nobody was in it. The game was going on and Bill was gone. The game stopped. They were going to put

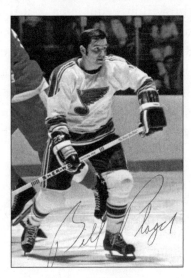

someone else in the net when he came back. He had gone into the school to go to the bathroom." Another time he got his tongue stuck licking the goalpost. The nets were made of iron posts with mesh or cloth tied to them. Billy saw light glistening on the post and, while play was at the other end, he licked it. "I can remember my tongue sticking to it and I'd be yelling, but no words, just screams," he says of this quintessential Canadian experience.

Billy quit playing goal, he says, after he "discovered it was far better to give the puck than receive it in the face." But his decision may also have been influenced by Scotty Bowman, at that time a young scout for Montreal, who told the family that Billy would make it to the pros only if he played defence or forward, because Montreal had plenty of up-and-coming goalies.

The Plagers each played three age levels of hockey every year. Billy remembers playing 122 games for three different age groups, his own and two older ones, when he was eleven. In the early 1950s when Kirkland Lake boys reached midget and juvenile hockey age or played for those teams, they got to play games in indoor rinks, and parents got as excited at the prospect then as now.

The boys were just as spirited as their mother. One night, Gus sent Billy to the boys' bedroom for some misdemeanour he'd committed. The punishment meant he couldn't play hockey that night – the worst fate he could imagine. Bob came into their bedroom and created a plan to throw Billy's equipment out the window, lower a rope, and let Bill scale down it so he could go to the rink. Billy got on the rope and Bob let go. The caper didn't go as smoothly and quietly as the boys had hoped. Bill recalls, "My mom yells, 'Gus, Billy just fell out the window.'" When the parents discovered what had happened, they let Billy go to play hockey but grounded Bob.

Playing hockey was also what the youngest Plager boy was born to do.

In one year, Edith lost her two eldest sons to hockey. (She also lost her brother, Carson Lewis, who went to the United States on a hockey scholarship. Hockey was in the family.) She did not want young Billy quitting school and leaving home. It would mean losing all three sons before they were even sixteen, and she couldn't stand the thought. She says of Billy, "He was the last boy and only fourteen. I thought he was too young." But Gus told her they "couldn't spoil their dreams."

Billy, who like Barc quit school after grade eight when he moved, remembers going to the Canadiens' Junior hockey camp in Ottawa in 1961. He got on a train in Kirkland Lake with his cardboard suitcase loaded with two pairs of jeans, a dress shirt, one other shirt, one pair of dress pants, and "twenty pairs of socks and underwear." His size 10½ skates were flung over his shoulders. They were far too big but he always stuffed socks in them for a better fit and shellacked the toes to make them harder.

"When we got to camp, they measured me for a skate and I was size 7½. When they gave me the new pair, I could hardly skate. We always had skates to grow into, never ones that fit."

Billy was sent from that training camp in Ottawa to Montreal. He remembers his cardboard suitcase falling apart in the rain when he arrived in Montreal but the team was "a class organization," he says. Cliff Fletcher, later an NHL coach and general manager, was a scout for Montreal at the time and an assistant to Sam Pollock. He met Billy at the train station and took him, as they did every kid, to Tony the Tailors. "They outfitted us in two tailor-made suits, fedoras, three pairs of pants, two sports coats, an overcoat, then took us to stores and got sweaters and pants. We felt good and we looked sharp."

Billy, built like a water barrel and just as solid, was sent to a junior team outside Montreal, in Lachine, where he boarded with people who wouldn't let him use their house, just a little room in the basement. His food was left in a milk box, and if he wanted more milk, it was a dime a glass. A lonely fifteen-year-old who couldn't speak French, Billy didn't want to tell anyone. "I was too young to know, too afraid to speak." But when he returned home at Christmas, weighing 155 pounds, down from the 185 he'd weighed when he arrived at camp, his mother was shocked. When he told her what had happened, she immediately phoned Montreal, and his boarding place was changed.

The next year, in 1964, he left Quebec and went to Peterborough to make, after board, $25 a week, up from the $20 he'd been making in Lachine. Billy says, "We played knowing we were not going to the NHL right away, but going to the minors first. You would have to be Bobby Orr not to go to the minors in those days."

He loved Peterborough, where older brother Barclay had been a star. He says, "We always credit Peterborough for our success. We were so scared of letting the people down in Peterborough we always wanted to win for them. It helped make us all get in the NHL, the fear of losing for Peterborough."

When Billy turned pro after three years of junior hockey, two of them in Peterborough, Sam Pollock gave him his first contract and sent him to Montreal's farm team, Houston, in the semi-pros, where future NHLers Danny Grant, Mickey Redmond, Jacques Lemaire, Pat Quinn, and Rogie Vachon were already playing against people like Phil Esposito, Derek Sanderson, Terry Crisp, and Al Arbour.

"Before sending us to the minors, we'd line up to talk with him [Pollock] about our future. He said to me, 'I like you, Bill, I'm going to give you what I gave your brother Barc, I liked him so much.'

"He gave me a $500 signing bonus and $3,000 to play for the year. I came home from Houston that year with $500." Bill had married a Peterborough woman and decided to return to Peterborough in the summer to work paving driveways.

His career wasn't as stable as those of his two older brothers as he found himself moving around minor-pro teams and NHL teams, even a journey to St. Louis playing with his two older brothers on Bowman's team.

Bill remembers Scotty Bowman coaching him in the NHL, where he played off and on with his brothers, Barc and Bob, for parts of four seasons in St. Louis. His toughest job was making the team when two of his brothers, the Big Bruisers, already held two spots on defence.

"We were having a good year [1970-71]. I was the top plus-minus player and got the nerve up to ask for more ice time. I was feeling good about myself, and Scotty even said, 'Yeah, we'll get you more ice.'

"I went home and told my wife I'd be getting more ice. The next day he told me to pack my bags – I was going to Kansas for two weeks to get more ice. I played five games in five nights, with plenty of ice," laughs Bill.

The St. Louis team had a rule that only a few specific players were allowed to own a house. Billy says, "They didn't want anyone to get too comfortable." He recalls that Barc – although he wasn't approved to do so – had bought a house, and although he and Bowman were quite close, this was one thing he wouldn't confide to Bowman. "Barc just kept telling him he had an apartment near Bob's," says Billy, who fondly remembers those days and how hockey has changed.

"Things were different then. Today's hockey is shoot and chase. It's not entertaining. We were defencemen and kept the blue line, forwards earned their way around you. Stan Mikita could get by anyone. He was great, better than Gretzky. Every team had three guys who could carry the puck."

Billy played in the NHL for nine years and still holds what he believes is the shortest apartment rental in NHL history. He was told in Minnesota in 1973 to rent an apartment for his wife and baby because he was staying in the NHL. They rented a place, but within forty-five minutes were told he was going back to the minors. That was Billy's pro life, up and down from the big league to the minors, moving his wife and children around, but loving every minute of playing hockey. He played in eleven different cities during his pro career. His only full year in the NHL was with Atlanta in 1972-73. He finally retired in 1977 and moved to Peterborough permanently, where he works at the Quaker Oats plant. He has been involved with minor hockey, helping coach several minor Petes teams.

The toughness of the Plagers is the stuff of enduring NHL legend. There was the time when Billy was playing for Minnesota and their parents had driven from northern Ontario to see their first NHL game. It was a big deal, getting to see all three brothers play, Billy for Minnesota and Barc and Bob for St. Louis.

In the first shift of the first period, Billy and Barc duked it out. They continued on the way to the penalty box, yelling at each other about how angry Dad was going to be. They fought again when they were in the penalty box and were kicked out of the game. Edith Plager went back to the couple's hotel room in disgust. Gus went upstairs to the rink's lounge, where he waited for the boys. He ordered bottles of beer all round while Billy and Barc still argued about who had started the fight. As the father and sons settled down with their drinks, another fight broke out on the ice and within a half hour, Bob walked into the lounge saying, "You didn't think you were going to have beers without me?" He too had been ejected from the game for fighting.

Barclay Plager died of brain cancer in 1988.

Bob was an executive with the St. Louis Blues in 2003.

Billy and his family live in Peterborough. His mother, Edith, lives with them.

BRYAN WATSON
Born in Bancroft, Ontario, November 14, 1942
Peterborough Petes 1960-63
NHL career in Montreal, Detroit, Oakland, Pittsburgh, St. Louis, Washington
WHA career in Cincinnati

Harold Watson and his wife, Doreen, raised their family – three sons and two daughters – in Bancroft, a town that was soon to become known as the Mineral Capital of Canada. More than 1,600 different minerals have been found in the area, which enjoyed a huge boom in the 1950s and 1960s because of uranium mines. At its peak, the uranium mills were processing 1,600 tons daily.

There was another tough rock growing up on Harold Watson's two-and-a-half-acre property. That rock was his youngest son, Bryan.

Bryan was smaller than most of the kids, but he just seemed always to want to play sports. "My first memory of skating is when I was three," he says. "I was falling all over the place. There was music playing, and I was loving it." This memory might be from visits the family made to the community outdoor rink in downtown Bancroft,

where music was played for public skating, or it might have been the indoor rink, where the adults skated and more organized hockey was played.

Bryan also remembers playing hockey outside at the age of six or seven when it was "so damn cold we would sit in a shack to keep warm while the others were on the ice." The boys skated on the nearby York River, and Doreen, Bryan's mother, recalls, "It wasn't deep. There was no current and it was the first water to freeze. Jack [a brother] and Bryan would always go there. Jack pulled him out of the river many times soaking wet. They'd go to another home to dry before coming home."

When Bryan started playing minor hockey, he was tenacious. Doreen says, "I don't know where he got that from, his tenacity and pugnaciousness."

A star player in Bancroft, he played any position, scoring goals at will, skating as if born on blades. He seldom took penalties or played what some call a dirty style. "He didn't do any of that when he was a kid. His dad would have gone at him, and given him a talking to," Doreen says with a laugh.

Bryan was always in an age group above the one he should have been in. When he was six, he was playing with and against ten- and eleven-year-olds. Bantam teams called him up when he was too young to play at that level. He was still one of the smaller kids in his age group, but his talent and drive were bigger than most. By the time he was eleven, he was attracting attention at tournaments held in places such as Apsley and Peterborough. He was usually named the most valuable player at these events.

In spite of these successes – or perhaps because of them – Harold noticed that some people involved in minor hockey were jealous of his son's ability. Bryan was once severely penalized when he shot a puck over the boards, a punishment far too harsh for the minor transgression. Harold also believed the team's coach didn't play him enough or use him properly and felt that he needed better competition. Harold's belief in his son was soon corroborated. At a Peterborough tournament, when Bryan was eleven, the Petes' coach, Baldy MacKay, suggested to Harold that Bryan should think of coming to Peterborough when he got older.

It seems that the Montreal scouts were everywhere watching kids play hockey. "No wonder they [Montreal] were so good," says Bryan, looking back. "My dad was in contact with Montreal. He got on the phone to them, and at the age of fourteen I became the property of the Montreal Canadiens."

Looking back on the decision now, Bryan isn't sure if he could make that kind of choice for his own child. "It was a gutsy move, but we talked about it," Bryan says. "He felt I had the right stuff. He was taking a chance but thought it would be better for me than staying in Bancroft and being held back." He adds in a matter-of-fact way, "I was born with this ability, my brothers and others weren't." Like the Plager boys in Kirkland Lake, Bryan left home at fourteen for hockey. He had the advantage, however, of having relatives in Peterborough. His maternal grandparents lived there and were happy to take him in.

Like other youngsters committed to Montreal, Bryan either had to go to school or work, and the Watsons weren't about to let him quit school. Doreen says, "They were supposed to go to church, too. I don't know if Bryan did, but the Catholic boys did. Letting him go was terrible. He was lonesome for a while. He'd come home some weekends and we'd drive to his games [to see him play]."

"The first few days I was pretty homesick," remembers Bryan. "The first days going home from school I had to ask directions until I got used to knowing where I lived. For the first month I'd go home to Bancroft every weekend, but after that I didn't want to go home." The teams he played for took over his life. He played Bantam church-league and all-star hockey the first season he arrived. At fifteen he moved up to the local Junior B team that the Petes sponsored, playing with and against players as old as twenty-one, and any position he was asked to, but mainly defence.

"It wasn't until Junior that we even thought he could play in the NHL," says his mother. Given that there were only a hundred or so players in the big league, and that he was smaller and lighter than most, the possibility was quite a stretch. Even the Peterborough Petes' players knew making it to the Montreal Canadiens would be extremely difficult. The Montreal rookie camps in Watson's day boasted the likes of John Ferguson, Terry Harper, Jacques Lapérriere, and André Boudrias, and the Habs' lineup had the Richards and Jean Béliveau as the basis for a solid winning team. Cracking that lineup would be more difficult than skating on cement.

But Bryan Watson had been dreaming of playing for the Petes ever since he arrived in Peterborough. He explains it this way: "Lots of people are born with athletic ability but some are born with a com-bination of heart, smarts, ability, and the drive. They have so much ability and the drive to be the best every night. That [sets them apart], that desire to be the best, that passion. Passion is the word that separates the guys. I had the passion. I loved it. I was born with it – and you have to have it."

He continues, "That was, and still is, a dream [for many kids], making it to the NHL. It was the best league in the world. . . . I was offered scholarships, but all I wanted to do was play pro. I turned down the schools. In those days if you went to college you could forget about playing pro. I think the NHL wanted to control you, and going to college was actually looked down upon."

Scotty Bowman, the Petes' coach in 1961, sent Bryan an invita-tion to attend the Canadiens' camp in Ottawa. A bus ticket came with the formal invitation, normally the only way you were allowed to attend camp. Bryan was successful and joined Bowman's crew.

"It was a tremendous experience. As young men growing up, Bowman would tell [us] that if we played a certain way, we'd win. 'What the hell is he talking about?' we'd ask, but he said if you believe you'll win, you will. He was so smart."

Bryan had decided by then that he'd rather play defence because defencemen got more ice time (although throughout his career coaches would continue playing him on both defence and as a forward). His calculation was justified when, once when he was with the Petes, he played an entire game on defence, never leaving the ice.

His forte, in spite of his small stature, was hitting. The Montreal Canadiens soon took notice of this tough young kid with the flaming passion. By the time he was twenty he had been invited to the Montreal Canadiens' training camp, along with two other Petes, Claude Larose and Jim Roberts.

All summer, he worked out, drank milkshakes, and did anything he could to get more size – he couldn't add inches to his five-foot-nine height, but he could put some weight on, he hoped. At the end of the summer, he had gained all of two pounds, weighing in at 160 pounds. Still, at one of the scrimmages at camp, it was enough to flatten Bernie "Boom Boom" Geoffrion, Montreal's big superstar.

In 1963, Bryan was sent to Omaha to play for a Montreal farm team there, but eventually he was called up for his first game as a Canadien. He was so excited he forgot to bring his skates and had to borrow a pair from another player, Bill Hicke. It didn't take long for Montreal's legendary sportswriter Red Fisher to take note of the pugnacious kid's style and label him the "basher from Bancroft."

Bryan played in the Montreal system for two seasons. "[Being with] the Montreal Canadiens was the greatest experience in my life. On and off the ice Montreal had discipline and you played to win." The desire to win was almost palpable. He says, "All you had to do was walk in the dressing room – it was unbelievable, the tradition."

When he went to Detroit in 1965, he says, the contrast was striking. "My greatest shock was being traded to Detroit, having Sid

Abel, then the coach, standing at training camp saying, 'Let's head for fourth place.' If anyone in Montreal had said that, the whole team would have skated off the ice. That was the difference."

Bryan was the first Bancroft native to play in the NHL – making for big news in Bancroft. He seemed to flourish in Detroit in a way he hadn't before. One of the biggest reasons was the move to forward, where coaches had him checking the other team's stars. He collected a raft of nicknames that reflected his role: Bobby Hull called him "Super Pest," the media dubbed him the "Shadow," and his team-mates called him "Bugsy" because he tormented them in his playful way. When he shadowed Bobby Hull during the playoffs in the 1965-66 season, he drew punches, harsh words, and angry flare-ups from Chicago's scoring star. Watson's face bore testament to his tough playing – he started looking like a pugilist who got more than he dished out.

That summer of 1966, Bancroft recognized his achievement by holding a parade for him. In return, he helped pay for the peewee team's all-Ontario championship jackets. Even though he was making only $10,000 a year playing for Detroit – the league average was $14,000 – he bought his parents their first colour television. Doreen still smiles when she remembers that.

He went back to Detroit for another season and more publicity as one of the best checkers, as well as one of the hardest-working and, yes, dirtiest, players in the league. But the following winter, in the season of 1967-68, he was back in the minors, in the AHL playing for Houston. Still a small player at 170 pounds, he continued to play with passion and gusto – he was chosen the MVP and all-star defenceman, and set a record for penalty minutes with 293.

He had an up-and-down career after that, moving between the NHL and the minors several more times. According to a story in the 1974 Hockey Sports Review, "there isn't a hockey rink anywhere in the NHL where fans haven't discussed the benefits of lynching Bryan Watson." In the hockey world, that's one of the highest compliments a player of his type could ever receive.

Off the ice, Bryan was not only thoughtful and thankful, but was also involved in helping others. In 1978 he won the Charlie Conacher

Memorial Award for his work with mentally disabled children and for outstanding humanitarian contributions.

Over Bryan's sixteen years in pro hockey, he played for fifteen different teams. He lost the scoring touch he had as a kid but he had mastered clutching, grabbing, and holding. Along the way he gained a rock-cut nose from the many fractures and a face with more stitches than a tailored suit that together somehow added to his cowboy good looks.

His longest NHL stay, from 1969 to 1974, was with the Pittsburgh Penguins. He was the league's all-time penalty leader until the Philadelphia Flyers brought in Dave Schultz in the 1970s. His final NHL appearance was with Washington in the 1978-79 season. In 1979 he joined the Edmonton Oilers as an assistant coach and briefly became the head coach.

"When I turned pro, defence was defence," he says. "Doug Harvey was offensive, then Bobby Orr changed the whole game. Before Orr and Gretzky, there were 1-0 games. I don't think it's any faster now, not faster than Bobby Hull."

Watson sometimes can be found now in the sports bar and restaurant he owns in Alexandria, West Virginia. The extra weight he carries would have been useful in his playing days. When he surveys the lunchtime crowd, he remembers the years when he was known as the Pest with satisfaction, and says, "I loved hockey until the last day I played. I could have played forever."

Bryan Watson lives with his wife, whom he met in Bancroft, and two children, in West Virginia.

DANNY GRANT
Born in Fredericton, New Brunswick, February 21, 1946
Peterborough Petes 1962-66
NHL career with Montreal, Minnesota, Detroit, Los Angeles

Barker's Point was once a tiny village – if you blinked ten times while driving into it, you'd be out of it. It was situated just east of

Fredericton, the capital city of New Brunswick. In fact, Fredericton, a small, beautiful non-industrial city of 50,000, with the St. John River running through it, gobbled up Barker's Point by amalgamation in the 1970s. But the redrawing of boundaries doesn't wipe out allegiances. Those who were born and raised there still know their hometown as Barker's Point.

Before amalgamation, there wasn't much to do in Barker's Point except work, go to church, go to school, or just hang out. Forget about staying home to watch television – television ownership was unheard of. The only viable option for filling spare time was playing sports.

Danny Grant had no trouble filling his spare time, no matter what season it was. By the time he was thirteen he was in track and field. He played soccer and rugby in the spring, baseball in the summer, football in the fall, and hockey in the winter. He played whenever, wherever he could. School, church, even meals, just interrupted the games.

With four brothers who were also active in sports, he always had competition, but none of them could match his passion. He played for as many as seven hockey teams per season. (Today, because of the rules of organized hockey, he would be restricted to playing for one team.) He played for his age-group team and for older teams – midget, junior, senior – whoever needed players. He would hang around the rinks looking for a chance to get more time on the ice and, sure enough, someone would always need a player. There were times he would score a dozen goals a game playing in the nearby Fredericton youth league.

John Doherty remembers those days. He was a Fredericton boy, a big strapping player nine years older than Danny. He sold Danny his first pair of CCM hockey skates, a pair of Tacks that Doherty had bought new for $57.50. He says, "The skates were more than two weeks' wages for some people. A few weeks after I bought them my dad got the bill. He woke me up one morning and told me to come downstairs. He asked me where my skates were and made me go get them. He took them in his hands, looked all around them. Finally I asked, 'What are you looking for?' He quickly responded, 'The motor. Anything that cost that much has to have a place for a motor.'" Danny paid Doherty the princely sum of $10 for the second-hand skates when Doherty was finished with them.

Doherty, now sixty-six and living in New Jersey, says, "We were just a bunch of guys we put together for the senior team. The Fredericton Merchants usually won the league and had the best team. We were called the Misfits. There was really no other name for us." The Misfits made it to the finals one year against the heavily favoured Merchants.

"We walked into the rink for [the] final game and I remember one guy saying, 'What are you guys doing here? Clown night was last night.' We got no respect." What they did have was Danny Grant.

"He had the ability to skate and score. If he got near the net, he would score. He was incredible and so young," says Doherty. He goes on to admit, "There were a lot of good players. I wouldn't say he was the best in the league, but he was better than most. He was our scorer. It seemed that every time we needed a goal he'd get one."

Reliving the game as if it were yesterday, Doherty says, "That night we needed one to win and he scored it in the third period. What a feeling! I was never prouder. We wouldn't have won without him. There was no way we should have beaten the Merchants."

Danny, with his moon face, calf-like eyes, and forever smiling face, played for the Barker's Point Aces (a.k.a. the Misfits) in 1959-60. He is registered as having played in 6 games, scoring 23 goals and 3 assists with no penalty minutes – at fourteen he was scoring almost four goals a game against grown men! The next two years he played with the Fredericton Bears and Fredericton Canadiens, keeping up the same scoring pace. It wasn't long before he came to the attention of people far away from Barker's Point. When he was sixteen, he got word that the Montreal Canadiens wanted him at their Junior A OHA camp in Peterborough. Danny had never heard of the place. He didn't even know what the Ontario junior hockey league was about.

"I never thought of playing hockey for money," he says.

The Boston Bruins were also after him. Their scout, Gerry Regan, wanted him at their camp in Niagara Falls. This was an offer Danny considered very seriously. Boston's team wasn't good whereas

Montreal had many good players, so he thought he'd have a better chance of playing more hockey with Boston.

The decision became easier when Montreal Canadiens players Dickie Moore and Phil Goyette came to a minor-hockey banquet in Fredericton that Danny attended. "They really impressed me. They were so classy, just top-of-the-line guys. . . ."

As usual, Montreal supplied the train ticket. Danny, who had never been out of the province, was one of four New Brunswick kids selected to go to the camp. In Montreal, Cliff Fletcher, a scout, met him and made sure he transferred to a train to Toronto, where he got on yet another train to Peterborough. Scout Scotty Bowman met him at the station. Bowman didn't say much, just took him to the Empress Hotel, the only hotel in the city's downtown, where the Leafs stayed for their training camps.

The rookie camp was good, Danny showed his stuff, with the result that the Habs wanted him for the Petes. Of the four New Brunswick boys who had been on that train from Fredericton, Danny was the only one who stayed.

Danny soon became an experienced traveller: the Petes played in places such as Montreal, Toronto, and St. Catharines. Although he scored only 12 goals in that first year, he fell in love with Peterborough, the people, and the team.

The fans recognized that he wasn't a scrapper when, in his first fight, he suffered a broken jaw and missed four weeks. (He would stay out of fights and the penalty box for the rest of his career – he averaged fewer than twenty-five minutes per year in the penalty box.) When he was injured again in his second year, he worried that his short career would be ended prematurely. By his third year, however, he was settling down. He scored 47 goals that year, and in the fourth year he popped 44 more.

It dawned on him only gradually that he might have a career in the NHL. "I never even thought about it until [I got to] Peterborough. Then I started seeing some of the guys I was playing with, and against, making it and I figured I was as good as or better than them, so maybe I could play there too." Shrugging his shoulders, he adds, "Until I was about eighteen, I wanted to be a Mountie."

With André Lacroix and Mickey Redmond, he was part of the top line in the OHA in the 1965-66 season. In 1966 he signed his first pro contract, a two-year deal for $10,000 per season. Danny spent a year in Houston in the Central Hockey League, an amazing league filled with talented players. On his team alone seventeen players went on to the NHL, including Yvan Cournoyer, Jacques Lemaire, Bill and Bob Plager, and Mickey Redmond.

In 1967 he became a Montreal Canadien. Montreal played the game the way he wanted to play. If you dumped a puck in, chances were you were soon on the bench or sent to the minors. Montreal wanted puck possession – you worked your way into the opposition's zone and the defence held the blue line. It was wonderful. He would have played for the honour of wearing their sweater.

The season after the NHL expansion of 1967, he was traded along with another former Pete, Claude Larose, to the Minnesota North Stars. Now he truly blossomed. He also started making far more money than Montreal had paid him. He didn't have an agent – agents weren't even heard of. The Montreal players all had to work at summer jobs to make ends meet. Once in Minnesota, he would never have to work in the summer again for as long as he played hockey.

That year, 1968-69, he won the Calder Trophy as the top NHL rookie. He played for Minnesota for six years and played in the All-Star Game three times. He was traded to Detroit in August 1974 and reunited with his old partner, Mickey Redmond, but Redmond was injured that year and Grant was later put on a line with Marcel Dionne.

What a line that was! Grant and Dionne were the most productive players on the team and Grant reached the 50-goal mark for the first time in his pro career. But the next year, at the age of thirty, he ruptured an anterior thigh muscle. It was a serious injury. He had been the league's iron man, playing in 566 consecutive games. But nobody is invincible. Although he tried to come back with the L.A. Kings from 1977 to 1979, he finally had to retire from the NHL.

Grant left behind him a creditable list of achievements. Besides his 50-goal season, the first by a Maritime-born player, he was the first Calder Trophy winner from New Brunswick, and the most successful Maritime hockey player ever. He was also the most famous player from Fredericton since Willie O'Ree became the NHL's first black player in 1960.

On leaving pro hockey, Grant moved back to Fredericton, where he was an assistant coach at St. Thomas University and coach at the University of New Brunswick. He also worked with the minor-hockey program there.

Danny Grant lives in Fredericton with his wife, Linda. He works for Enbridge and helps raise money for various area charities.

ANDRÉ LACROIX
Born in Lauzon, Quebec, June 45, 1945
Peterborough Petes 1964-66
NHL career with Philadelphia, Chicago, Hartford
WHA career with Philadelphia, New York/Jersey, San Diego,
*   Houston, New England*

The winters are cold in Lauzon, Quebec. You can feel the wind in your bones through your jacket, but if you skate hard and long enough, you're sweating so much you have to remove your coat. It's not the cold that gets you, but the thirst.

It's not much different there from any other cold Canadian city, except the dominant language is French in this tiny town of 15,000 people (since it amalgamated with Lévis it has close to 40,000 people) situated on the southeast shore of the St. Lawrence River.

André Lacroix was born here in 1945, one of fourteen children – seven boys and seven girls – who lived in a six-bedroom home where his father did his best to make sure they always had food on the table. Their father delivered oil on horse-drawn wagons, later worked at shipbuilding, then owned a repair shop–gas station. There was never any money to spare. André's mother was a great cook who prepared hot meals three times a day, at breakfast, lunch, and supper. "We would come home for lunch – we all did in those days," says André. He also remembers his father's old pickup truck. "He'd turned the

André Lacroix, fourth from right.

engine off when he was going downhill to save on gas." Frugality was important, as was church. André grew up in a traditional Catholic family where weekly Mass was mandatory.

André has no idea why he fell in love with hockey and no idea when it happened. He was the only one in the family to play. "[One] brother was a year older. When we were in school we used to play against each other but he really didn't have the same interest I did. He became a priest. I try to tell people I have no idea how I learned to skate or how old I was. Some people say they can [remember learning to skate] but I have no memory of it.

"I had an old Hespeler stick that cost about $1.50. You couldn't take slapshots in case it broke, because you wouldn't get another one. If it broke we put nails in it, [or] wired it so we could still use it. . . .

"In the summer we would play ball. I never owned a bicycle. Who could afford that? But I'd always wait for November, the first snow-fall, the first ice. I just loved that."

That first ice didn't last very long. "Maybe some of November, but that ice would melt and you'd wait for more ice by December, which would last until the end of February."

Hockey was fun, and André was the best in the town, even the best in his township, but like many other Canadian kids, he lived to play hockey, not to become a hockey player. However, the more André played hockey, the more he began to realize how good he was.

He could skate circles around anyone in Lauzon. He was always the leading scorer, no matter what age group he was playing against.

He was twelve when he first played in an indoor rink. His team was going to the provincial championships, and because the tournament would be held in an indoor rink, the team went to another town to practise indoors to get acclimatized.

"I didn't like it. I couldn't breathe," André recalls. "I was used to playing outdoors in the fresh air. I still remember trying to breathe."

André's team won the championship and for the next three years, up to midget, continued to win. The midget team never lost a game and the still-small André (he eventually grew to five-foot-eight and 160 pounds) was the leading scorer, always with more assists than goals. "I always loved getting assists," he says.

As far as he can remember, no one taught him to play in these early years. "In midget we had a [school] principal as a coach. He didn't know much about hockey. The players basically ran the team and won. I remember the principal was going to leave a guy off the team [and replace him with] someone he thought was better who lived outside the area. I said I'd leave if the other kid played. He kept our kid. We just played all the time. I played on the power play, shorthanded. God gave me a talent, and I just kept using it."

Soon he was being invited to play in Quebec City for more competitive teams. It was no small matter to cross the St. Lawrence River by ferry in order to play, but (with his parents' help) he did it.

André, the youngest child, believes he was spoiled. "I remember asking for ice-cream cones before supper and getting really upset if I didn't get them. And when I was playing for the Montreal Junior Canadiens . . . my parents [would be] making this two-hour drive from Lauzon to Montreal. Two hours then was like ten hours today. I'd be crying, waiting for them to come to the Forum. I was fifteen and disappointed as I waited because I was spoiled. . . . I'd cry before every game waiting for them and cry after every game when they went home."

By the time Lacroix had turned sixteen, the Canadiens reckoned that he was one of the best in Quebec, maybe the country, and they signed him. The following year, after his first year as a junior, Pollock asked him to sign a C form, the document that would make him Montreal Canadiens property, for $100. As far as Lacroix was concerned, "it was a contract for life with the Canadiens. Sam Pollock came to me and said I had to sign it. I told him I wasn't going to sign it. I had been a big fan of Jean Béliveau, he was my hero. Jean Béliveau had not signed a C form and played in Quebec City, so I wasn't going to sign. I went to Quebec [instead of signing with the Habs].

"Pollock told me if I didn't sign they'd send me to Peterborough. I didn't know where Peterborough was, but I knew it was regarded as a farm team for the Montreal Juniors. He was trying to scare me. I had no English and Peterborough had no French. I still refused."

Players did not buck management in those days – they deferred to it. They didn't talk back or ask questions. They did as they were told. The seventeen-year-old Lacroix's act of rebellion was extraordinary. "I went to Peterborough," he says. "It was the biggest and smartest decision I ever made.

"When I went there I learned how to speak English. The coach [Frank Mario] was French. I started hanging around a bowling alley, just like in Lauzon, and a pool hall. A Greek family helped me learn some English. I started speaking short sentences and reading newspapers, listening to learn words. . . . The Greek family taught me about verbs and nouns, past and present tenses. I got to the point when I talked English I thought in English and when I talked French I thought in French."

Lacroix didn't go to school because there were no French schools for him to attend. Instead, he got a job in a clothing store where, somehow, with his limited English, he was able to sell clothes to English people! "I listened to people and picked up words from that," he says. "I paid much attention to what was going on and learned a lot. It was a great decision. Those junior years were the best." When he got to the rink, the dressing room was full of people speaking English. "I had a hard time understanding. I was the only French guy and I wanted to be accepted so I concentrated on my hockey. I decided to do my best to be the best. I figured if I was the best of the best, it would help me be accepted." His linemate Danny Grant admired his friend's determination and says, "When he came to camp he couldn't speak English, and by the end of the season he was giving an English interview to the local radio station."

Lacroix also experienced culture shock and homesickness along with the language barrier. "I remember going to lunch with the guys and they said they would have some sandwiches. Sandwiches? I was always used to having hot meals. I had never had a sandwich before." In spite of it all, he was determined to prove Sam Pollock wrong. "I had made up my mind in Peterborough to show him he made a mistake. I didn't care what city I played in, I was going to show him and have a good year. I thought he had sent me to Peterborough so I would be miserable. I concentrated on hockey."

Lacroix started to play on a line with Grant and Mickey Redmond. They clicked immediately. "It was great having Mickey and Danny to play for. I'd just tell them to get in the open and I'd get them the puck."

André recounts how he used to analyse games. "Even when I was a kid I looked at the game differently. I never watched the game: I'd watch the players like Béliveau, Keon, and Richard. They were the centres and I'd learn from watching them. I told my linemates I'd find them. I played the same way as Gretzky did later. . . . I basically had eyes in the back of my head. Even when I was twelve, when I received the puck, I always knew what to do next. Danny was up and down his wing – he skated like Cournoyer. Mickey was young, a great skater, and could shoot the puck. They could both shoot. I always made sure my wingers got as many goals as they could because I'd get the assists. I couldn't care less about scoring goals. I could handle the puck, Danny had size, Mickey had speed, and we had success."

They had so much success the entire line was selected to the OHA's first all-star team, the only time that has happened in junior hockey. All three of them were in the top ten in league scoring.

"The Grant-Redmond-Lacroix line was the premier line of junior hockey," says former Petes defenceman Billy Plager. "They could do it all: they could read plays, shoot, hang on to the puck, and they hated to lose. Our job was to protect them."

André was so good that he won the Red Tilson Trophy twice, in 1965 and in 1966, as best player in the league.

In 1967, after graduating from the Petes, Lacroix played for the Quebec Aces in the AHL and was far ahead of anyone else in the league's scoring race. The Aces' fan club appreciated him so much they bought him his first car. The day after that presentation the Philadelphia Flyers called him up for a game in Pittsburgh. The game was a 1-1 tie, Lacroix scoring the Flyers' only goal, on a break-away. The next night the team won 7-4; again, André got a goal and, this time, three assists. The next day Philly asked him to stay.

"I was thinking of going back [to the AHL] because I was leading the scoring title and the fan club had just given me a car. But I stayed in the NHL. It was the right decision."

André always negotiated his own contract. Philly offered him $18,000 a year, he wanted $25,000; they settled at $22,000. By 1971 he was being paid $35,000. Then the World Hockey Association came calling, offering to double his salary. He accepted the offer but made sure he had a clause in his contract making him a free agent whenever the coaches changed or the team moved.

He was the WHA's leading scorer in 1972-73 – the new league's first scoring champion. He got 106 assists in 1974-75 – a record for him and the WHA.

That year he was nominated for an award as Canada's French Athlete of the Year, up against Guy Lafleur and Marcel Dionne. He and his parents went to the banquet in Ottawa. The announcement from the podium was that Lafleur was the winner. André accepted the decision gracefully, saying, "I was just glad to be nominated." But that wasn't the end of the story. A reporter told him he felt he should have won the award. Lacroix replied that that was nice of him but added, "You can't win them all." The reporter repeated, "No, I think you should have won it." The reporter had asked other reporters how they voted and it appeared to him that the majority of the votes were for Lacroix. The next day, award officials called André to say that a mistake had been made, and that he really had won the award. Lafleur had to return the trophy and $1,000 prize.

Lacroix played in all the WHA All-Star Games and was the all-time leader in games played, most assists, and most points. He played for five different WHA teams without ever being traded because of his insistence on the free-agent clause. He retired in 1979, hoping to coach hockey, but it was not to be.

Summing up his career, Lacroix says hockey was a game, a passion, a "gift from God, and I loved to play it, that's why I was so good." It's also why today there is a rink in Lauzon, Quebec (the first indoor rink in the village), named the André Lacroix Community Centre, after the only kid from that small town who became an NHL player. He was also one of the few junior players of the time who dared to say no to Sam Pollock and be glad he did.

André Lacroix lives in Oakland, California, where he operates a skating rink and various hockey programs. Unlike his parents, he and his wife have only two children. Although they are adults now, André telephones them every day.

MICKEY REDMOND
Born in Kirkland Lake, Ontario, December 27, 1947
Peterborough Petes 1963-67
NHL *career with Montreal, Detroit*

DICK REDMOND
Born in Kirkland Lake, Ontario, August 14, 1949
Peterborough Petes 1966-68
NHL *career with Minnesota, California, Chicago, St. Louis, Atlanta,*
  Boston

Eddie Redmond quit playing hockey shortly after moving to Peterborough from Kirkland Lake in 1953. He brought with him his wife, Mae, and two young sons, Mickey, six, and Dick, four. He had taken a job managing TPT, the company that would later sponsor the Petes and have their emblem on the team sweaters until the 1960s, but the real reason for the move was so he could coach (and play defence) with the local senior hockey team.

Peterborough was a hotbed for hockey when he arrived in the 1950s and the Redmond boys were going to play. There was never

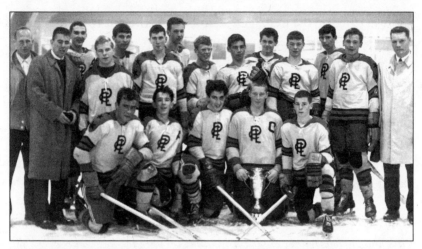

Dick Redmond, with trophy, as captain of a Peterborough all-star team. Assistant captain is Dennis Patterson, now head scout for the Philadelphia Flyers.

any doubt about that. They were not only going to play, they were going to excel.

Mickey excelled as he grew. From the time he was ten until he was fourteen, it wasn't unusual for him to score twelve goals in a game. His upper body strength was amazing. Nobody was stronger, nobody could shoot harder. He was so good that Scotty Bowman let Mickey practise with the Petes when he was only thirteen. The junior team in Oshawa almost got him to play there the following year, but Mae wouldn't let him leave home. In Mickey's house-league games, he was on the ice for most of the game – the teams were small, with just enough players for two lines. Many times he'd score all his team's goals.

When he was only fifteen, the Peterborough Petes – now without Bowman – put him on their team for the 1963-64 season. It was the right decision. That year he was third in team scoring, with 21 goals and 19 assists.

In his third year, 1965-66, he was hooked up with the kid from Quebec, André Lacroix, a playmaker the likes of which Peterborough had never seen before, and the right winger from New Brunswick, Danny Grant, both older than Mickey. Lacroix had two of the best shooters in Canada on his line and he made use of them.

There was something about the way Mickey played that puzzled Lacroix. "He'd always be going to the boards and I'd want him to get to the open ice." Finally, Lacroix took Mickey aside. Mickey explained that his dad had always told him to play wide to the boards. Lacroix told him to forget his dad, just get in the open; he would get him the puck.

This was the best line the league had ever seen. Mickey filled the nets that year. He had 92 points in 48 games, and his line had 308 points. When he was nineteen, Montreal signed him, and he was with Montreal from 1967 to 1971, playing sparingly for the Canadiens, but winning two Stanley Cup championships before being traded to Detroit for Frank Mahovlich. He blossomed in Detroit. In his first three years he scored 42, 52, and 51 goals, at a time when a 50-goal season was rare, and was named to the All-Star Team twice.

In 1973 he signed a $1-million contract over five years, a huge sum for that time. In the second year of the contract, he ruptured a disc. He tried to continue to play, but just couldn't skate. His career was over at twenty-nine, just when he was at his peak. He stayed in Detroit and became the team's television colour commentator. He also ventured outside the hockey world to start his own travel agency.

In February 2003, he had part of a lung removed because of cancer. The fifty-five-year-old was back in the broadcast booth two weeks later. He had missed only one game.

And what about his brother Dick? Dick also was a star in Peterborough, another hard shooter, a tough kid with a mean streak, but also with a particular fondness for fun. He was Minnesota's first-round pick and played defence in the NHL for Minnesota, California, Chicago, St. Louis, Atlanta, and Boston.

Eddie Redmond died in the 1990s. He had been active on the executive of the Peterborough Petes, serving as its president at one point. Mae died in 2000.

Dick lives in Toronto with his family and still plays on NHL oldtimers teams.

Mickey lives in Michigan with his wife and four daughters, aged twelve to twenty-seven.

The Redmond family still owns a farm in the Peterborough area.

JOEY JOHNSTON
Born in Peterborough, March 3, 1949
Peterborough Petes 1964-67
NHL career in Minnesota, California, Chicago

At the ages of thirteen and fourteen, Joey Johnston was the Petes' stick boy, standing behind the bench and watching Danny Grant, André Lacroix, and fifteen-year-old Mickey Redmond put on scoring shows. It wasn't until the next season – 1964 – that Joey joined the club for three games and the following year became a full-time Pete.

Joey certainly didn't have the same bloodline Redmond had. Neither his father, Johnny, nor his mother, Kay, had ever been on skates. Johnny had been a farmer and trapper before moving into the city to work at the General Electric factory. His father may not have had hockey genes to pass on to his son, but he had a strong work ethic to bequeath to him – in thirty-nine years of working at GE, Johnny never missed a day. After Kay and Johnny married, they bought a two-storey brick house in the south end of the city, close to the Catholic church, the GE plant, and a park. King Edward Park, with its ice rink in the winter and ball diamonds in the summer, became the babysitter for the Johnston clan – older brother, Tom, Joey, a sister, Mary Ann, and four younger brothers, Ray, Wayne, Jim, and Paul.

Both parents worked hard to support and care for their large family. Kay cooked three meals a day – a hearty breakfast, a hot lunch, and then a big supper. Dick Meredith, who lived around the corner from the Johnstons, ate there quite often. "You wouldn't believe the potatoes on that table. And everyone had to do dishes when they were done."

The family was careful with money. Kay made clothes for John, herself, and the children from scratch, and when the children were school age, she worked full-time shifts at GE for ten years before slowing down a bit and taking a part-time job at Zellers, while continuing to prepare the daily hot meals. Johnny ran the finances and believed in paying cash for everything – including their house. He never had a credit card. He made sure the children worked for

everything they got. There was no allowance for the kids: if you didn't work, you had no money.

Kay says, "The children always worked. Joey just loved to work. He'd shovel snow, cut grass, and deliver papers."

Joey remembers how tough it was to get money from his dad. "One time we were at the Civic [Arena] and I asked him for 25 cents, because I think the fries were 15 cents and a pop was 10 cents. He asked me when I was going to pay him back. I never asked him for money again.

"When I signed a one-year minor-league AHL contract for $14,000, Dad said that was more than he had ever made at General Electric in a year."

Kay says Joey was a good student, but he readily admits he didn't apply himself. He couldn't wait for recess so he could shoot cards. The kids would flip hockey and baseball cards against a wall to see whose card came closest to the wall. The winner would take all the cards. The big argument would be whether to allow leaners (cards leaning against the wall) to count. These hockey and baseball cards were treasures that came in packages that included pink bubblegum coated with powder.

Religion was a big part of the Johnstons' life. Every night after supper the whole family, and any friends who were visiting, would gather in the living room to say the rosary. "I learned the rosary there," recalls Dick, a Protestant, with a laugh. Every Sunday morning the family walked the three blocks to church. Joey and Tom were altar boys for three years during elementary school and went to church every day to serve Mass.

Like so many kids in those days, Joey and their friends developed their hockey skills on a backyard rink – in this case the rink Dick's father made. The two boys were playing there just about the time that Dick's second teeth had come in. Joey wound up for a shot but missed the ball and hit Dick in the mouth with his stick. "I'll never forget it," remembers Dick. "Joe goes, 'Ah shit, I think I broke your tooth.' I went into the house kind of happy about it and my mother started crying."

(As an adult, Dick joined his father in a denture therapy clinic that he operates today.)

"We played on that rink until we were about eight or nine, then King Edward Park became our home. Hockey was our focus; it was our whole life," remembers Dick. "Someone would always end up crying, and usually Tommy would start something. He started swinging his stick when he was about six."

Johnny Johnston always came up with used skates for the boys. Joey and his family can't remember his first pair, but they were undoubtedly bought used. "My first new pair of skates wasn't until bantam when I was about thirteen," says Joey. "They were new black Bauers. I remember them because I always wanted a pair of new CCMs." Another kid had CCM skates and Joey used to envy him having those skates. "I said I'd get a pair of those some day, but even in Junior B, when I did get some CCMs, they were hand-me-downs from the Petes' players."

Before Joey got into organized hockey at the peewee level, he was content with being a "park bum" or playing hockey in the driveway. His parents didn't push the boys into hockey, but they were never against it. When the boys did start playing, their father drove them everywhere.

Two leagues were in operation, city and church league. At the end of the year, the all-star teams from each league would play off to decide who would represent Peterborough in the Ontario Minor Hockey Association playoffs.

In Joey's first year of peewee house league, he remembers scoring one goal and "not knowing any of the rules, especially [about] penalties." In his second year, he scored twelve goals and thought he was ready to make the all-star team. His brother Tom played on the church-league peewee all-star team and Joey wanted to make it too. "You always wanted to make the all-star team because that meant you got to play another game every week," says Joey. "I can remember getting cut from the team; the tears came down that day. I thought I was better than a lot of the guys who made the team. Maybe it made me try harder."

"Joe . . . wasn't afraid of anything and would never give up," says Dick. "The only fear I ever saw him show in anything was the fear of losing."

As Joey got older, he'd go to his uncle's farm in the summers, haying, cutting grass, and painting fences. And he started to grow. In his last year in peewee, at age twelve, he was five-foot-nine and weighed close to 165 pounds, much of it muscle. "The next year I scored 144 goals and made the all-star team," he recalls.

Joey's size soon made him an intimidating player. He also had a mean streak that stayed with him throughout his career. "Joe was big and strong, the biggest guy out there, and he had so many skills. He could skate, shoot, and stickhandle. He could do it all," remembers Peterborough resident Bill Dobbin, who played against him. "He just dominated, even in all-star. He was head and shoulders above everyone. I remember one poor goalie – Joe would just come in and blast a shot at his head. Then the next time Joe would come in and slide the puck under him.

"Joe was tough, aggressive, and players feared him. He also played most of the game. If he wasn't on as forward [mainly playing centre at that time], he'd be on defence."

Dick Meredith says, "He would irritate people. He was intelligent. Whether he was playing outside or inside he would irritate you to get you to make a mistake." One of Joey's favourite moves was sticking the end of the stick blade into a player's ankle bone. Dobbin says it was much more enjoyable playing with Joey than against him. In those days there wasn't much high-sticking, but it was rough and things were usually settled with fists.

Joey says his size helped, "but I also wanted to play so bad. It was in that third year that I got really gung-ho. I had been playing with kids older than me for the last two years and it really improved my skating. I was dominating in that third year."

"Joe could shoot," says brother Tom. "He had a real heavy shot and was a good skater, but the big thing about him was that he could take a pass." In house-league games, Joey was taking shots from centre ice and scoring. He had such a hard and accurate shot that the goalies would sometimes just get out of the way.

Joey not only had a mean streak, he had a hot streak. He hated to lose. He admits, "I had quite a temper – or should I say, I didn't react very well to having a goal scored against us."

That was putting it mildly, remembers Tom. During one bantam game, Mickey Redmond scored on Tom, who was in goal, from centre ice. "Joe came right down the ice and suckered me," says Tom, his brother and teammate.

On Saturday mornings the boys would walk to the Civic Arena to referee younger children's games, arriving at seven and staying to ten. They were paid a dollar a game, but got the money only twice in the season – at Christmas and at the end of the season. In the summers, as he grew older, Joey moved from farming to take on jobs in the construction field that would make him stronger.

Joey didn't get much in the way of teaching or coaching when he was playing hockey, but he learned from his mistakes. He would watch the Petes' practices after school; it was easy for him to get to their rink, since he lived across the street. When two pucks would go over the boards, Joey would chase after them but only one would go back on the ice. He needed the pucks for his shooting practices.

That practising and his obsession with the game paid off. By the time he was fifteen, he had graduated from stick boy to player with the Petes, only for a few games, but enough to impress the Petes' brass. His first game was on a line with Mickey Redmond and André Lacroix. In his second year, he was known more for his penalty minutes than anything else. In 1967, a new coach arrived in Peterborough – Roger Neilson. Neilson knew that Joey was about to turn eighteen and wasn't going to stick around Peterborough and attend school. He had been selected eighth overall by the New York Rangers in the amateur draft the previous season. Neilson was convinced Joey was going to sign a pro contract, so he traded him to Kitchener to get something for the next year. At least, that's the story that was reported at the time. Joey says now that the truth was that he had been in a car accident as a result of drinking. Neilson had a rule that anyone caught drinking was gone.

Joey did sign a pro contract in the AHL and moved to Omaha and Buffalo in the 1967-68 season before going to Memphis the following year. That season, 1968-69, he joined the NHL, playing for the Minnesota North Stars in eleven games. The next year he was in the minor pros again with Iowa, then in Cleveland for the 1970-71 season, before being traded to the NHL's California franchise when he was twenty-two. The new team, the California Golden Seals, was owned by the colourful Charlie Finley, who had the team wearing white skates. Joey signed for $100,000 a year and flew his parents to California to take them to Disneyland. In his third season and twenty-four years old, he was the team's captain and an all-star. He had also married a Peterborough girl, and they had two daughters. Life was good – until 1975.

In the summer of that year, he was home in Peterborough and had been celebrating a friend's impending marriage at a stag held near the city. He had been drinking all night and left the party early in the morning. His van left the road and hit a pole. Joey was hospitalized, in critical condition.

That summer he had been traded to Chicago for Jimmy Pappin, but when he tried to go back to pro hockey, it was clear the effects of his injuries were too severe for him to continue playing. He had played 331 NHL games, scoring 85 goals and 106 assists and getting 320 minutes in penalties. At the age of twenty-six, he was done with hockey.

Johnston returned to Peterborough and drifted. He and his wife divorced. He turned to alcohol. Who knows what causes some people to wake up from a nightmare when others never do? Joey did wake up. He quit drinking – he hasn't consumed alcohol in close to twenty years – and began building a new life. He is now a jack of all trades, building anything you want out of wood. It's hard work and the hours are long, but he seldom has time on his hands.

In 2004, at the age of fifty-five, he was still playing recreational hockey, and on the ice that mean streak still shows up now and then.

DALE MACLEISH
Born in Lindsay, Ontario, June 27, 1948
Peterborough Petes 1965-66

RICK MACLEISH
Born in Lindsay, Ontario, January 3, 1950
Peterborough Petes 1967-70
NHL career in Philadelphia, Hartford, Pittsburgh, Detroit

The town of Cannington, often described as being in the heart of Ontario, was founded in the 1840s by Irish and Scottish Protestants. The little community had been expected to grow with a rail line that connected it to other centres such as Orillia, Oshawa, and Lindsay, but the expectation was not fulfilled. The rail line is long gone, and today most of the people who live there – blue-collar workers and senior citizens – either work for or used to work for General Motors.

In 1958, when Dale and Rick MacLeish were ten and eight years old respectively, the population of Cannington was 1,000, down from 1,500 before the Second World War. The boys' father, Garnet,

Al McPhail Collection

From left:
Dale MacLeish, Rocket Richard,
and Rick MacLeish in Cannington
charity game.

worked on the line at Oshawa's General Motors, travelling forty-five minutes to and from his night-shift job.

There wasn't an organized hockey league in Cannington then – there weren't enough kids to form one. A few teams were put together for kids thirteen and older, but they allowed kids like the MacLeish boys to play, even though they were several years younger. Dale remembers playing bantam hockey with fourteen-year-olds when he was only eight. "There weren't enough teams so they let me play there. Eventually there were lower-age-group teams and I went back to peewee after bantam and still had two years in peewee."

Both boys scored goals easily. Al McPhail, a high-school teacher who was involved in local hockey, wasn't concerned when people said the boys might be too young or too small to play with the older boys. "If they wanted to play hockey, they could play," he says.

By the time Rick was ten he was playing for several of these local hockey teams and getting calls to play for other all-star teams in the area, including Peterborough's peewees when they went to the Quebec winter carnival and played in Canada's most prestigious peewee hockey tournament.

Hockey was a community affair. The boys' maternal grand-parents, the Nicholsons, lived next door, and because of their great love for hockey, they were involved in the minor-hockey system and

would lug local kids around to various rinks in the area. Drivers
didn't have to worry about equipment taking up much room in the
car, though. Many of the players wore their jerseys and other equipment to the game and didn't have much else. There were no helmets
– "just a stick and whatever they could afford." The Cannington
minor-hockey organization supplied goalie pads, which cost $26.
Each player had to pay $5 to play the season, a dollar of that cover-
ing insurance. When they went to tournaments, they were billeted
at the homes of the home team's parents.

Al McPhail describes the conditions in which the boys played in
those days: "Our ice surface was natural, as were most of the area
arenas. There was always a conflict in ice scheduling with the junior,
senior, juvenile, and midget teams." In addition, the rink's icemaker
was a prima donna, says McPhail. "He didn't like anyone using the
ice before the senior games, so the kids lost ice time there. He also
didn't want teams practising before games."

In the 1950s and early 1960s, McPhail did the scheduling and
managing and even stepped in to coach whenever he had to. Parents
of kids on the team were not allowed to coach. Minor hockey officials wanted hockey to be fun for all the kids, and not to be just about
winning. But it was hard not to win with Rick on your team. He
scored 270 goals as a twelve-year-old peewee in the 1961-62 season.
The *Hockey News* called him the best peewee hockey player in Ontario
that year. McPhail says, "Rick could always anticipate plays. He was
a natural player from the beginning. I think that's a built-in thing.
Dale was good too, but Rick just seemed to know where that puck
was going all the time."

In spite of that, many people say Dale was a better hockey player,
but he admits, "My attitude was to have fun. That hurt, because I
always liked to have fun before, during, and after games. Rick was a
bit more serious about the game."

Rick, who later earned his professional living as a winger, played
defence as a young player in Cannington.

"He could . . . pick up the puck and go," says McPhail. "He was
a tremendous skater. His grandmother was an excellent skater and
he might have got that from her. He was compact, not a stringy kid

like the others. He had this terrific wrist shot. He could slap the puck, but you weren't allowed to then.

"How good was he? We were a D centre [the rating for small community hockey centres – the smaller the community, the smaller the calibre rating usually was] in minor hockey. We went to the final in a big Brampton tournament, the grand final of the AAA clubs. [Rick] was a one-man band. I remember we lost the game when some water on the ice stopped one of [his] shots in the crease."

In the early 1960s, the old rink was torn down and Cannington got its first artificial ice surface. Federal and provincial money was available for cultural buildings, so Cannington applied for "a meeting room, with a rink" and got the funds. It turned out that there wasn't enough water at the new location – the well ran dry when they tried to flood the rink. Townspeople would be out volunteering late at night, pumping water from the river and creek to make sure there was an ice surface. With the new facility, local kids could now expect to play a game and have a practice every week, but the rest of the time was for unstructured hockey – at least four or five hours on school days and up to ten hours on weekends. Play, play, and play. No adults, just the kids.

Young Rick would give instructions at some games. When one of his buddies played goal, he told the team not to let anyone take shots on him. Rick would make sure they didn't. "The goalie wasn't the best of skaters and Rick protected him. By the end of the year, he had five or six shutouts, but he wasn't getting any shots," remembers McPhail.

"Another thing Rick did was try to make sure nobody scored on his team when he was on the ice. He also made sure that other kids would get shots on goal. He'd pass it to them to try and get them to score. I think that really helped his hockey. He was always looking and passing."

Rick was so far ahead of the other kids that he was being scouted by other centres at a young age, especially during his spectacular peewee year.

"The other centres would always want to sign him to a card so they would get money from the junior teams if they signed him. [It] always upset me that the minor-hockey organizations the kid played in didn't get a thing," said McPhail. It also upset him that Cannington adults would recruit out-of-town players so their local teams would win championships. Dale and Rick had left Cannington by the time this started happening, but a younger brother, Tom, was still playing there.

"I didn't think [it] should be win at all costs. Kids' hockey isn't about that, it's about so much more than just winning. I thought bringing in ringers was wrong. Others disagreed, so I left minor hockey." McPhail, eighty-one in 2003, looked back on this time with no bitterness. He had plenty of other things to do: run for council, teach, help run the high school, and support the local New Democratic Party.

For his part, Dale, the first MacLeish to play for the Peterborough Petes, doesn't remember being scouted, but "they thought I could play Junior C at fourteen and fifteen." He says, "Roger Neilson, a Montreal scout, called one day in 1965 and said the Petes had drafted me. It was some kind of secret draft and they thought I'd probably be playing for their affiliate C team in Chatham, but I went to Petes' camp – I just got on a bus and went – and made the team.

"It was probably a mistake. I would have got more ice [time] in Chatham and learned more about [what it meant to live away from home]."

Joey Johnston and Dale were the only rookies on a team that was picked to win the Memorial Cup in the 1966-67 season. It was loaded with NHL-bound players, such as André Lacroix, Danny Grant, Mickey Redmond, Billy Plager, and Garry Monahan.

"We just felt fortunate [to play for the Petes]," says Dale. "We thought we were lucky to have a chance to play for a team that was connected to the NHL."

Rick stayed in Cannington until the following year, when he signed to play Junior C hockey in nearby Sutton, before following Dale to the Petes. Dale ended up playing in Chatham when the Petes went on a hunt for younger players, which included his brother.

Dale was drafted in 1967 by the Toronto Maple Leafs, twenty-second overall. He muses, "Can you imagine the money I would get today if I got drafted that high?"

He went to Tulsa Oilers of the Central Hockey League for the 1968-69 season, then played in the East Coast League for Jacksonville, Salem, and Roanoke, and later in the Southern Hockey League in Charlotte, ending his minor-pro career in 1976.

"Rick had the drive," says Dale. "I was more a happy-go-lucky guy. Redmond and Grant were great role models. They'd do anything to win and had great shots. I was a faster skater than Rick, but he could do more thinking" – "Million-dollar legs, one-dollar brain," his father used to joke of Dale.

When Rick joined the Petes, he made an immediate impact, leading the team in scoring and winning the MVP award. In his second year he had the most points and most goals and won three team awards. But he wasn't always winning Neilson's heart: he got fines for being overweight, among other things. Neilson once fined him $5, or a dollar for every pound he thought he was over the limit. MacLeish wasn't his only target as he went on a war against flab. The extra weight didn't bother Rick. He was the Petes' top scorer all three years he was with the team, and in his final season, 1969-70, he had 45 goals, 56 assists, and a whopping 135 minutes in penalties. He was not only the team's top sniper but its tough guy as well. He may have been the best all-round player the Petes have ever seen. He could score, pass, check, and fight.

Rick was drafted by Boston in 1970, fourth overall in the NHL draft, and was dealt to Philadelphia for Mike Walton. For the first time in his life, goal-scoring didn't come easily. Philly was patient, but his lack of production in his first two years meant a trip to the AHL's Oklahoma Blazers. He played twenty-six games for the NHL club that year, but the following year was playing for Richmond Robins in the AHL. In 1972-73 his chance to establish himself in the NHL arrived. He lined up with Bill Barber and Gary Dornhoefer and became not only the team's first 50-goal scorer, but the first expansion-team player to score 50 in a season. He also got 50 assists for 100 points in his first full season as a Flyer.

He loved playing in the playoffs even more and led the team in scoring both years they won the Cup. He played in the All-Star Game three times and is a member of the Flyers Hall of Fame.

The Rick MacLeish goal that lives on in Flyers fans' memories came during the last game of the Stanley Cup championship in 1974, a goal he scored in the first period of the game to put Philly ahead 1-0. Nobody imagined it was going to be a memorable goal when he scored it so early in the game, but the periods moved on and the minutes ticked away and the kid from Cannington had scored the goal that won the Stanley Cup.

Rick was traded by the Flyers in 1981 to Hartford. Injuries began to plague him, and he moved on to Pittsburgh and Detroit before retiring in 1984 at the age of thirty-four. The Cannington Kid comes home every year to see family and friends when the town holds a fund-raising golf tournament in his name. Cannington doesn't have a golf course, so it's held in a nearby town, but lunch and prize ceremonies are held at the Cannington Legion. Rick has been away from home a long time, but when he sits down at the Legion, he knows he's home, in the village where it all began, not far from MacLeish Alley.

Dale MacLeish lives in Lindsay, Ontario, and he manages a rink in Sunderland.

Rick MacLeish lives near Philadelphia, where he runs his own financial business.

CRAIG RAMSAY
Born in Weston, Ontario, March 17, 1951
Peterborough Petes 1967-71
NHL career with Buffalo

Work hard and good things happen. It seems like such an easy philosophy but we know it isn't always true. So when we find an example of it working, it somehow restores our faith. Craig Ramsay showed it can happen.

Craig Ramsay (top row, first player on left) when he was on the peewee team.

Craig, born in 1951, grew up in a small home on a dead-end street in Thistletown, Ontario. Thistletown was then a little village near the city of Toronto halfway between Weston and Woodbridge. He lived there with his parents, Bill and Barb, and two sisters, Laura (who became one of the best squash players in Canada) and Jill.

Craig's first taste of hockey was on the driveway, where Laura and some neighbourhood kids would play. He remembers his first time on skates: "It was at the Woodbridge arena. I was only five and could hardly make it around. I held on to the boards."

When Craig was around the age of seven, his mother took him to the nearby outdoor Pine Point rink (a roof was added later) where the ice surface was divided into thirds for some organized but informal hockey. His shin pads were wooden slats, he wore old gloves, and his skates were two sizes too big so he'd get a couple of years' use out of them. Craig's mother insisted he wear a floppy hat with earflaps. His first real organized hockey came a year later, and some of the players remembered him from the year before: "Hey, you're that kid with the hat."

Still just a runt with straight, short, dark-brown hair and impish little eyes, he was becoming more immersed in the world of hockey. He wasn't very good, but he loved playing it nonetheless. He tried some other sports – softball and golf – but hockey was his game.

It must have been with a heavy heart, then, that the eight-year-old felt he had to turn down an offer to join a hockey team. His mother remembers the telephone call from the manager of the team who was making the offer. She heard Craig say, "I don't think that my parents can afford that." He had just been told that it would cost $10 to join the team. He had overheard his parents talking about the cost of a new home they were building and needing to "stretch a dollar." His mother quickly assured him they could afford the fee, and he was able to join house-league hockey.

That first year the team played one game a week with a practice thrown in once in a while. His first coach, the only one he had in minor hockey, was his neighbour, Burt Turney, a former pro hockey player who turned out to be the hockey mentor Craig needed.

At the age of eleven, Craig went to his first all-star tryout for a North Etobicoke team coached by Turney and organized by Nick Durbano, father of future NHL enforcer Steve, who cut Craig. Craig was disappointed, especially since he'd been invited to try out. "I told my dad, and he called coach Turney, who told him not to worry but bring me out for the next practice." Turney hadn't known that Durbano had told Craig not to come back, but Turney wanted him on the team. Craig admits now, "I wasn't all that good and didn't play all that much. We only had two lines and four defence, one goalie. I played centre."

Craig's friends Wayne Butt and John Simpson were the best players on the team. Craig remembers them "trying to win the scoring championship. Here I was just hanging in."

"There was one time I wasn't happy. I didn't play much and my dad noticed. [He said], 'If you'd like to play more, you must work harder.' For a kid that was something," remembers Craig. "I knew I could not score all the goals or win all the faceoffs, but I knew I could try harder than anyone else."

There were other lessons Craig learned. When he was in grade four, he was part of a small group known as the Get in Trouble Gang. "We'd get in a little hot water, [and] they'd make us stand under a clock at the school. Other kids would walk by, see you standing there. Then my report card came home saying there was 'room for improvement in Craig's behaviour.'

"My mother said, 'You'd best stop that or there'll be no hockey.'" It wasn't long before the Get in Trouble Gang had to get along without Craig.

Another time, while he was playing in a game, he got to kill a penalty. "I heard all the parents yelling to shoot the puck down the ice, so I did. When I came off the ice, coach says, 'If you've got the puck, they can't score. Hold on to it.' I became adept at holding it and freezing it."

Both his mother and Craig vividly remember a turning point in his hockey, although his mother's memory is a bit different from Craig's. Craig says, "We won the King Clancy tournament that year [possibly in the 1964-65 season]. We were winning 3-2 with thirty seconds left. I won the faceoff in my own end and took it to the boards and wouldn't give it up."

Mrs. Ramsay's recollection: "He ragged the puck for two minutes. My eyes saw spots. I was so nervous."

The more Craig played, the more he realized that hard work, and not just talent, would make a better hockey player. It certainly began working for him. "I became adept because I was encouraged to do it. . . . I learned to take a hit, make a play, not be in a rush. The most important thing was that if [something] didn't work, that was okay. Coach never yelled if you did something that he asked [even if it didn't work out]."

"Coach Turney was teaching us to do everything. We had a small team with not many players. He gave us the opportunities to try, and there was quality ice [time] for us all."

Mrs. Ramsay clearly enjoyed the delight her son took in hockey, even though it was a game she knew little about. She recalls, "Craig would tell us every detail, every little detail, even from road-hockey games. He was so little, so shy, but when it was about hockey he knew every minute detail. We as parents just went along with the rest. We didn't know what was going on." She remembers it as a fun time. Other teams in the league had sponsors, but Craig's team was sponsored only by the parents who went to all the games.

In bantam, the team moved to the more competitive Toronto Hockey League and won the championship in the 1965-66 season. Craig was scoring goals and gaining confidence. The next year, at fourteen, he was playing midget, and Craig became the team's best player. He was the leading scorer and a dominant force. One team he didn't like playing was the Woodbridge midget team. "If you got into the third period and they were winning, the hockey was over. It wasn't stop time so the coach [Roger Neilson] would have them ice the puck or change players, one at a time, to run out the clock. I hated that."

"Parents were starting to talk about Craig in midget, saying he would go somewhere," remembers Mrs. Ramsay. "They said he would get picked. We didn't know what they were talking about. We knew so little about hockey."

Craig was just as naive. "I knew nothing about scouts. I remember a man approached my dad and said he could get me a scholarship. I thought that was good, it sounded like a great deal.

"That summer [1967] I was golfing with a friend and he said I was drafted to the Marlies [Junior A team]. I didn't know anything about a draft. I asked my dad when I got home and he didn't know either. I had watched some junior hockey on television and thought those guys were too big for me to ever play. As for the NHL, I never dreamed of the NHL. I thought I'd be a teacher."

But Craig was curious about how good he really was. He tried out for the Marlies' system: "They cut me. I was the 127th player and they cut me on the first tryout. I was gone." But before long, he got a letter saying the Peterborough Petes had taken him. "I didn't know about Peterborough's tradition but I thought it would be neat to go to training camp. The camp was a weekend before the veterans arrived, and I'd also miss a day of school.

"I asked my parents, and they said whatever I wanted to do would be fine with them. They drove me to Peterborough and I stayed at a local hotel. I had three shirts and two pairs of pants." His mother had also bought him new skates, the wrong size. "I never assumed I could play junior. I thought the players were so big. But my friend Wayne Butt said I could make the Petes. I stepped on the ice and the first guy I meet is Paul Epping. He's huge. He's a monster." Epping, a Peterborough boy, was about six-foot-three on skates and 195 pounds; Craig was four inches shorter and forty-five pounds lighter, his thin muscles gripping his skinny frame. His face was thin, too, and there was something about the way he smiled, showing his small teeth, that gave his face a look of perpetual wonderment. Despite their size, however, Craig soon found out "big guys weren't going to catch me."

Craig was prepared to stay for the two days. Neilson called to tell him he was staying for a week. "I was flabbergasted, but another week off school was great. I called my parents and they said, 'Whatever.'"

His first game was at home against the Toronto Marlies, the same team that had cut him. "I had to be at the [rink] by 6:00 p.m. for an 8:00 p.m. game with a shirt, tie, and jacket. I didn't have anything. I came early with my hockey jacket done up tight. One of the trainers, Frank Gurney, saw me, and since then it's been a joke – 'the kid with no tie.'"

All Craig remembers of that game is taking the first faceoff against Terry Caffrey. Peterborough lost the exhibition match 8-4. At week's end, he had his bags packed and his parents came to get him. The Petes had offered him a position with the local Junior B team, but he was sixteen, didn't want to play in the old Peterborough rink where the B team played their games, was homesick, and didn't think he was capable. At home, he played B hockey for the Etobicoke Indians at the start of the 1967 season.

If Craig thought the Petes' training-camp players were huge, the Etobicoke Bs were even bigger, with players up to twenty-one years old. It was here that Craig, whose only coach had been Burt Turney, started getting jabs from coaches.

"Coaches would see me at practice and think nothing of me. They'd wonder why I was even there. Then when they saw me in a game, they'd be buddies. That first practice in Etobicoke the players tried to kill me, [and] the coach wasn't happy with me. I wasn't a good practice player, I never have been. But after the first game he loved me." Later, in the autumn of 1967, after playing ten games with Etobicoke B team, Craig got the letter from Neilson that changed his mind.

"My parents put me on a bus," he remembers. "I took a cab from the Peterborough bus terminal to the Memorial Centre. I remember to this day a guy, who turned out to be Jack Gibson, met me at the door of the rink and said, 'Don't tell me you're Ramsay! You're another little guy.' Another man, the Petes' trainer, Bob Delahaye, reinforced that with 'Great, another midget from Toronto.'" (Craig got the last laugh when he later married Gibson's daughter, Susan, "the best thing that ever happened to him," according to his mother.) "I couldn't play that Sunday so I watched from the stands. It was such excitement, a great rink and great crowd."

Craig's first game was against the Kitchener Rangers. "[They] were huge. They had these sweaters that had to be sent back to get bigger ones. They had guys like Don Luce and Mike Robitaille. They were bigger than the New York Rangers. I remember just stopping and staring when they came out to warm up. I'd never seen so many big people."

To make matters worse, he started the game at centre against Walt Tkaczuk, a junior star and future NHL great. "He beat me on the draw all night. They were a very good team and the Petes weren't."

While Craig was trying to settle in in Peterborough, his father had been transferred to Montreal, and the family would be moving in a few months. Craig's homesickness was increasing. (During the move to Montreal, his collection of hockey cards, coins, and *Weekend* magazine posters disappeared. The loss still hurts. He says, "I hope whoever stole them enjoyed them because I certainly did over all those years.") School didn't help ease the longing for home, although Ramsay was a good student. He had attended a newer school in Thistletown but the school he attended in Peterborough was an old brick building, much of it dating back to the turn of the century. The city's oldest school, it was also the most prestigious, because many of the town fathers, lawyers, and business people had attended.

The homesickness got so bad that Craig almost abandoned the team and went home. But he fought back against his depression and took advantage of what the old school had to offer. He joined the high-school rugby team, where playing was the "toughest thing I've ever done."

Craig almost quit the Petes again when a college came calling to offer him a scholarship. "I agreed to meet [the representative] one night. Roger found out about it. He picked that night to call curfew and I was fined $10. I came in to talk to Roger, and [in the end] the Petes offered to help with my education. It was then that I tried to make it in hockey. I figured I could always go to school [later]."

By the time he was eighteen he was one of the league's top players, no longer a shrimp but a sculpted athlete who had grown from teen to man. After he met Susan Gibson, he started staying in Peterborough year-round, instead of going to Montreal for the summer.

Through those years in minor hockey and with the Petes, Ramsay kept his work ethic and his passion. But his practice-game dichotomy continued. "I was different, stronger, more competitive during games. My job was to play against the best player – players like Gilbert Perreault – and keep them off the scoresheet. It was the competition that drove me." (He also was quite recognizable on the ice when he became one of the few junior players to wear a helmet after he'd been hit by a puck in the head at a practice. Soon after this incident and before the league actually did it, Neilson made helmets mandatory for all his players. Mickey Redmond had worn a helmet two years before this. The helmet of his day was more like strips of leather.)

On the Petes' bus trips, Ramsay would do something that had drove his parents nuts. On the drive home, he would sit and talk with Neilson about the game, every detail of it. He knew the Petes' system inside out. He had played every position with the team, except goalie, and had become one of the best defensive players in the league, as well as one of the top scorers. He knew the system so well he coached a game when Neilson was serving a suspension.

Petes executive member Herb Warr asked Neilson why a player had been chosen to coach the team that night. Warr remembers Neilson's answer: "He knows how the team plays and he is the most knowledgeable person to put behind the bench."

The Peterborough Examiner had already endorsed Ramsay: "His leadership qualities are such that he is the unofficial assistant coach of the club."

Neilson had suggested to the *Toronto Star*, "I wonder if the NHL scouts appreciate what a splendid hockey player Ramsay really is. Maybe he's not the high scorer like some flashy players, but anyone who can check the way he does has to have a good chance in the NHL."

When Ramsay scored 100 points for the Petes that season of 1970-71, he reached a standard achieved by only two other Petes (André Lacroix and Rick MacLeish), but the fans, 2,886 of them that night, treated it with silence. Neilson expressed his dismay to the *Examiner*'s reporter. "He is a guy who has played four years here and always gives 100 per cent. If this had happened in St. Catharines, Ottawa, or Montreal he would have had a five-minute standing ovation. It is hard to understand the fans here. Lacroix and MacLeish were ultra-offensive players. Ramsay is more of a defensive player but it is still something for him to score 100 points in one season."

But the pro-hockey world was paying attention. Ramsay was rated one of the best players in the league, along with Marcel Dionne, Richard Martin, and Murray Wilson. He was drafted nineteenth, went in the second round behind players like Guy Lafleur, Dionne, Martin, and even tough guy and old teammate Steve Durbano.

Ramsay played for the Petes from 1967 until 1970-71. He was the team's captain in his last year, never finished lower than sixth in team scoring, won the team scoring championship once, received the President's Trophy for best combining scholastics with hockey ability (he had an 80-per-cent average in school), and was acknowledged as the team's best checking forward.

In 1971, Craig joined the Buffalo Sabres, staying with the team until 1985, including ten consecutive seasons without missing a game from 1972 through 1982, and boasting eight 20-goal seasons. In 1985, he received the Frank Selke award for the NHL's top defensive forward. In 1986, he became Buffalo's assistant manager and went on to be an assistant coach in Florida from 1993 to 1995 and Ottawa from 1996 to 1998, and also a coach in Philadelphia from 1999 to 2001, before becoming assistant coach in Tampa in 2002.

The determination Craig showed as a youngster, when he realized that he might not be the best player but he could work harder than anyone, was put to the test in 1993. That determination, with skilled medical help, saved his life. For most of his adult life, he had struggled with stomach problems, mainly ulcers, but just when he was about to join the Florida team, an ulcer exploded. Doctors didn't think he would live, but he underwent several operations, one of which was the complete removal of his stomach. Doctors attached his intestine to his esophagus. He has been able to continue eating regular, but much smaller, meals. Shortly after the procedure, he lost forty pounds, but he has gained it all back, and now, other than taking daily B12 shots, he lives a healthy life. It's tough to keep a good man down.

Craig Ramsay lives with his family in Tampa, Florida, where he is assistant coach for the Tampa Bay Lightning, who won the Stanley Cup in 2004.

BOB GAINEY
Born in Peterborough, December 13, 1953
Peterborough Petes 1971-73
NHL career with Montreal

In Bob Gainey's family, he's known for two things: his determination and his tidiness. He was one of those kids who would succeed at whatever he set his mind to. He was also one of those rare children who made his bed. At home, he liked things to be neat and organized – a trait he inherited from his father – but he soon showed that on the ice he could be experimental and daring.

At five, he had his own pair of skates – a used pair bought by his dad, George, a big strapping man who worked at the Quaker Oats plant and ran his own delivery service on the side. His father strapped the skates on his son's feet, took the boy to an outdoor rink, and watched as the youngster skated away. Of the boys in the family – Bob has two brothers and four sisters – he was the one who took to hockey in a big way. "None of the other children showed a great deal of interest in sports, but Rob was a fanatic," says Mrs. Gainey. An old

Marlow Banks

chum, John Swann, remembers how, at the age of seven, Bob talked Swann's father into buying his son his first skates: "He just kept telling my dad that [I] really should have a pair of skates."

Bob was growing confident on skates, but by the time he was six he was hit by a bone disease that put a scare into the family. Their doctor told them he might have a permanent limp, but Mrs. Gainey, a devout Catholic who made sure the family went to church every Sunday (Bob was later an altar boy for two years), turned to prayer for help. Almost like a miracle, the bone problem was gone. With the illness behind him, Bob took full advantage of the opportunities to play sports in his neighbourhood, where it seemed there were base-ball, road-hockey, basketball, touch-football, and softball games going on all the time.

In the summertime the boys were also fond of swimming at the local community pool, where ten cents would let you join dozens of other children in a chlorine-dosed outdoor pool. Bob's sister Maureen remembers, "When Rob was in the pool he would be diving off the high board. He was just a kid, but always an athlete and miles ahead of us."

In winter, of course, hockey took over. "I remember my first game in the Civic Arena," says Bob. It was a mite game in 1959. He was six, and playing defence for his church, Immaculate Conception, in the local church league. "The games were always on a Saturday and were only a half-hour long. They would only flood the ice after

Bob Gainey (middle row, second from left) and his Grade 8 basketball team.

four games. They used shovels and barrels then. If you were to be on during that game [when they flooded the rink] it would only be about ten minutes because the flood would take twenty."

While the family had a small black-and-white television set, Bob wasn't much for sitting around watching it. Still, he must have watched enough hockey to know the names of the players. Swann says, "We talked about the NHL all the time. When we were playing, we were always guys who played in the NHL. We all wanted to play in the NHL but none of us knew how to get there." In spite of that, he adds, "Hockey wasn't something that consumed your life. When winter was over, the next sport season began."

When the young Gainey kid wasn't on skates, he worked as a bat boy and scorekeeper at the ballpark, helped put the courts down at the tennis club, and caddied at the golf course where, as a teen, he would get a summer job. Wherever he went, he usually walked or rode his bicycle. He also had a newspaper route, delivering the local newspaper to eighty customers.

When he was about eight, Bob was asked to try out for a local all-star team and made the team as a high-scoring defenceman. That meant a practice and game a week and some tournaments that were always scheduled around school holidays. Taking the kids out of school for hockey was out of the question. Old friend Steve Sullivan played on those all-star hockey teams with Bob and remembers him as being awkward. He says, "The funny thing is, I used to always think I was a better hockey player than Bob. We'd play shinny on the outdoor rinks and he certainly wasn't a superstar. I never would have thought at age twelve that I'd be able to say later I chummed with a Hall of Famer. He didn't stand out until midget."

Bob remembers, "From about eight to thirteen there was a period where it got different. There were other interests besides hockey. Some of our group splintered off. Those wanting to continue in hockey did so with the support of some good people. For me it was a combination of things. No matter how much I wanted to do other things, I wanted to do hockey more. I wanted to play hockey more than go to school or hang out with friends or play basketball."

The basketball reference is important. Bob, a tall, gangly teen with brown curly, swirling hair that he wore in bangs, was an excellent basketball player, and he made the high-school team. But when the coach told him he'd have to dedicate himself to one sport, basketball was out.

In his midget year, his hockey coach, Red Wasson, moved him to forward. There was no clever planning behind the move. Wasson explains simply, "We needed a forward." By then, Gainey had, indeed, become a dominant force with size – six feet and 185 pounds – his powerful skating style, fearlessness, bashing, and excellent hockey sense. Gainey was instrumental in getting the local midget team (his regular team), as well as the juvenile team that called him up to play for championships in the 1969-70 season. He covered the other teams' top forwards, such as Rick Middleton, Eric Vail, and Don Lever, and also scored the winning goal in the juvenile championship. By this time Bob was considered one of the bigger players. He could not only play with and against the top players, he was one of them.

In 1971 he helped lead the Peterborough Junior B team to the Canada Winter Games gold-medal championship after it qualified by winning the Ontario Winter Games.

When he signed with his hometown Peterborough Petes in the fall of 1971, the team fit his style perfectly. Roger Neilson believed in putting together team parts, not just using scoring stars to lead the way. He knew the team needed a checker, a skater, a shooter, a fighter, and a defenceman, and he used various personalities, skills, talents, and strategies to mould them into a good team that knew its opponents. "Being in Peterborough, playing for the Petes with a coach like Roger who structured the Petes in team play, fit my style. That was good for me," remembers Bob.

Gainey soon made his mark. He was named the team's most valuable player in his first full season, and he played an important role in getting the team to the Memorial Cup final. He wasn't the team's leading scorer, but he was certainly the team's leading hitter and checker. In fact, he told reporters, "I don't like it when any guy who I'm supposed to be checking scores," and he liked that challenge. Unfortunately, Gainey was injured before the final with a compound fracture of the forearm and wrist. Neilson knew that losing his leadership, determination, skating skills, toughness, and checking ability would hurt the team. It did, and the Petes lost.

Petes executive member Herb Warr considers Gainey one of the best Petes he has ever seen, certainly the best two-way player ever. "There was nothing flashy [about him]. He'd go up and down the wing. He took checks and gave them back. He didn't give an inch."

Former teammate Mike Fryia always thought Gainey would go before anyone else on the team in the NHL draft. "Some thought it would be Bob Neely, but it was just the way Gainey played. He could read plays so well and had speed and the size, but I never saw a guy miss so many breakaways. He must have had fifty one season with the Petes," Fryia recalls, laughing at the memory.

Another former teammate, Bill Evo, says Bob was "always a leader. Even then he had something special, He was controlled, careful, physically talented. He was a tremendous hockey player that only comes along once in a while. He seemed to be always in control. He was one of the guys who seemed to always make the right decision on and off the ice."

In 1973, after two more-than-twenty-goal seasons with the Petes and becoming a team assistant captain, he gained the attention of Sam Pollock, who saw something other managers and scouts – including his own – weren't seeing. He insisted the Habs draft the kid. Gainey was Montreal's first draft pick and eighth overall. His father heard about his draft selection on his transistor radio at work while Bob heard it from a phone call in Peterborough. That draft year was the same year the World Hockey Association had formed and had its first draft. Gainey wasn't even picked by the new league even though Bob Neely, Colin Campbell, and several others were.

The Habs' pick was a surprise to most people. Montreal goalie Ken Dryden would later admit he thought the Habs had drafted Bob Neely. Gainey was also surprised and a bit disappointed because he wasn't sure he could make a powerful team like the Habs.

Gainey was nineteen when he went to the Montreal Canadiens' camp. He figured Pollock must have seen something in him so he thought he'd give it his best shot. Luck played a role because two of the Habs young stars, Marc Tardif and Rejean Houle, had decided to bolt to the new WHA. Gainey had never lived away from home – unlike many other players his age who had left home to play junior – and was now moving to the home of the Canadiens. Two of his friends drove him there. They watched an Expos game before dropping Bob off at a Montreal hotel. One of those friends, Jack Scriver, remembers they had to yell to point out to him that he had forgotten his skates. Bob remembers it differently. He says, "They almost drove off with my skates."

It didn't take Bob long to prove that Pollock's instinct was right. In a game against Boston, Gainey smacked league star Bobby Orr into the boards. He showed he could skate with him and wasn't afraid to hit him. Under a former Petes coach, Scotty Bowman, Gainey learned his role well. He learned it so well that when the league created the Frank J. Selke Trophy for its top defensive forward, Gainey won it in its first four years.

During his time with the Habs he married Cathy Collins, another Peterborough native. They would have four children.

Gainey also helped his team win the Stanley Cup five times, once while he was the captain (the third Peterborough native to become captain of an NHL team). He also won the Conn Smythe Trophy for MVP in the 1979 playoffs. His skill was noted beyond the ice rinks of North America and one observation propelled him into superstar status. In 1976, Soviet national coach Viktor Tikhonov described him as the most technically perfect player in the world.

After starring for sixteen years with the Habs, Gainey retired in 1988 and moved his family to Epinal, France, where he was a player-coach for the local team for a year and immersed himself in French culture. The following year he came back to the NHL to coach the Minnesota North Stars and took that team to a Stanley Cup final. From there the team moved to Dallas, where Bob was coach and general manager, taking them to a Stanley Cup win as general manager. In 2003 he was back with the Montreal Canadiens, this time as general manager.

Red Fisher, senior hockey writer for the Montreal *Gazette*, has covered the Montreal Canadiens for decades and has seen everyone from the Richards to the present-day players. He once wrote about Gainey: "No player I have ever covered in this business has ever worked harder, hit harder or played through as much pain. No player I have ever known has led better by example."

Bob Gainey lives in Montreal, where he is general manager of the Montreal Canadiens. His wife, Cathy, passed away in 1995 with cancer. His son Steven plays hockey in the Philadelphia Flyers organization. Two of his daughters were in college in 2003, and the eldest had earned a postgraduate degree.

STAN JONATHAN
Born in Ohsweken, Ontario, September 5, 1955
Peterborough Petes 1972-75
NHL career with Boston, Pittsburgh

As you drive into Ohsweken, a village on the Six Nations reserve near Brantford, Ontario, you know why you're here, and maybe that's why you feel like you're trespassing. You're another white man come to steal something from an Indian. Today, it's memories you're stealing – memories of one of the toughest, if not the toughest, fighters the National Hockey League has ever seen.

Marlow Banks

Stan Jonathan has a face of leather, like a brown baseball mitt with character. If his face has taken a few hits, he has given far more than he received, but it's his barrel chest that has been his trademark. Deceptively, it makes him look overweight – even during his playing days he looked that way. He's short at five-foot-eight, but don't let that fool you. Stan Jonathan is a big man around this country.

Stan, a full-blooded Tuscarora Indian, was born on the reserve in 1955 in a house no bigger than twenty-five by thirty feet, with two storeys and four bedrooms – not a lot of room for Stan's parents and their fourteen children.

Earlier in the century, his grandfather, a hereditary chief, played full-contact lacrosse with no pads, nation against nation, using just sticks and a ball. The reserve had a minor lacrosse system, and Stan played organized lacrosse before he played hockey. By the time Stan was five years old, he was working in the summers, picking tobacco or berries. "All of us had to earn our keep," he says.

It was an outdoors life in other ways, too. For example, whenever adults came to visit their parents, the kids had to leave the house. "That was the law; all the kids outside so the adults could talk privately about their business. And it's still that way today."

An older brother had had the family's first hockey skates. Stan's parents bought them on credit at Canadian Tire. They were too large for Stan's brother when they were new, and they were three sizes too big for Stan when it was his turn to wear them. Like many parents, Stan's bought the skates too large on purpose, so the boys would grow into them and fewer pairs would be needed. Stan remembers some nights in peewee and bantam hockey when his brothers were playing at the rink on the same night and would pass the equipment down to a younger sibling to use in the next game.

Stan didn't really start to skate until he was eleven years old, when he played organized hockey, making him a late starter compared to most other kids. He played two years of peewee, two years of bantam, and then, with only four years of hockey behind him, joined the Waterford Junior B team, where he met Brantford's Doug Jarvis. Walter Gretzky was the coach and Wayne was the stick boy.

Stan loved playing defence, a position he played until he moved to Peterborough, where he became a forward. Roger Neilson explained to him that the team already had plenty of great defencemen, so there was little choice but to move up.

The Petes weren't the only ones with an eye on the tough kid from Six Nations. The Sault Ste. Marie Greyhounds told him they were going to pick him first in the draft and wanted to know if he would go there if they did. He says, "I didn't even know where it was. They had to know by noon that day so I looked at the map and said no. I wanted to play in Hamilton or St. Catharines, someplace close. My parents weren't royalty. They had one car and they wouldn't [be able to] see the Soo games." Peterborough was a lot closer than the Soo, so Stan was glad when he was drafted by the Petes instead of a city even farther away.

Before he arrived in Peterborough, Stan was working summers as an ironworker, a job that had paid him more than $150 a week clear, almost as much money as his new junior coach, Roger Neilson, made. To all intents and purposes, the seventeen-year-old was already a man. He had his own car, which he had bought with his own money. He had cash in his pocket. And, unknown to the Petes, he had a wife and child back home.

Stan kept his family a secret, eventually telling only one close teammate. "There was talk that players would be sent home in that situation, but I didn't fear that. It was just none of anyone's business." His wife sometimes came to Petes games to cheer him on.

Stan developed a close relationship with his second Peterborough landparents, the Garveys. It was a tough time for him to be away from home. Not only was his new family back on the reserve near Brantford, but his own mother and father were in the process of separating. Stan had been the oldest boy at home and was able to return to the reserve a few times to help his parents.

Mike Kasmetis, another player who stayed at the Garveys', was there for one year with Stan. "He was incredible. He was very proud of his heritage, even had a freehand drawing of an Indian chief on his car. . . . We had no idea then that he would become as tough as he did but he was so strong." Kasmetis says that Stan marched "to the beat of his own drum." He adds, "He either hated you or loved you – there was never a grey area with Stan – and thank God he loved me."

He goes on more seriously, "I remember when I came to Peterborough I was fifteen and so homesick, so homesick. But Stan wasn't. It didn't bother him at all. We were there with twenty-year-olds but it didn't bother him ever.

"Stan's philosophy was, whatever was his was yours and whatever was yours was his. He used to drive me to school in his Mustang, but he wasn't much for going there himself."

"I only went to school for sports," admits Stan, but "the Petes wouldn't let you play much school sports."

He says he actually was homesick his first year, but that was before he moved in with the Garveys. He almost quit several times. "I wasn't playing much. One time we were playing in Toronto at the Gardens and a group of people from the reserve came to watch me play and I [was] on the bench [for most of the game]." He almost went home with the group.

Stan's physical prowess was incredible. Kasmetis remembers a demonstration of his strength off the ice. They were helping the parents of teammate and close friend Paul Evans move from one side of the street to the other side. Stan strapped a fridge on his back and walked across the street with it. "He was a good guy and [would] do anything for you," remembers Evans, who also went on to play pro hockey. Paul was the only teammate he had confided in about Stan's child.

Another friend and teammate was Mike Fryia. Fryia says, "He was a super guy, lots of fun. You helped him, he helped you. He had plenty of nicknames: Merle [he loved country singer Merle Haggard], Burnt Tennis Shoe, and Chief." (He'd later be called Bulldog.) "He made a fortune on hits. Roger used to pay guys for the number of hits, not much, but Stan would always be out there hitting."

Stan kept to himself. Socially he felt awkward but he found freedom on the ice. He wasn't a great skater, but he worked harder than anyone, and although he was shorter than most of his team-mates, he was as big as a bear in strength and heart. Paul Evans played with him throughout junior and says that whenever Stan got into a fight the team usually felt sorry for the other guy. Peterborough hockey observers have often compared him to current Toronto Maple Leafs tough guy Tie Domi. However, former scout Gary Darling leaves no doubt about his opinion: he says Stan would "eat" Tie. They could both throw and take punches, but Tie would sometimes smile when he was punched in the head and mock his opponent while he fought him. He treated fighting like entertainment. But Stan never smiled at his opponents, never patted their heads: he fought for keeps. J.J. Johnston, a former Petes teammate and now a Dallas Stars scout, comments, "He had a good career for the way he played. He was the equalizer. He knew the role and didn't mind doing it. He's the toughest player I ever played with or ever saw fight. The thing was he liked to fight. I liked him on my wing – he took care of everything."

Former teammates remember a night in Hamilton when Stan had his front teeth knocked out. It was a night Dave Norris will also remember. He was the one who delivered the cross-check that damaged Stan's smile. Jonathan wanted to get Norris but Neilson wouldn't let him back on the ice. The two teams were playing the next night as well but Neilson wouldn't let Jonathan on the ice when Norris was there.

At this point, versions of the story differ. Some say Neilson finally relented, others say Stan just jumped on the ice when he saw an opportunity. No matter, Norris and Jonathan went at it at centre ice. Players say they have never seen a hockey fight like it. The two went toe to toe. "Stan's head was a like a beachball, and when the fight was done Norris couldn't open his eyes," says Kasmetis.

In his first season with the Petes, 1972-73, Stan scored 14 goals, had 35 assists, and 107 penalty minutes in 63 games. It wasn't an unusual number of penalty minutes; in fact, it was the same number as teammate Bob Gainey. (Roger Neilson's team featured in a lot of brawls. In one playoff game against the Marlies the team accumulated 18 fighting majors – 170 penalty minutes, more than Jonathan had in the entire year.)

In Stan's second year with the Petes, he was fifth in team scoring with 19 goals, 33 assists in 70 games with 127 penalty minutes. Every year his skills improved. He could score, but most importantly, he could get the scorers the puck.

The next year he was fifth again, with 36 goals, 39 assists, 130 penalty minutes, and he made the second all-star team. He was selected eighty-sixth overall in the NHL draft in 1975.

It was his strength, determination, and ability not only to fight but also to come up with the puck and score points (he was a twenty- and thirty-goal scorer) that attracted the attention of Harry Sinden, the Boston Bruins' general manager. Sinden told Gary Darling, Boston's chief scout, that he wanted Jonathan and to take him in the fourth round. Darling says, "I took someone else in that round and Sinden snapped. Luckily, [Stan] was still available in the next round and we took him." Darling, like others, was surprised at Stan's NHL success, but says he was the best fighter he has ever seen.

After leaving Peterborough in 1975, Stan played in the IHL for Dayton. The team won the Turner Cup that year and Stan was on the first all-star team. In 1976 the pugnacious left winger went on to play for Boston, where Don Cherry described him as the toughest player he had ever seen. In 411 games over his eight-year career, he scored 91 goals and had 110 assists and 751 minutes in penalties. He's also part of an NHL record that may never be broken. He was one of the eleven Boston players who scored 20 goals or more in 1977-78, a feat never equalled. He had 27 goals. It's a shame he's known best as a fighter. He was the team's MVP in 1977-78 and the NHL's shooting-percentage leader with a 23.9 per cent average.

After six full seasons with Boston, the team sold his rights to Pittsburgh in 1982 for "future considerations." He played in nineteen games there but with little success, and he retired.

Reflecting on how he learned to play hockey, Stan says, "I always played with older guys and watched them to learn. I learned most . . . from the players I watched, not the coaches. Look at the Petes' coaches then – none of them [had] played pro hockey. I'd ask them to show me what they wanted me to do and they couldn't. I'd watch Gainey and Jarvis and learn from them. They knew how to play the game, and I could learn by watching them, not the coaches."

After he retired from hockey, he and his wife moved to a comfortable home on the reserve, where their two children are fourth-generation Jonathans. Every winter Stan makes a rink for his grandchildren on his grandfather's old homestead. "I try to tell the kids here and on other reserves I visit to leave the reserves. I hope I get through to one kid, one kid gets the idea that they can achieve off the reserve, but it's hard to. There is so much politics for Natives off the reserves."

After retiring, Stan tried to come back to play for the Brantford seniors, but only played one game. He still plays NHL oldtimers hockey.

Stan Jonathan lives in Ohsweken, on the Six Nations reserve, with his wife. His two adult children also have made their homes there. He works as a handyman, supports aboriginal causes, and instructs aboriginal youths in hockey schools.

BILL EVO
Born in Royal Oak, Michigan, February 21, 1954
Peterborough Petes 1971-74
WHA career with Michigan, Baltimore, Edmonton, Cleveland

When Bill Evo was growing up, education was the last thing on his mind. All he wanted to do was play hockey. Even though his grandmothers emphasized the importance of education to their

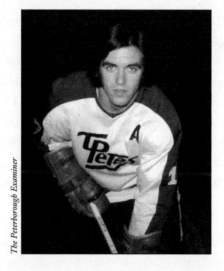

The Peterborough Examiner

grandchildren – both grandmothers had graduated from university – Bill's head was full of skates and sticks rather than books and pencils. Although Bill lived in Royal Oak, Michigan, his Canadian roots were clearly still visible in his great love for hockey. His father's family originally came from Montreal, and his mother had been born in Dresden, Ontario.

The closest indoor rink was across the border in Windsor, Ontario, and most of Bill's minor hockey games in the 1950s and early 1960s were played outside. "We'd sometimes play our playoffs in the Windsor arena. We'd get there early and go up to the top seats, jump on paper coffee or pop cups to make them bang, to hear the echo through the empty building. I loved that echo. I loved that rink. I always felt it had this Canadian feel to it.

"When we had to play in Windsor, we'd sometimes be running late, and my father would get us to change into our equipment in the car while we were going through the [border] tunnel. When we got to the rink we'd run right in it."

As Bill grew into his teens, the lanky, beefy, brown-haired boy turned into a tough hockey forward, one of the bigger, better players in the area, but his skating was weaker than Canadians of the same age. He just wasn't getting enough ice time to improve the way Canadian kids did, but with outdoor rinks and local games, he worked at getting better. A family friend, Fern Spooner from Blind River, was working in the States and helped Bill, showing him crossovers and the more technical side of skating. By the time he was fourteen, he was playing on all-star travelling teams. A midget team he played for was the Dearborn Fabrication team, where he skated alongside Mark and Marty Howe, sons of NHL great Gordie Howe. The team were national champions, winning games by scores like 22-1 – a close game would have 7-1. Bill played either left wing or right wing, wherever the coach put him.

In 1969 Evo went to play in an Ontario Junior C league alongside twenty-one-year-olds who were "drinking, smoking, talking to women, staying up past 11:30 p.m. on school nights, and it was all approved by my dad." He scored 36 goals that year and "took the gloves off" a few times. The scouts began to notice. One came from Preston (which was amalgamated into Cambridge), Ontario, to watch him play and see if he'd be interested in playing Junior B hockey there. "I told Dad I wanted to play junior in Canada, where you got free sticks and skates. It was the big time, and it's all I wanted to do when I was a teenager.

"My parents wanted me to get an education, but I wanted to go to Preston and my dad [finally] agreed. He didn't tell my mom I was leaving until the night before I left, and she cried her eyes out." At the age of sixteen, he got on a bus that took him to the tiny town of Preston to play with kids up to five years his senior. Despite the differences in age, his talent shone. The muscular, good-looking Evo, now six feet tall, was second in team scoring, as well as rookie of the year. Things weren't as sunny at school, though, where he was failing. He was skipping school and was "the antithesis of what our parents had taught us. I was hanging around the pool hall and got good at snooker."

Bill's goal was to play for Kitchener. When Roger Neilson, who'd been keeping an eye on the young American, came with an offer from the Peterborough Petes, Bill didn't know what to think. "I didn't know much about Peterborough. I wasn't exposed to its reputation."

Neilson went to Michigan to visit the Evos and then he drafted Bill, making him the first American-born youth to play regularly for the Petes.

Bill says, "I wasn't overly gifted but I worked hard. So the next fall [1971], once again my parents put me on a bus, this time to Peterborough. I commuted by bus a lot and learned a lot. I grew up quickly. I'd sit in bus depots and men would proposition me. I was alone, naive.

"Hockey guys get street smarts quickly. It's not knowledge acquired from schools. Junior guys played hockey and school wasn't important. That is until meeting Roger. He insisted you [go] to school full time or have a full-time job. You weren't going to sit around all day watching *The Price Is Right*."

Meeting Neilson changed Bill's life. He soon became familiar with Roger's philosophy: "Lazy mind, lazy on the ice." He says, Neilson "straightened me out, got me on the right road academically. I wasn't getting A's, but I was passing. On the other teams, I didn't care if I passed, the players just had fun and could do whatever they wanted. Roger wanted us to be complete people. He wanted to make a difference in our lives."

When the Peterborough Petes made it to the first World Junior Championship, the young American found himself playing for another country, Canada, in yet another country, the U.S.S.R. Strangely, he found himself scoring a winning goal against the U.S.

Back in Peterborough, after a bad experience with his first land-parent, Bill found a stability and reality he had been lacking. He didn't give up the good life entirely but he was more focused. He actually studied for exams. His hockey improved too, but it was not without frustration. He was playing behind Bob Gainey (a tough act for just about anyone to follow) and he wasn't getting on the ice as much as he'd like. "I knew I wasn't going to beat him out, so it was frustrating. I even called the University of Michigan to see if I could go there. But Bob got injured and I scored two goals when he was out one game so I stuck."

Bill had just 17 points in his first season, but in the next two he had 51 and 52 points and kept his rugged ways with two 100-plus penalty minutes.

Teammate Mike Fryia remembers Bill fondly as "one of the craziest you'd ever meet." He intends that as a compliment: "crazy" meant wild things like dressing up in drag for a Petes' Halloween party. "Crazy as he was," says Fryia, "you kind of figured he'd be something like a lawyer. If he couldn't be a player, that's what he wanted to be."

Although the Detroit Red Wings drafted Bill in 1974 in the third round, he decided to play in the World Hockey Association, because the Michigan Stags were offering him a one-way contract that Detroit wouldn't match. The WHA, however, was far from stable and he ended up with four teams (Michigan, Baltimore Blades, Edmonton Oilers, and Cleveland Crusaders) in two years. Then in 1977 he went to the Pacific Hockey League, where his San Francisco team, the Shamrocks, won the championship. While playing minor pro in 1979 he decided to quit hockey and go back to university. "I told a brother and sister I wanted to be a lawyer and they all laughed, [but] that just put fuel on the fire."

Bill was accepted at the University of Western Ontario in London, where he graduated with his B.A. degree in one and a half years, half the time it usually takes. "I buried myself in my books," he says. When he discovered he couldn't practise law in Ontario unless he was a Commonwealth citizen, he switched to the University of Detroit. "They'd have to kill me to take away my U.S. citizenship," he says firmly. "My dad was a war veteran and I love this country."

After he got his law degree, Bill specialized in corporate and contract law, but remembering his time as a younger player, he identified a niche. In his last year of junior hockey, many agents had approached him and "some didn't have a clue what they were talking about." He began representing NHL players such as Petr Klima, Lee Norwood, and Jason Woolley.

Then, twenty-two years after being drafted in the third round, forty-fifth overall by the Detroit Red Wings, Bill Evo finally joined the NHL as a Red Wing. At the age of forty-one, he became the club's president. While working as an agent, he had met Detroit Red Wings owner Mike Ilitch and eventually the idea of Bill joining the club came up. He said to Ilitch, "One day I'd like to run this organization."

It seemed like a perfect fit. A Michigan boy, a former player, a lawyer, a player agent, and also president and general counsel for the Red Wings' alumni. Why not? He was appointed president, but the fit wasn't quite as perfect as it had seemed. After a year, Evo resigned because of "internal differences with other management members" – in other words, they didn't get along. He made his mark, though. During that one year he signed former Peterborough Pete Steve Yzerman to a long-term deal and the team had a record of sixty-two wins.

It had taken Bill rather a long time to see that his grandmothers were right to insist on an education – he just had to get the sports out of his system first.

Bill Evo lives with his Peterborough-born wife in a suburb of Detroit, where he practises law.

COLIN CAMPBELL
Born in London, Ontario, January 28, 1953
Peterborough Petes 1970-1973
NHL career with Pittsburgh, Colorado Rockies, Edmonton, Vancouver,
  Detroit

GARY GREEN
Born in Tillsonburg, Ontario, August 23, 1953
WHA career with Vancouver
Coached Washington in the NHL

Tillsonburg, a little tobacco town in southwestern Ontario near London, is a three-hour drive from Peterborough. Even though it's such a small place – with a population of about 9,000 in the 1950s and 1960s – it has given us two important additions to the cast of characters that make up the drama of modern hockey: Colin Campbell and Gary Green.

The two Tillsonburg-born boys had one other thing in common: their love of sports, especially hockey. In other ways, they were different: Gary grew up on a farm with parents who had little interest in sports; Colin grew up in the town, where hockey dominated his

Colin Campbell was captain of the Tillsonburg team. Gary Green is in
top row, third from right.

father's life. Gary had a busy voice – he was a chatterbox; Colin was
a quiet prankster.

The Campbell family – Jack and Gwen Campbell and their two
daughters and two sons – lived in a three-bedroom bungalow on a
corner lot near the quiet downtown. Jack, who worked as a hydro
linesman, wanted the boys to play hockey. Colin started playing
when he was six.

"He wasn't enthusiastic at first," says Gwen, now retired and
living alone following her husband's death more than a decade ago.
She is still in the same, but expanded, house Colin grew up in. "Colin
always wanted to make sure he got home for noon to watch the car-
toons. He never watched hockey then. He got more interested when
he was seven or eight."

On his parents' two-hundred-acre farm, about fifteen miles from
Tillsonburg, Gary Green and his brother and sister skated and played
shinny on a frozen creek that ran through the property. Gary wanted
to play hockey as soon as he could. "Dad wouldn't let me [when I
was] five. Before I could play hockey I had to take figure skating for
a year. He was smart, but I didn't want to do it. Once, in one of their

carnivals, I was an astronaut and had to wear some bubble over my head." He remembers this with distaste even now. Around the age of seven, Gary and brother Randy were finally allowed to go into Tillsonburg to play organized hockey, and that's how Colin and Gary met.

"Colin and I played together that year and all the way up," says Gary. They also played baseball together in the summers. "Colin loved to go out to our farm and I loved to come into the town. He had a little lake across from his house that froze and we'd skate on that." The parents made it their goal to give the kids as many opportunities as they could. Gary took piano and drum lessons as well as vocal lessons while he was growing up. He entered public-speaking contests and thrived on them. "A lot of the other farm kids didn't get those opportunities. We milked cows and did chores, but not like our friends, who had to do it all the time."

"He had no fear getting up in front of people and speaking," says his father, "while I would shake like a leaf."

When Gary was twelve, his father thought he was old enough to get to town by himself. "He took me to the end of the driveway, stuck out his thumb, and said, 'That's the way you hitchhike.'"

Colin attended the public school in town with the rest of the neighbourhood kids while Gary attended a two-room school near the farm. "It was the same school his dad had gone to in Delora and even the same teacher," says his mother, Margaret. One of the teachers recognized that Gary had a good singing voice and entered him in a competition, which he won. He began singing at church services, and then at weddings and other functions for money. He entered the Stratford Music Festival two years in a row and won the gold medal twice, both times beating out John Avery, who went on to become an international opera singer.

"We never pushed him into singing or competing," says Mrs. Green. "He wanted to do it and we didn't want the kids just doing one thing." He also worked hard at playing the drums.

When he was a teenager, Gary was in a rock band that practised at the farm – "It didn't bother any neighbours but it rattled our walls," his parents remember.

Colin's life was sports. When he was in grade six, he wrote a composition saying he was going to play in the NHL. His mother says, "I told him not to plan on that, but he wouldn't listen." In his teen years he was on the high-school track team and made the provincial finals in the 400-yard run. "He had short legs but he could run," says his mother. He also played football for the high-school team.

Like most kids in the area, Colin and Gary worked on the tobacco farms in August. The town delayed school to bring in the harvest every year.

The Green boys continued to bring home good marks from school. "They knew if they didn't do well in school they didn't play sports. We told the kids all along they would graduate from high school even if they were forty," says their mother.

One of Gary's fondest memories is of the weekend Colin's aunt took the boys by train to Maple Leaf Gardens to see a Junior A game. Gary says, "I was obsessed with hockey, but not like Colie. I was doing so many other things, but he paid the price, spending more time than the other kids lifting weights . . . less socializing and more concentration on getting better at hockey. . . . A lot of us wouldn't do it. He lifted weights, practised, studied the game. He ate it, slept it, and breathed it. He was the strongest guy I knew growing up." Both boys were the same height – five-foot-nine – and their short stature was seen by some as an obstacle.

When they were still preteens, the two of them would show up at the Tillsonburg rink every Saturday morning at 5:30 to referee hockey games. They'd let themselves into the rink with the key the manager had given them. Gary remembers, "The rink was dark. Colie and I would skate with just pucks, sticks, and helmets. We hardly had any light at all, just what shone through the windows when the sun was coming up. He'd always be terrorizing me. Somehow he could see in the dark better than me. We'd play chicken in the shadows on the new sheet of ice."

They'd referee from 7:00 until noon for fifty cents a game, then go for a hot dog at Colin's place, then back for public skating or pond hockey and referee again from 7:00 to 9:00 at night. Gary's mom would pick him up at the end of the day.

Gary wasn't interested in being a coach, he just loved to play. However, when he was fifteen, he was asked to coach a bantam house-league team that couldn't find a coach. "In hindsight that was ridiculous. I was only a year or two older than the players and knew nothing about coaching."

As far as school was concerned, Gwen says, "Colin was a fair student. He wasn't planning to keep going to school. His mind was on hockey – he didn't talk about it, he just did it. You knew where his mind was." And he hated to lose. "Cameron [Colin's brother] did too, but Cameron would forget about it quickly. Colin would break his stick and he'd get home and go to his room mad. Jack wasn't like that; I don't know where he got that from."

By the time the boys got to midget, Colin was starring for the team as its top defenceman. Gary was a good hockey player, a winger, but wasn't as focused. He didn't get drafted by a junior team.

Colin's mother says, "Jack had told the boys all along if they were going to play team sports, they couldn't miss a practice or game unless they were really sick, and that included vacations or holidays. He wanted that commitment when he coached and he expected his kids to have that commitment. Colin had to work harder because his dad was a coach."

Colin was drafted by the Peterborough Petes in 1970 after hockey scout Paul Goulet recommended him to Roger Neilson. Goulet took Colin to Peterborough's training camp that fall of 1970, when he was only sixteen. He told his family, "I'm not coming home again."

His mother says, "He had his mind made up."

She continues, "Jack went up to the training camp. He didn't think [Colin] would make it but [he] was so determined. We knew a lot about the Petes' reputation. When Colin made it, my daughters used to drive me all over the province to watch him play. We certainly never thought he'd be in the NHL."

Meanwhile, Gary was taking a different road from his buddy. He had tried out for the Chatham Tier II team and was cut. He was heartbroken. After all those years of pond hockey, shooting pucks at the garage door on the farm, ball hockey in the basement, he had been cut.

Gary was still determined to be a hockey player, so he decided to try a different route. He went back to juvenile in Tillsonburg, worked part time, played in his rock band, sang at weddings for $25.50 a gig, and, whenever possible, hitchhiked to see his friend Colie play for the Petes. He'd arrive on a Wednesday night, stay with Colin's landparents, go to the Thursday-night game, and hitchhike home the next day. Sometimes on a Wednesday night, when Neilson rented ice, Gary would play shinny with Colin and Petes teammates Bob Gainey, Ron Lalonde, and Bob Neely.

Along with all this activity, Gary and his parents were thinking about Gary's future. His parents wanted him to go to college – in fact, they insisted on it. Gary was looking for a university when a University of Guelph coach called to see if he was interested in playing for their hockey team. The next two years, from 1971 to 1973, were busy ones for Gary. Summers were especially busy – not only did he continue his university courses (he majored in psychology), but he also worked at a hockey school that Neilson started in Tillsonburg. He did a lot of driving to meet his work commitments and get back to school. His determination and intelligence helped him earn his degree in two years.

Life was hard in the hockey arena, too. For his first year of university hockey, Gary sat on the bench most of the time. "I didn't like it. You don't learn anything on the bench. I worked hard at it, hard at practices, and I'd still be on the bench. They had the old college thing about rookies not playing. It wasn't fun. It was frustrating, I didn't play until the next year and then I became a brawler. I think I started one of the biggest brawls in the league. It was so bad, the opposing team's athletic director had to come on the ice to break it up, which was not a good idea on his part."

Meanwhile, Colin was doing what he had to do to survive in hockey. A defenceman who gave as hard as he received, he was one of the most popular players on the Petes during the early 1970s. It was a great time to be a Pete – the team was the Ontario champion and missed winning the Memorial Cup by only one goal in 1972. The next season, 1972-73, with people like Bob Gainey, Doug Jarvis, Stan Jonathan, and Bob Neely on the team, Colin was their captain, an honour shared with goal-scoring star and Peterborough native Doug Gibson, the first time the captaincy had been shared. While Gibson was setting Petes scoring records, Campbell was back on defence, making sure the other team didn't score. He was also one of the leaders in penalty minutes, although he wasn't known for toughness off the ice. He also was wearing shoulder pads for the first time in hockey. He had never felt comfortable wearing them, but in an early game with the Petes Neilson touched him on the shoulder and noticed he wasn't wearing pads. Neilson couldn't believe it, and sent him to the dressing room to put some on. Colin admits now he was relieved because the hitting had become a bit too much to take.

Bonnie Coombes, his landparent, says that Colin "was really independent. He knew he wanted to play hockey or be involved in hockey. He knew he wasn't big enough, but he worked hard and Roger told him to learn enough about the game so he could always work in some other area of hockey.

"He absorbed everything, learned from anybody. He wanted to be a player first, but he always wanted to do something in hockey. He wasn't the five feet, ten inches shown on his driver's licence and he knew his shortness might hurt his hockey playing career, but, God, he was determined."

Colin would spend hours with Neilson in his office. "Colin always knew what was going on," remembers former Petes teammate J.J. Johnston. "He'd want to know what was happening.

"He was a quiet guy who made it on strength. He was a strong skater. He was short . . . but he was effective. He kept the game simple and knew his strengths."

Another teammate, Bill Evo, remembers having a run-in with Colin shortly after Evo joined the Petes. Always a practical joker, Campbell was squirting water in the locker room and soaking people. Evo took exception and tossed Campbell's jacket into the shower. A fight broke out between the rookie Evo and the veteran Campbell.

"He was such a strong guy, the strongest guy on the team, but I didn't care," says Evo, who could be accused of nerve or stupidity for taking on the more experienced Campbell. "Colin later came on the bus and apologized and we became good friends." (Campbell loved, and still loves, practical jokes. At Greg Millen's wedding, for instance, he cut the heels off the groom's shoes. Colin was his best man. "He just wanted to make sure he wasn't the shortest one in the wedding party," laughs Greg.)

Craig Ramsay was a veteran and the Petes' captain when Colin was starting out with the team. "He was so tough, small, studious. He wanted to learn the game. . . . I always assumed he'd coach after playing, he was so involved in the game."

A combination of all these qualities made the NHL scouts take notice. The Pittsburgh Penguins drafted him in the second round in 1973, and the World Hockey Association's Vancouver Blazers in the team's first draft picked him fifth overall. He chose the Blazers, who offered him a better financial deal. Gary Green remembers, "I flew to Vancouver to see Colin play at the end of the Blazers' year. Colin had this new Monte Carlo car. We packed his stuff after the last game and decided to go non-stop to Peterborough. The deal was we'd only stop to eat and use the washroom or get gasoline." They made it in two days with Gary doing most of the driving.

"Colin was a terrible driver. . . . Colin finally took over, just fifteen minutes from Peterborough, and he got a speeding ticket. All that way and he gets a ticket," laughs Green. "We could barely open our eyes. We got there for the traditional Petes Thursday-night hockey game. They were in the playoffs." The next day they went home.

Colin Campbell spent most of his eleven seasons in the NHL with the Pittsburgh Penguins and Detroit Red Wings, with stops in Vancouver, Colorado, and Edmonton. He played in 636 regular-season games, scoring 25 goals and 103 assists and racking up 1,292 minutes in penalties. After he retired as a player in 1985, he became an assistant coach with Detroit for five years before joining the Rangers as an assistant coach in 1991. In this role, he and Dick Todd helped coach Mike Keenan take the team to the Stanley Cup title in 1994.

At the end of that season, Keenan was fired and Campbell replaced him. He took the Rangers past the second round of the playoffs every year he coached until he, too, was fired, in 1998. But his hockey career wasn't over yet. The NHL was looking for a director of hockey operations, to be responsible for discipline and game officials. They were looking for a former player, one with credibility among players and coaches, as well as a student of the game. Campbell, with his experience as both coach and player, and his first-hand knowledge of the NHL, was the obvious choice. A player who had had almost 1,300 minutes in penalties over eleven years, far more than the average player, was now in charge of league discipline. His first suspension was delivered to a member of the Petes' alumni, tough guy Matt Johnson, who had to sit for twelve games and was fined $100,000.

Over his first six years as director of hockey operations, Campbell had given out more suspensions than anyone in NHL history. And in the year 2000 he suspended his former coach, Roger Neilson, because Neilson threw a stick in the direction of a referee. Campbell sat Neilson down in his office and handed out the discipline, just like Neilson used to do to him when they were together with the Peterborough Petes. Two years later, Colin Campbell was one of the people mainly responsible for organizing a dinner in Neilson's honour in Toronto, the same day it was announced Neilson was to be inducted into the Hockey Hall of Fame.

In 1974, after Gary Green graduated from the University of Guelph with a B.A. in psychology, he still couldn't get hockey out of his mind. He was asked that year to try out for the Vancouver Blazers of the WHA, but coach Joe Crozier sent him to the East Coast League.

Gary was getting ready to get some stability into his life. He was all set to move his wife down to Virginia in preparation for the hockey season, but before taking this step, he asked the team manager how secure his job was. "He just laughed and said he couldn't guarantee any security; security was for fifty-goal scorers.

"I went back to my room, looked in the mirror at my five-foot-nine, 180-pound body, and did a reality check. I was making $300 a week and I was disillusioned. I went home." Gary applied for the director's job at a Belleville hockey school. "They thought I was twenty-five or twenty-six [he was twenty-one]. They saw my degree, saw I had played pro hockey, and they hired me."

His role at the hockey school was to get more people to attend and to get the school a higher profile while also learning as much about the game as possible. He drove all around the country and into the States, promoting the school by taking flyers and programs to every city and town he could. He drove to Philadelphia seeking out Flyers coach Fred Shero, known as one of hockey's greatest innovators. He met more and more hockey people. And then, in 1975, he organized a symposium in Belleville, featuring hockey's great coaching minds, including Shero, Bob Pulford, David Bauer, Billy Harris, and Roger Neilson. He set a hefty admission price – $150 per person – and he paid the participants $500 and expenses.

He had no idea if it would work. It was a big risk for the young man with little money and no backing to take. He hoped he would break even or, just possibly, make a bit of money – the symposium was, in fact, the first of its kind.

It turned out to be the biggest break of his life. Boris Kulagin, who had coached the Soviet teams in the 1972 and 1974 summit series, read about the symposium and sent a telegram asking for permission to attend or at least get transcripts.

Gary was bowled over. This respected, experienced, and highly qualified coach was *asking* to be invited. In secrecy (because they didn't want the media swarming the place and feared the U.S.S.R. would frown on Kulagin making such an appearance), Gary made arrangements for the Soviet coach to attend the meeting, even renting a small plane to pick him up at the Toronto airport. "He spoke at the symposium through an interpreter. . . . Needless to say it was a huge success," Gary says.

That spring Gary went to Peterborough to ask Neilson if he needed an assistant coach. He was willing to commute from his Belleville job at the hockey school to help. Coaches in junior hockey didn't have assistants. Gary says, "Roger said no, but when I told him I'd do it for free, I became the first assistant coach in junior hockey."

Not only was he an assistant coach, but he was also selling advertising for the Petes' program and helping Roger try to get more fans

into the arena. At the end of the year the Petes' executive, realizing
the role he played, paid him the only pay he'd get for the job – a
$1,000 one-time stipend.

Meanwhile, Gary was still working at the hockey school and
living in a rented townhouse in Peterborough. His wife, who was able
to get a job teaching in Peterborough, soon joined him from
Belleville. Roger would stay with them overnight after their long
scouting trips instead of driving to his house outside Peterborough.

"I was helping Roger [in] his best years, when he was at his most
innovative and creative. . . . People didn't realize, but he was not just
a great coach but a great marketer. He always wondered how to get
more people into the building," Gary says.

Gary went on to become coach of the Petes in their most glorious,
Cup-winning year. Then, at the age of twenty-five, Gary left the
Petes to take the head-coaching job with the Hershey Bears in the
AHL. Just after Green made a verbal commitment to the Bears,
Boston Bruins GM Harry Sinden called offering him a job with the
Bruins. As much as he wanted that NHL job, Green kept his word
with the Bears.

After only fourteen games in Hershey, Green was promoted to
the NHL Washington Capitals to become the youngest head coach
in NHL history, but they missed the playoffs in the first year, and the
next year he was let go.

Green was frustrated with the way the NHL operated. He found
he had no real control over the players. In 1981, disillusioned, he left
the NHL and went into private business, taking on speaking engage-
ments, running hockey schools, planning arenas, and covering more
than a hundred games a year as a television commentator. He moved
his family to Florida permanently in the 1980s for business reasons –
though the attractive climate played a part in the decision. In 2002,
he coached a Canadian team to the gold medal in the annual Spengler
Cup in Europe. In 2003 he was asked back and once again led Canada
to the championship. He still has the urge to coach and has often been
tempted to go back to the NHL, but hasn't found an offer that suits

him. "I don't live my life with regrets, but I have one major regret. I could have gone to Buffalo and coached with Scotty Bowman. I really regret not doing that."

When Colin Campbell was drafted into the NHL from junior in 1973 there was no big draft event. You usually heard about the draft from a phone call or on the radio. Almost thirty years later in 2003, Colin's son Gregory was drafted (after his Kitchener Rangers team won the Memorial Cup) by the Florida Panthers in a glittering program televised to Canada from Nashville. Colin was there not only as an NHL vice-president but as a proud father.

Colin Campbell lives in Tillsonburg with his family.

Gary Green lives in Florida with his family.

DOUG JARVIS
Born in Brantford, Ontario, March 24, 1955
Peterborough Petes 1972-75
NHL *career with Montreal, Washington, Hartford*

Doug Jarvis was raised in Brantford, a small southwestern Ontario city, in an unpretentious red-brick bungalow that his parents have lived in since 1968. Doug and his older brother, Howie, played sports – especially house-league hockey – on the outdoor rinks in the neighbourhood parks. Because Howie had the only goalie pads in the neighbourhood, he was usually the goalie. Doug was only six years old when he started skating, tagging along to the park with Howie to play all day. The hockey was informal, but every park had a hockey team and these teams, composed of kids of all ages, played shinny against one another.

And of course there was road hockey. The street had plenty of kids, and Howie remembers with a laugh that even though he had the goalie pads, "Doug was sometimes the goalie because he was the youngest and we were older."

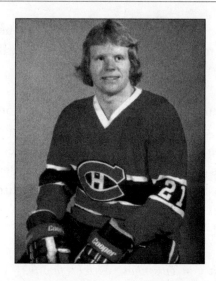

His mother, Millie, remembers one night when Doug was watching a Montreal game on television. "He looked up at me and said,
'Some day I will play for that team.' I said, 'That's up to you' and
nothing more was said.

"Doug had this self-discipline in any sport he played, and he
played them all," says his mother. These sports included football,
baseball, lacrosse, and hockey, and, in fact, he loved football and was
a running back on his high-school team. His parents remember Doug
running for the winning touchdown in a football playoff game and
then getting him in their car to drive to St. Catharines, about an hour
down the highway, for a Junior B hockey game. He missed the first
period but still got two goals.

Doug was raised in a devout Christian household. During his
high-school years his religion became even more important to him.
"By dedicating my life to Christ, I have him here by me at all times.
Christ can make the difference. He's what's important in life," he has
told people.

When Doug was about fifteen, and already five-foot-nine and
170 pounds, he caught the eye of Petes scout Paul Goulet, who lived
in Brantford. Roger Neilson started coming to his games, too. A year
later, Doug, with his creamy skin and red-blond hair accentuating
his choirboy looks, could have played hockey in Chatham for a
Tier II team close to London, but his dad believed he was too young

to leave home so he played for the Waterford Bs, a team located near Brantford. During the summers, Doug worked at a glue factory and a horseradish plant, among other places. His parents had no thoughts of their son playing in the NHL but they were willing to support him in following his passion in these early years. They drove him, and many of his teammates, to hockey and lacrosse games in the car that "God gave us to do those things," as his father says.

When the Petes drafted him in 1972, he was ready to go. Making it easier for him was the fact that he would be able to board in Peterborough with his uncle and aunt (the Wilkins). Another attraction was the university. Doug's marks had always been above average, so gaining admission was not likely to prove difficult. Physically, this quiet kid didn't fit the stereotype of the hockey jock: he had all his teeth, few scars, short hair, a nice smile, and a small frame.

Jarvis joined the Petes in the 1972-73 season. He made up for his small size with tenacity and an ability to win faceoffs seldom seen in a kid so young. In his first year, he scored 20 goals and 49 assists, and took only 14 minutes in penalties. Former teammate and current Dallas Stars scout J.J. Johnston said Jarvis "wasn't very big, but size wasn't very important then. Strength was more important."

Mike Fryia, another teammate, remembers a night when the Petes played in Sudbury. Neilson had a stalling tactic that certainly didn't appeal to the fans but ensured that the team held on for a win. "Neilson's plan was to have Jarvis take the draws and then ice [the puck]. There were more than a hundred draws and Jarvey won most of them. The crowd was booing, but we won the game 3-2.

Landparents Reverend and Mrs. Wilkin say Jarvis would come home after games some nights and be so tired he'd just "sink into the bed." But no matter what time he came home after a Saturday-night game, even if it was 3:30 a.m. following a road trip, the next morning he was at church. Another Pete and former linemate, Bill Evo, says, "He just worked hard all the time, not only at hockey but spiritually and intellectually. He earned great respect. Some of the guys would tease him [about his Christianity and wholesomeness] but we'd always respect him. He was always seeking the best in himself."

Jarvis wasn't too homesick when he first arrived, but he was always in touch with his family, and they would usually drive to Peterborough for the games. Doug was never a worry for Roger Neilson but he did break curfew once: he missed Roger's call by a few minutes when he returned home late from a birthday party for a member of his Bible-study group.

After Bob Gainey left the team for Montreal in 1973 Doug took a leading role with the Petes. He led the team in scoring, made the all-star team, and won the league's most gentlemanly player award while finishing fifth in league scoring with 45 goals and 88 assists for 133 points while taking only 39 minutes in penalties.

He spent a couple of years taking part-time courses at Trent University and found "good balance" in Peterborough with hockey, his Christian life, and his studies. When Neilson had the University of Waterloo test his team's fitness in the 1974-75 season, Doug's results were incredible. He led the team in almost every category: the ability to accelerate and skate at high speed; the ability to maintain a fast pace for the duration of a shift; the ability to perform over the duration of three periods. In the heart-rate testing, he never reached a point where he had to stop.

Doug had also led the Petes to a bronze medal in Russia at the first world junior championship, in which the Petes represented Canada. The team was thumped 9-0 by Russia in that 1974 tournament, which became the forerunner to the present-day World Junior Championships. That same year he was named one of the top three junior players in Canada and Neilson described him as one of the best all-round players in junior hockey.

When the Toronto Maple Leafs drafted him in 1975, Doug thought he might one day play against former teammate Bob Gainey. But Roger Neilson had told Scotty Bowman and Sam Pollock that Doug Jarvis, despite his small stature, was the best centre in the world. They had locked that opinion away, and when Toronto took Jarvis in the draft, Pollock craftily told Leafs owner Harold Ballard about Jarvis's Christian background, knowing that Ballard didn't like the "Christian players." Pollock offered to trade top draft choice Greg Hubick to the Leafs and said he'd take any of five young players they were willing to trade. Fortunately for Pollock, and probably because he'd mentioned Doug's Christian ways, Jarvis was on that list, and Ballard threw him in without consulting Leafs management.

So rather than playing against him, Doug joined old teammate Gainey in Montreal, where they hooked up as the best penalty-killing unit in the league and its best defensive forwards. They relished the role and went on to help Doug's father's favourite team win the Stanley Cup four times from 1976 to 1979.

Gainey stayed in Montreal for his entire sixteen-year career, but Doug was traded to Washington in 1982, then to Hartford three years later. He was playing for Washington when he won the Frank Selke Trophy in 1984 for the league's best defensive forward and for Hartford when he won the Bill Masterson Trophy in 1987 for perseverance, sportsmanship, and dedication to hockey.

Jarvis showed his consistency by playing for thirteen seasons without missing a game and playing in 964 straight games, scoring 139 goals and 264 assists between 1975 and 1988. He is the league's iron man, and still holds the record for most consecutive games played.

In 1987 he started the season in the AHL with the Birmingham Whalers and became their head coach during the season. After retiring as a player in 1988 he became an assistant coach with the Minnesota North Stars. In 1990, when Bob Gainey arrived in Minnesota as the team's new head coach, the familiar face from his Peterborough and Montreal days was already there. In 1993, the duo moved with the Stars to Dallas, where Doug was the assistant coach and Gainey became the general manager of the team. The two of them took the Stars to a Stanley Cup title in 1999.

In 2003 Doug was hired as head coach for the Hamilton Bulldogs of the AHL, a Montreal Canadiens farm team, headed now by old friend Bob Gainey, who was named the Habs' general manager the same year. Doug's job is to develop the players for the NHL team, and winning would be a bonus.

Doug Jarvis lives in St. Catharines, Ontario, with his wife and two children.

GREG MILLEN
Born in Toronto, Ontario, June 25, 1957
Peterborough Petes 1974-77
NHL career in Pittsburgh, Hartford, St. Louis, Quebec, Chicago,
  Detroit

Greg Millen was an only child, born in 1957 and raised in the Don Mills area of Toronto. Both his parents worked outside the home: his father, Ted, was vice-president of Philco Ford, a large subsidiary of the Ford Motor Company; his mother, Barb, was an executive administrator for Sears. Although both parents had some interest in sports in their youth, neither had continued in the hockey his father had played or the figure skating his mother had been involved in. In the summer, Greg didn't play many organized sports, but his parents loved the outdoors, and so did Greg. In the winter, Greg's father made an ice rink in their backyard. Many of their summer weekends were spent boating.

When he was five, Greg joined organized hockey, first as a forward, then as a goalie, with the Don Mills Civitans team. Greg doesn't remember his first game, but his parents do. They realized they were going to be putting his equipment on for the first time ever so they had a practice session the night before. His mother says, "We

put on all the gear the night before so we would be sure we knew how to do it. We had to get him up at 4:00 a.m. for a 5:00 a.m. Saturday-morning practice, just to have the time to put it all on. [In the morning] he was sleeping. By the time we got his equipment on, he was like a board and his dad carried him to the car." She laughs as she remembers the fuss.

Greg's dad had been told goalies had to be good skaters, so Barb thought it might help Greg to take figure-skating lessons. When she suggested it to him, she says, "he just looked at me and said, 'Are you kidding?'" That was the end of that idea.

The Millens were lucky in one respect. Greg's uncle managed a Toronto sporting-goods store and they got Greg's equipment from him at a good price. Goalie equipment didn't come cheap. He didn't wear his first goalie skates until peewee, however. Hockey got a bit more serious when he was about eight years old and started trying out for all-star teams. He still went to the park to play. "I'd go outside all day long on weekends. Some kids would stay only a while but I'd stay all day. I'd have to be home when the street lights came on, but many times I'd get in trouble [for being late]."

One day, when he was twelve, and still serious about hockey, his mother asked him, "Did you ever think you'd like to make hockey your career?" He didn't hesitate with his answer: "Would I ever!"

Although hockey took up most of his time, Greg had found another love. "It's fair to say if I hadn't found hockey I would have pursued a career in music," he says. Both his parents could play the piano. Mrs. Millen remembers Greg wanted to play guitar but "his fingers were too small. He couldn't play piano, but he wanted to play the drums. We got him a set through the Sears catalogue. He'd prac-tise on his own and I took him to drum lessons every Saturday. He learned to read music and played in the Don Mills orchestra at high school. He also eventually learned to play piano by ear."

But hockey got in the way.

The biggest peewee tournament in the world is held annually in Quebec City. It's by invitation only – yet Greg went to the tourna-ment in three consecutive years. One of those years he was playing for the Toronto Shopsy's team. He recalls, "We had beat the Toronto

Nats and got to the final of AAA. We were winning 1-0 with 15 seconds to go in the final game of the tournament and the other team got two goals to beat us." Greg wasn't in goal for that game, but he remembers that the winners would have won special winter boots. "I wanted them so bad. I was so sour."

Greg kept making the all-star teams but people "all the way up were saying I was too small for a goalie." He tried out for the elite Toronto Marlies squad in 1968. The Marlies were the team to play on at that time because they paid for all the ice and equipment. "[The Marlies minor teams] always wanted to cut me. Every year at tryout time one guy, George Legge, would say I was too small but the coach, Paul McNamara, would always keep me." Being called too small was just an added incentive to prove they were wrong, Greg says. Each year Greg would display his excellent goaltending, but each year he had to fight to make the teams.

Greg's father also remembers the Marlies' tryouts. "For the first peewee [tryout] Greg had somehow cut his finger on a screen door just when we were leaving. . . . It was quite a cut. I bandaged it. The cut was on his catching hand but he went to the tryout and made the team. I took him to the York Hospital right after and the doctor really hassled me for not bringing him to the hospital first because it could get infected. He stitched it up and things were fine."

The Marlies memories are great ones for Greg. "The best memories are of going to practice in the morning and playing subway tag all the way home. You'd run past the door and leave your teammates to get into the next car."

His favourite Marlies memory, though, is playing for the under-age Junior B team, which was the same age as the midget Russian team that was touring Canada in the 1973-74 season. The game attracted 10,000 people to Maple Leaf Gardens. Just to be playing in the game was a thrill, but winning made it even better.

However, not everything was rosy. Greg wasn't growing – he was almost five-foot-nine – and the Junior Marlies passed on him in the draft. "I was bitter. I thought I was better than the one they took. He was good, but I was better. [Then] the Petes drafted me. I didn't know much about them. . . . I knew they had two good goalies. I didn't think

I had much of a chance to beat out two established goalies but I said I'd give it my best shot. I'm not sure I was dreaming of pro hockey at the time, but I was plugging away at it."

Another area that wasn't always rosy was school. Greg's marks sometimes suffered. "Greg has to put more effort into math and less into hockey," one teacher wrote on his grade-twelve report card. "Greg's output has not changed since I taught him in Grade 10 . . . he must worry less about hockey and more about his school marks," wrote another.

Greg hoped hockey would be different in Peterborough. One thing that was different was that Greg, now sixteen, got his driver's licence. Because his father worked at Ford, he was able to get his son a car. The good-looking teen with the long brown wavy hair started a new life. Other than not liking the first high school he went to there – he transferred in his second year – Greg didn't have many problems with the move. He got on particularly well with coach Roger Neilson.

Millen flourished, but the team didn't. In his second season, 1975-76, the Petes failed to make the playoffs for only the second time since they were founded. A bigger disappointment hit him that summer after he returned from a trip to the west with the Peterborough high-school band. Each player on the team got a letter from Roger informing him he was leaving the Petes to go to Dallas of the Central Hockey League as coach and general manager.

In part, the letter read:

It has always been our policy to urge each player to do his best at school. It is my hope that you will continue your education in order to keep alternative options open to you. It is not in your best interests to become completely dependent on hockey dictating your future.

Also, it is my sincere hope that you will maintain the highest degree of moral character in the years ahead.

Your friend, Roger

The new coach, Garry Young, was a former NHLer. Greg had a great year in the 1975-76 season and Young said following one game:

"I've said all along that Greg is the best goaltender in the league, [and with him] stopping 36 of 37 shots and having the best average in the league at 2.75, my belief is reinforced." He was playing in the twelve-team league with players such as Ken Linseman, Dwight Foster, Mike Gartner, Bill Root, Ron Wilson, Doug Wilson, Dale McCourt, Ted Nolan, and Ron Duguay.

Greg was picked by Pittsburgh in the sixth round of the 1977 NHL draft. He was nineteen, engaged to be married to a Peterborough girl, and ready to play hockey. But the thrill of his life quickly turned into bitterness. After he arrived in Pittsburgh, he was cut from the team and sent to Kalamazoo, where he was cut again. He was suddenly without a hockey team. He couldn't even return to the Petes because they had filled their roster.

He decided to quit hockey and go back to school. He was going to register at the University of Guelph, but returned to Peterborough. He says, "I was living at [my future wife's family home] and I did something I have never done. I'm not good with my hands. I sat down and built a birdhouse. I can't build anything and it was a horrible birdhouse. . . .

"The Petes were trying to help me and [they] let me know that the Sault Ste. Marie juniors were interested in me. I was determined to give hockey up, but my dad said, 'Why don't you just go out there and have some fun?'" Fun? Greg had forgotten why he played the game.

"I went to the Soo and it changed my whole world. They didn't have any structure, nothing like the Petes. There was no discipline, no tradition, and there was no pressure on me. I just decided to have fun and I loved it."

The team – which included Wayne Gretzky and Craig Hartsburg in its lineup – had just fired its coach when he arrived and had no replacement, so Greg took over practices. "I'd call Roger for drills," he says.

Still, the team couldn't continue without a coach, no matter how much fun Greg was having. He and other team members were getting angry, and when an executive meeting was being held, the team charged into the boardroom. All the players were there, even sixteen-year-old Wayne Gretzky. "We basically told them we'd all quit the next day if there was no coach by noon." The team hired Paul Therrien. (He's the answer in a trivia quiz: "Who was the first coach to bench Wayne Gretzky?") The Soo made the playoffs, won the first round, and played Ottawa in the semifinals, taking them to an eight-game series (ties weren't broken by overtime) before getting beaten out. Ottawa then played the Petes, and when the Petes were victorious, Greg told his former teammates, "We wore them out for you."

But for Greg, the experience had been a big turnaround. "I was totally rejuvenated. There had to be some fun in the game and I had found it." He went back to Pittsburgh, the team that had drafted him in 1977.

The next summer he returned to Peterborough, but this time for a much happier event than building birdhouses – he and his fiancée, Ann, were married in her hometown. Greg went on to a great NHL career, playing fourteen years in Pittsburgh, Hartford, St. Louis, Quebec, Chicago, and Detroit before retiring in 1991. Not bad for a guy "too small to play."

Greg Millen and his wife live near Peterborough with their four children. He is a CBC Hockey Night in Canada *analyst.*

WAYNE GRETZKY
Born in Brantford, Ontario, January 26, 1961
Peterborough Petes 1976
NHL career with Edmonton, Los Angeles, St. Louis, New York
  Rangers
WHA career with Indianapolis, Edmonton

Most hockey fans know the story of Wayne Gretzky's years as a kid and in the NHL. But not everyone remembers the time he spent in Peterborough playing for the Petes. Yes, the Great One was a Peter- borough Pete. Only for three games, but if his father, Walter, had had anything to do with it, he would have been a regular with the Petes, instead of playing his junior hockey in Sault Ste. Marie.

The Peterborough Examiner

Walter Gretzky knows his hockey. He knew about the Petes' great tradition not of just winning but also of treating players the way parents want them to be treated when they are away from home. Gary Green, a coach with the Petes, recalls that Walter told him he was thinking about sending letters to all the junior clubs telling them not to draft his son because he was going to Peterborough or nowhere.

In Toronto, Wayne played Junior B hockey with the Seneca Nats, a team affiliated with the Petes. When Petes' coaches Garry Young and Gary Green needed players, they called up players from the Nats.

In November 1976 they called up Wayne. The Petes had had success with many Brantford boys, such as David Foster, Stan Jonathan, and Doug Jarvis, probably because the Petes' head scout, Paul Goulet, lived there. Goulet scouted all around Ontario but he knew the Brantford teams especially well.

Gretzky was fifteen when he was called up to play a game in Peterborough on November 27 against the Soo Greyhounds. He had already been picked out as someone to watch, so a huge contingent of hockey media was there to cover his first Junior A game. For Peterborough fans, it was just another game – just over 2,000 people attended.

Petes trainer Dick Todd remembers that day better than the night. "We couldn't find a helmet small enough to fit his head. There was nowhere in Peterborough with a helmet that small. We had to stuff it with Styrofoam, that's why the helmet looks tilted," says Todd. "[Wayne] was frail and weak-looking, but every game he played he showed you something more."

That night he passed the puck to the Petes' Tim Trimper to earn his first point in the OHA in a 5-4 win over the Greyhounds. Another Petes player who became a part of the growing stock of Gretzky trivia was Steve Peters. The under-age Peterborough native was chosen in the midget draft ahead of Gretzky.

Gretzky played twice more for the Petes that season. In his three games, he had three assists. The Soo drafted him in 1977. He played one season there, scoring an amazing 70 goals and 112 assists in 64 games. The rest is hockey history.

Wayne Gretzky lives in the United States with his wife and children. He retired from the NHL in 1999 and now is an owner of the NHL's Phoenix Coyotes.

STEVE LARMER
Born in Peterborough, June 16, 1961
Peterborough Petes 1977-78
NHL career with Chicago, New York Rangers

JEFF LARMER
Born in Peterborough, November 10, 1962
NHL career with Colorado Rockies, New Jersey, Chicago

The Larmer boys, Steve and Jeff, learned to skate in the backyard rink that their father, Don, made for them in a residential neighbourhood in Peterborough. When Steve was five, his parents signed him up for mite hockey in the church league. Right away he began scoring goals and was so good that his parents were asked to have him try out for an all-star team. It was for six- and seven-year-olds, but league officials thought he was good enough to compete with the older children.

Jeff (left) and Steve Larmer. Both played on a Peterborough all-star team.

That first year he scored two shorthanded goals at the Mississauga paperweight (six-year-olds) tournament, which the team won. He impressed everyone there not only with his skating but also his ability to raise the puck from the blue line and into the net. The other kids couldn't raise the puck at all.

The same year, his team played in a tournament in Brampton. His teammate and still close friend Cal Sweeting remembers that everyone was talking about Steve and Wayne Gretzky. Gretzky's team didn't make the final, and Peterborough won it, with Steve scoring eight goals in the tournament, three in the final game. He was named the MVP. Steve remembers his coaches had them in a "relaxing atmosphere, we just played hockey for fun."

Next year he played with boys his own age, but with a year of experience under his blades he was the best player on a team of good players. However, a bout of back pain kept him out of hockey for six weeks. It was frustrating, but he followed doctor's orders, stayed off his skates, and the pain disappeared. As soon as he could he was playing again. His parents never pushed him to play sports; they didn't have to. "It was a perfect atmosphere at home. They let us make our own decisions, and if we got out of hand, they stepped in."

Jeff remembers his older brother was always patient at games. He was never in a rush to get rid of the puck or ball and he seemed to be able to analyse situations very quickly. He also remembers he would get most of Steve's old equipment. While their parents usually bought the boys new skates, other equipment came to Jeff in the form of hand-me-downs. "I loved getting it, I'd always be eyeing it, even years later I always preferred my equipment loose and broken in."

When they were ten, Steve and Jeff sometimes got themselves to games or practices by taking city buses, lugging their equipment around with them, but usually their father rushed home, gulped some food, and drove the boys himself.

By the time he was eleven, Larmer's shot was becoming hard. School friend Gabby Killen remembers, "Steve, Jeff, and I were playing hockey in the backyard. Steve was taking some shots. I had on these shin pads that you use for road hockey. You weren't supposed to use raisers, but one thing always led to another. Steve let go a shot and shattered my knee."

The boys loved to listen to hockey games and would sneak a transistor radio into their room. When they were eleven and twelve, they listened to the games being broadcast from the Soviet Union when the Petes represented Canada in the first world junior championships.

By the time Steve was twelve and playing in peewee hockey, he was travelling to tournaments in places such as Brampton, Burlington, and Prescott. The players were always billeted with local families. "You'd be nervous about billeting at first, but these people opened their doors to us and it was part of the memories," says Steve.

Although his later fame came from playing wing, Steve played centre throughout his minor-hockey days, while Jeff played the wing.

"[Steve] hated to lose," remembers Cal Sweeting. "As a kid it didn't matter what sport it was, he always had that desire to win and

Steve Larmer
as an underage Pete.

he'd get angry about losing. He might not have shown it, but he got
even quieter when his team lost."

Steve says he "always tried to learn from watching the great
plays or mistakes and asking myself what I would have done in
that situation."

When Steve was fifteen, Gary Green asked him to try out for the
Petes as an under-age player. (The team knew they would lose him
the next year in the OHL draft.) Green remembers Steve telling him
he was going to the national junior lacrosse championships out west.
Green was stunned that the kid wasn't excited at the prospect of
trying out, but when he returned as a lacrosse champion, he got to
camp and made the team.

Both Steve and Jeff said by the time they were drafted in junior
– Steve by the Niagara Falls Flyers in 1978 and Jeff by the Kitchener
Rangers in 1979 – both were ready to leave home. Steve had saved
up to buy a 1974 Malibu and drove that to training camp. The teams
they went to weren't as strict as the Petes – they weren't required to
go to school or even have full-time jobs. The Larmer boys took

advantage of the freedom, but both finished high school with relatively good marks.

Steve's team made the playoffs that year but was beaten out by the Peterborough team that went on to win its first and only Memorial Cup. Jeff and Steve, virtual scoring machines who both made the OHL all-star team, were the best brother combination to be born and raised in Peterborough.

Jeff was a prolific scorer in junior with the Rangers, getting 108 points in his second season, 1980-81, in 61 games and 95 the following year in 49 games. He led all OHA playoff scorers and helped his team to the Memorial Cup in 1981. He played five seasons in the NHL with the Colorado Rockies, New Jersey, and Chicago. He also went overseas in 1994 to play in Switzerland, Britain, and Germany. His pro career stretched from 1981 until he retired in 1994 from the Milwaukee Admirals of the IHL. After leaving hockey, Jeff went back to school, got his degree, and is now an elementary-school teacher.

Steve left junior, having posted a total of 331 points in his three years with Niagara Falls after he was chosen 120th overall by Chicago in the 1980 NHL draft. He went to the AHL, playing in Moncton for coach Orval Tessier, who had also coached Jeff on his Kitchener junior team. Moncton won the Calder Cup in 1981. The next year, Tessier went to Chicago and brought Steve up, putting him on a line with Denis Savard and Al Secord. Steve played in the NHL in 1982-83 for Chicago and won the NHL Calder Trophy as rookie of the year, scoring 43 goals and 47 assists in 80 games. He didn't miss a game – playing 884 games in eleven straight years, setting the Chicago iron-man record until he sat out, demanding a trade. He retired in 1995, one year after his team, the New York Rangers, won the Stanley Cup. He had five NHL seasons with forty or more goals. He played for Team Canada in 1991 scoring the winning goal in the Canada Cup and was in the NHL All-Star Game in 1990 and 1991. In all, he played in 1,006 regular-season NHL games, scoring 441 goals and 571 assists. In 1990-91 he set the Chicago club record for points by a winger at 101.

Steve Larmer lives in Peterborough with his wife and daughter and works for the National Hockey League Players' Association.

Jeff Larmer lives near Collingwood, Ontario, with his family and is an elementary-school teacher. In 2004 he became the father of triplets. He and his wife now have four children.

GREG THEBERGE
Born in Peterborough, September 3, 1959
Peterborough Petes 1976-79
NHL career with Washington

Greg Theberge was born on the east side of Peterborough, across the river from downtown and only two blocks from two outdoor hockey rinks. That area had been a village until 1904, when it joined Peterborough. Many of its residents still refer to it as East City, the Capital of Canada. It's their way of saying it is the best village anywhere and not really part of Peterborough, the city. Greg's mother was the daughter of hockey great and Peterborough resident Dit Clapper. She and Greg moved into her father's house after she and her husband separated, so Greg grew up in his grandfather's place, which he describes as "a big sprawling mansion in its day."

Rob Kayser was a neighbour of the Clappers in the 1960s. "I always remember Uncle Dit as a bit bigger than life," he recalls. "When he came to the house on Saturday afternoons, he always seemed a lot taller and broader than my dad. He'd always come by to visit and usually shared a whisky with Mom. Most Saturday nights he would come by to watch *Hockey Night in Canada* with us. One memory is the first time we watched Bobby Orr and Uncle Dit said, 'Watch this kid, he is one of the best.'"

Greg says, "I can remember he'd have Milt Schmidt, Charlie Conacher, Red Sullivan, Hap Day all over to the house for cards. I was so young, I'd sit upstairs instead of going to bed. All I could hear was them laughing and see cigar smoke creeping upstairs.

"He was a like a father to me. He took me to my first skate at the old Civic Arena where they used to divide the rink in half for the little kids. He'd take me to my church-league hockey games. He'd always stand there watching and never said anything until one day I'll never forget." Greg, then about nine years old, and another boy started fighting, with Greg on the bottom getting pounded and "crying my eyes out. . . . He [Clapper] jumped right on the ice, took us by the scruff of the necks and pushed us into the penalty box. He said, 'You get in there, you guys are too young for that stuff.' Nobody said a word. He walked off the ice and went back into the stands. He was some disappointed."

By the time he was twelve, Theberge had moved away from Peterborough to play minor hockey for Wexford in Toronto. But he was so good in his teens, he was drafted by an OHL team: the Peterborough Petes. "There was a lot of hype about me being Dit Clapper's grandson. Garry Young was the coach and they offered me [Dit's] number 5. I didn't really want it. I wanted my own identity and took number 7."

One night, the Petes played against the Soo Greyhounds, and Greg came up against a highly regarded junior, Wayne Gretzky. "I asked Dit what he thought of him. He was intrigued by him and couldn't figure out how he could be so good. I told him I thought Gretzky was too small and I'd look after him that night." Clapper was in a wheelchair by this time, having suffered a series of strokes, so he didn't go to the game. Theberge came home a bit embarrassed. Gretzky's team had won 7-4, and four of those seven goals were scored by Gretzky. Clapper didn't rub it in – he just smiled.

Greg had the record for assists by a Petes defenceman until Larry Murphy broke it. He played two full seasons with the Capitals, then played in the minors and in Europe.

Greg Theberge lives in Toronto with his wife and children.

LARRY MURPHY
Born in Scarborough, Ontario, March 8, 1961
Peterborough Petes 1978-80
NHL career in Los Angeles, Washington, Minnesota North Stars,
  Pittsburgh, Toronto, Detroit

Larry Murphy remembers his first hockey draft in 1966 almost as if it were yesterday. His father, Ed, had asked him if he wanted to go and play hockey. "I said sure," he says, even though he'd never been on skates, had never gone through the ritual or the struggle of putting socks over shin pads, gartering socks, fixing the jock strap, forcing the sweater over shoulder pads, slapping a puck along the slippery ice. But after his parents helped him get through all this, including lacing him into an older brother's too-big skates, off they went with the five-year-old Larry, who was to try out at a local Scarborough rink with a group of six-year-olds. He was chosen last, but it was the last time he'd ever be chosen last.

He can still describe what the tryout entailed. "You'd skate from the blue line to the end boards and do circles. They picked you based

Larry Murphy, wearing the hat, and the Don Mills midget team in Europe.

on how well you did. I didn't fall, I could lean on the boards, but once I was out on the open I was in trouble."

How could they know there was a future National Hockey League star on the ice? But the coach picked the right position for him. "The coach had me playing defence. I guess defence was my natural position at that time," Murphy says, laughing at the memory. "I could only go up to the blue line and had to stay there until the play came back down. I wanted to play so it didn't bother me. I was happy to be there – besides if I went to the other end my shift would be over before I got back."

His mother, Doris, remembers these first hockey moments vividly. "I was so embarrassed, but said, 'Look how strong he is on the skates. He must have strong ankles to stand up that straight for that long.'" To which Murphy responds, "I know, Mom, you were the first to know I had potential."

But it was what happened off the ice that Doris and Ed Murphy remembered best. "When he came off the ice and we were going home, he knew what everyone [had done]. Even though he just stood there, he could describe everything that happened on the ice," says his mother.

After Doris and Ed Murphy were married, Ed was moved to Scarborough to work as a contract inspector for Bell Telephone, a job he held for forty years. Their first son, Richard, was born four years before Larry. Although Richard did play some minor hockey, he quit in peewee. But Larry was in love with sports. Frozen toes and lack of action wouldn't stop him from playing every Saturday. His skating improved over the next few years, in no small part because of the back-yard rink that his father made for the boys, and because of Ed's insis-tence that Larry practise basic skills, like skating backwards.

Ed also built Larry a board with a net outside so he could shoot pucks, not so much to make sure he practised his shooting, but to save their garage door. His father wouldn't allow him to take slapshots, believing he should master the wrist shot first. Larry didn't take a slapshot until after he was twelve.

Larry's second year of organized hockey was in house league, where he graduated from defence to centre. By his third year of hockey, the park's outdoor rink was covered over by the city, and Larry's team moved inside to play. This third year was the year Larry Murphy started to blossom.

On the way home after a game, his parents would talk only about the good plays, and Larry would talk about what happened on the ice, still remembering all the details. His mother says, "It was the next day that Ed and Larry would talk about the things Larry might do better, but never after a game. Ed had a real passion for the game, but he never put pressure on the kids."

By eight, at ninety pounds, Larry was getting some of his father's size (Ed was more than six feet tall and 250 pounds) and playing tyke, scoring twenty goals as a centre. Hockey wasn't his entire life, though. "Larry was an A student," says his mother. He also took violin lessons. He was so good in music, says his mother, that a teacher wanted him to join the school choir "but he never told us about this until years later because he was afraid we'd make him join."

By atom hockey at age eleven, playing defence again for the Marlies, he was described in a newspaper as the "hard hitting Bobby Baun type" of player. His team also beat Wayne Gretzky's Brantford team in a tournament, in overtime.

Larry tried out for the Marlies for his minor bantam hockey but they cut him, so he went to Don Mills, where he played centre and defence. "This was a significant point in hockey for me," says Larry, because he got to spend time playing both forward and defence, then started leaning toward playing defence full time. He also discovered he could play with and against anyone.

Before this he had dreamed what many Canadian kids who play hockey dreamed about: playing in the NHL. "But we didn't play the game with that as the ultimate goal. I just loved playing the game."

The next year, in 1976, he tried out as a centre for the Don Mills midget team as a bantam-age player. The coach said he wasn't going to make it as a centre but suggested defence. The team, made up of mainly second-year midget players, was capable of going all the way and was moulded for that purpose. The coach had talked most of the second-year players into staying with the midgets rather than playing for the Junior B team. Coach Don Booth wanted the team to take a shot at the Wrigley national championship. "Coach Booth wanted me on the team as a defenceman so my mind was made up after that, that to be successful, that would be my position," Larry says. At fifteen years old, Larry was the youngest kid on the midget team, but he was also one of the bigger boys – already more than six feet and 200 pounds.

Size *was* a problem when it came to Larry's equipment. He had to go to the Bauer factory in Kitchener to get skates made especially to fit him because his feet were so wide. When he was twelve he had to go to the Junior A teams to get a helmet big enough to fit his oversized head.

Larry had also inherited his father's temper – rarely seen, but that made it all the more impressive. Larry's temper broke out on the ice only occasionally and the opposing player usually regretted having provoked it, but the big teen learned to control it. It was seldom seen in that final midget season of 1976-77. The team was aiming high, with the goal of winning the national championship. It won the provincial championship in a final tournament game against Steve Larmer's team, right in Peterborough. Then it was on to Moncton for the national championship. They played and won in front of four thousand people, giving them the right to represent Canada in the Czechoslovakia and the Soviet Union tournament games for two weeks.

The next year, Larry was still midget age. He moved to the Seneca Junior Bs, where he got plenty of exposure for the OHL. His parents knew by this time he had a legitimate shot at playing in the NHL.

The junior draft was held at the Royal York Hotel in Toronto in 1978. Larry says, "I had no idea where I was going to be drafted. I remember that winter going to an OHL playoff game in Oshawa. My brother, Rick, had scored some great tickets with the seats right in front of the glass. Oshawa was playing Peterborough. I've never admitted this before but I was pulling for Oshawa.

"I remember watching the game and looking at the players. They were so big, so fast, it just seemed so far away."

He didn't know then that Peterborough was his destination. Petes scout Paul Goulet, who discovered more hockey players for the Petes than birds find worms, met with him. "He wasn't your typical hard-assed hockey scout. He was such a nice person," remembers Larry.

His parents were glad Peterborough had drafted him. "Peterborough was close to us and the team believed in schooling," says Doris Murphy. It helped that the Petes had once been a farm team for Ed's beloved Montreal Canadiens. The Murphys never missed a game in Peterborough and would travel all over Ontario to see Larry and the team play. He would always look up in the stands, from the time he was a kid to junior, to see if his parents were there.

"Peterborough was so well run. It had a structure in place set up by Scotty Bowman, then Neilson added to it. We never had any issues. The guys didn't get in trouble, the team did their homework, and it was unacceptable to lose, but lots of fun with no opportunities to go astray," he says. They gave him $20 a week and more the further they went in the playoffs. "One week we got $50. That was like winning a lottery." (Larry had learned to earn, and look after his money. When he wanted to go to a Catholic high school instead of a public school, he had to work all summer installing air conditioners to get the tuition.) He played his usual role of defenceman that year, steady and true.

In his first year with the Petes, they won their one and only Memorial Cup. The next year, coach Gary Green left the team to coach in the pros and Mike Keenan, a Junior B coach from Whitby, was brought in. Keenan gave Murphy more offensive responsibilities, and Larry repaid the trust by breaking the Petes' record for assists by a defenceman, set by Dit Clapper's grandson Greg Theberge, getting 68. Keenan also took the team to the Memorial Cup.

It was fourteen years after he had been picked last in the Scarborough tyke draft at the age of five, but Larry Murphy's hockey skills commanded some respect. In 1980, following his second year with the Petes, he was picked fourth overall in the NHL draft and was on his way to Los Angeles, California, and a big culture shock, to play for the Kings. It was there he set what is still the NHL record for assists by a rookie with 60. He also scored 16 goals, but it wasn't enough to win rookie of the year. That honour went to Peter Stastny in a controversial win. Stastny was in his thirties and had played for the Czechoslovakian national team before sneaking into Canada to play for Quebec in the NHL.

In his fourth season in L.A., Larry was traded to Washington, where he stayed for six seasons from 1983 until 1989, then to Minnesota until being traded to Pittsburgh in the 1990-91 season, where his team won the Stanley Cup twice and he stayed for four seasons. Toronto got him in 1995, and the fans didn't understand that while he wasn't flashy, he did his job and did it well. The Leafs, during his second season in 1998-99, traded him to Detroit, where he went on to win two more Stanley Cup titles. In Larry's last NHL season, 2000-01, his father, Ed, became ill with cancer. Larry drove from Detroit to Barrie, where the Murphys had retired, every week of that hockey season to be with his dying father.

When Larry Murphy retired from the NHL in 2001, he left behind him an impressive record. He played twenty-one years in the league – the last Peterborough defenceman who played that long was the legendary Dit Clapper (but Clapper had switched from forward to defence in his career). Larry scored 1,216 regular-season points playing in 1,615 regular-season games and 215 playoff games. His teams won the Stanley Cup four times, he played six times for

Team Canada, in six NHL All-Star Games, broke Bobby Orr's record for most points by an NHL defenceman, broke Tim Horton's record for playing the most games by a defencemen (later broken by Scott Stevens), and was second behind Gretzky for games by an active player when he retired. He was the third all-time leading defenceman in scoring, behind Paul Coffey and Ray Bourque, when he retired. He describes the key to his success: "I wasn't a fighter. After four fights I knew that wasn't going to be the key to my longevity. I had to find a way to play the game and stay in the game. I loved the game, that was number one. I had passion and ability to think through the game. I prided myself on that. I wasn't fast. I wasn't the hardest hitter. I didn't have the hardest shot, but I could be in the right place at the right time."

Larry Murphy lives on a farm near Detroit, Michigan, with his wife and children. He is a television hockey analyst in Detroit. In 2004 he was inducted into the Hockey Hall of Fame.

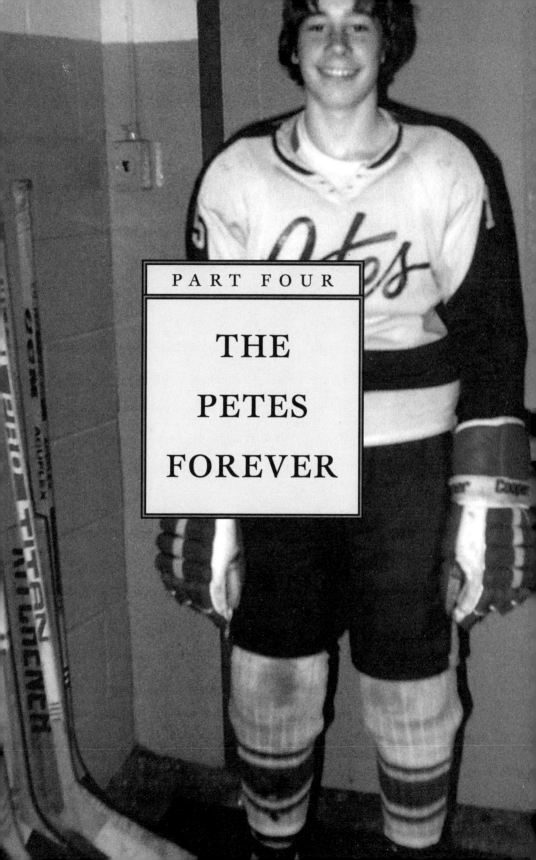

PART FOUR

THE
PETES
FOREVER

The Players' Coach

Dick Todd isn't the household hockey name that coaches Scotty Bowman, Roger Neilson, Mike Keenan, and Gary Green are, but the Toronto native is the most successful Peterborough Petes coach in the history of the team.

Some might say that assessment depends on how you measure success. Gary Green coached the Petes for only two years, but he took the team to the Memorial Cup final both times and won the team's only Memorial Cup. That is success.

Dick Todd's success is less obviously spectacular, but remarkable just the same. He helped put more than thirty players into the NHL during the twelve years he was coach and general manager, people such as Steve Yzerman, Bruce Shoebottom, Dave Reid, Doug Evans, Kris King, Randy Burridge, Terry Carkner, Tie Domi, Mike Ricci, Bob Errey, Kay Whitmore, John Druce, Ron Tugnutt, Jody Hull, Luke Richardson, Bill Huard, Jassen Cullimore, Jason Dawe, Chris Pronger, Cory Stillman, and Matt Johnson. Those few don't even include the eight years before he was coach when he was business manager, trainer, and scout with coaches Roger Neilson, Gary Young, Gary Green, Mike Keenan, and Dave Dryden.

Junior coaches are supposed to win games and develop character players for the NHL. These are usually players who can both play hockey and stand the pressure, be team players and keep their noses clean while they're in the public eye. That's why the kids want to play

Roger Neilson (left) and Dick Todd.
Neilson was Todd's best man at his
wedding, as well as his coach, mentor,
and friend.

at that level and why parents support them. Dick Todd is a great example of what a junior coach should be.

Todd never had a losing season during his tenure as coach. His winning percentage was more than 60 per cent. His teams won three OHL titles, putting them into the Memorial Cup three times. While he was trainer, the teams were in four Memorial Cup finals. That's seven Memorial Cup rounds while he was a member of the team. Nobody has ever matched this record.

If more evidence of his success is needed, his teams won the gold medal in the World Junior Championship when he was an assistant coach with the Canadian juniors, and when he was head coach. He was also with the New York Rangers as assistant coach when they won the Stanley Cup in 1994. Not bad for a baseball player who left a job in a grocery store to take up a position as team trainer, for which he had no previous experience.

Going into unknown territory was not unusual for Dick Todd. In 1955 in Toronto, he was only ten years old when a buddy asked him to go to the baseball tryouts with him for eleven- and twelve-year-olds. Dick made the team, which was coached by none other than twenty-two-year-old Roger Neilson.

Young Dick's mother was in poor health, and his father spent most of his time looking after her, so Roger took the boy under his wing. The baseball team won the city championship with an unblemished record of 36-0, which is what happens when you play or practise six days a week. (Roger tried to stay away from Sunday play.) In turn, Dick helped Roger deliver his hundreds of *Globe and Mail* papers from Monday to Saturday.

"[Roger] intuitively knew what to say and how to make a lonely ten-year-old feel good about himself," says Dick about Neilson. "He quickly became my coach, mentor, surrogate parent, and very special friend. I often attended church with Roger, and he helped me develop a set of values I have carried with me throughout my life."

But Dick was not a carbon copy of Roger. Their personalities and interests were quite different. While Roger was a committed Christian from the time he was twelve, Dick picked up only the values. Roger not only preached fitness, he was fit; Dick could take it or leave it. And while Roger was a "gee whiz" type of guy, Dick certainly was a bit looser with the language.

Baseball wasn't the only sport Dick and Roger had in common. Dick also played house-league hockey in the winter as a goalie, but didn't play for any of the many teams Roger coached. Dick wasn't good enough. "As I got older (sixteen and seventeen), I went to Roger's hockey practices on Saturdays when he was coaching the Bick's Pickles midgets and the Junior Bs in Aurora. I travelled and scouted with him. I had started to play forward in house league and I kept bugging Roger to [let me] play for his team. He finally said he would use me to kill penalties to give his players a rest, but he warned me that the first goal scored against while I was on the ice, I was out of there." Dick, a tall, gangly, brown-haired kid who wore glasses, hoped to prove to his mentor the move was justified.

Dick played for four games, getting on the ice only to kill penalties, just as Roger had promised. In the fourth game, he was skating up the ice on a two-on-one and flicked the puck over the opponent's stick to his teammate. "All the guy had to do was flick the puck back over to me, but he shot the puck at the net and missed. The puck went around the boards and we were caught deep. The other team went down and scored.

"Roger had the gate opened up at the end of the rink and I was gone."

By the time he was eighteen, in 1962, Dick's talents seemed to lie far away from the hockey rink. He was such a great baseball pitcher that he had scouts talking with him and he eventually signed a contract with the Pittsburgh Pirates. That was an amazing feat for a Canadian kid in the 1960s, long before the Expos and Blue Jays were in Canada. He was sent to the semi-pro league in Quebec, and one night was called upon to pitch in cold weather without warming up. "We went into extra innings and I kept pitching. I couldn't lift my arm the next day." After a Toronto doctor told him it was a torn rotator cuff, he went to a specialist in New York City, who confirmed the injury and asked, "Are you any good at hitting or can you throw with your left? Because your right arm is done."

Dick subsequently pitched for some senior teams, switching to a "submarine," underarm style of pitching, but his pro-baseball dream was over. He took a job in a Toronto grocery store, and by the time he was twenty-one he was a store manager. Four years later, the grocery chain said they wanted to promote him to supervisor. He says, "I looked at my manager's job and I was working sixty hours a week. A supervisor worked eighty hours, weekends and nights, and I didn't enjoy the thought of that."

That's when he heard about a trainer's job with Roger's Peterborough Petes. He talked with his wife about a possible career change, and then phoned Roger to see if he could be considered for the opening. Roger said yes. "I took a hefty pay cut. I was making $15,000 to $18,000 with bonuses and came to Peterborough for $7,000. I was married, had a baby daughter, but the cost of living was better there," he says. He was taking over a job that three part-timers had been doing in the hours outside their full-time jobs. The job was seasonal, but the Petes agreed to let Dick take on extra responsibility for selling ads and looking after the books in the off-season so he wouldn't have to go on unemployment insurance.

"I created huge savings for the team and made good purchases in the first year [1973]," he says. "We were the first team in the league to drop Sherwood sticks and go to Titan. They lasted longer and cut our stick purchases in half."

While he was doing this, he also took a course with the St. John Ambulance first-aid organization and learned a lot from the team doctor. "He taught me how to stitch guys. I sliced my finger once and the doctor stitched me up and showed me how to do it."

Mike Fryia was a second-year player when Todd arrived. "He was a super guy," says Mike. "We'd always take advantage of the new guys. We had this homemade whirlpool and we'd overflow it with bubble bath. He'd just go nuts. He had to learn fast. I remember the first guy he stitched was Brad Pirie. The last trainer we had would only take a minute to stitch a cut, but it took Dick an hour for two stitches on an elbow. I remember I broke a knuckle. Dick looked at it and poked it with his finger, and I just screamed. Imagine poking around like that."

Terry Bovair, who also played with the Petes in the 1970s, a few years after Fryia, also remembers one of Dick's stitching jobs. Bovair's elbow was cut during a practice but he didn't want to go to the hospital because some of the players were going out to socialize afterwards – a big deal because they didn't get to do it very often. "Dick got some needle and thread. The next day the wound was oozing, and I went to see the team doctor who asked what Dick had used. Turns out it was a needle to stitch a glove, a needle far too blunt. All the doctor did was laugh. I think I was Dick's experiment." Bovair still has a scar on his right elbow where the skin hangs down.

"Dick was the first person to meet me at the Petes' dressing room," remembers Bovair fondly of when he first joined the team. "Right off the bat he set the tone. He fixed me up with some old equipment. He was a great guy, a player's friend . . . who kept people loose." Bovair was with the team for three years and later coached with Todd for seven years.

Experienced former Petes trainers such as Ken Dales and Gunner Lynch showed Dick how to sharpen skates, although one player, Bill Evo, remembers that when Dick sharpened his, "I went out on the ice [and] I fell flat on my face. He had basically ruined the blade."

Greg Theberge, another Petes player when Todd was the trainer, remembers how well Todd and Neilson worked together. When

Roger needed to delay the game, for example, Dick, whose pockets were full of gum, would dump the gum on the ice. Roger and Todd "were so much unlike each other," says Theberge. "When you were making poor decisions, [Dick] would put it into perspective for you."

In 1976, when Roger and Dick had been working together for three years, Roger told him he was leaving the team for a coaching job in Dallas. Dick was devastated and worried about his future with the Petes. One of the main reasons he had come to Peterborough was to work with Roger, but since his arrival he and his wife had fallen in love with the town. Todd served another year as trainer under Gary Young, then two years under Gary Green as trainer and assistant manager-coach. Green gave him more responsibility and input with lines and players. Dick says, "Gary had connections, great connections, all over the place. He could meet people at a social and remember names and everything about them. It helped bring in some good players."

Todd also spent a year as the team's business manager under Mike Keenan. "Mike was very volatile. He and I would disagree and fight all the way home on the buses. He [was ready] to trade anyone." Because Dick talked Keenan out of making a number of rash decisions that would have essentially dismantled a winning team, "his dad told Mike he owed me a big debt and should repay me some day." Keenan made good on this suggestion, later hiring Dick as an assistant in the NHL.

When Keenan said he too was leaving the team, Dick recommended Dave Dryden, a former NHL goalie, a teacher, and brother of NHLer Ken, as the new coach. "I thought he'd be perfect for the job," says Dick. Dryden was hired, but he didn't work out – none of the Petes' former-NHLer coaches, Ted Kennedy, Gary Young, or Dryden, lasted more than a year with the team – and was fired during the 1981-82 season with no designated successor in place.

(The club executive issued a press release in November saying they wouldn't be firing Dryden: "His job is safe despite the team's poor start, clubhouse hassles, and sagging attendance." The next month he was let go when players threatened to quit.)

The Petes' executive put Dick behind the bench as a stop-gap until they could find a coach. "I had no desire to be the coach," says Todd. "I loved the kids and was always fearful of coaches being fired. I had a wife and daughter to support, and we were happy in Peterborough. If I was fired, then what?"

Dick was told he would coach until Christmas. "I said yes, as long as I could have my trainer's job back if they ever fired me as coach."

Dick used what he had learned from watching the other coaches – Neilson, Green, Keenan, Young, and Dryden – especially from watching the latter two fail. "The first time [I skated onto] the ice as coach, I was nervous. I felt more comfortable behind the bench, but as time went along I thought I could do the job."

Petes executive member Pat Casey said he "didn't even know if Todd could skate" when they hired him. "I remember what he said every year: 'Can I have my trainer's job back if you fire me?' He was always on a one-year contract."

Dick had immediate success with the team, winning five consecutive games, and the executive decided to keep him on as coach and general manager. Ed Rowe, who was on the club's executive at the time, says Dick "had a way with players that nobody else had. They loved him. He treated them all the same, treated them to improve them, not to run them down. He was an athlete and had a positive attitude. He was a disciplinarian, but he was part of the fun. He had a good hockey mind. The kids would do anything for him and he could handle them well." Doug Evans was on the team the first year Dick coached and says of him, "He took a lot of pressure away. He allowed guys to play the way they are capable of playing and made the game fun. Dick had a knack of taking your mind off the game."

Dick used all four lines, treating all the players equally. It was another reason the superstars on the Petes were not always the top scorers in the league. They had to share their ice time with three other lines, unlike some other coaches who relied heavily on their top scorers.

Todd took a team with a losing record at Christmas (17 wins, 19 losses, 1 tie) to a winning record (36 wins, 29 losses, 2 ties) at the end of the regular season and got past the first round of the playoffs. After his first partial year as coach, an assistant was hired. Jacques Martin, who later became coach of the Guelph junior team and was the Ottawa Senators' head coach from 1996 to 2004, came on board.

Once Dick began full-time coaching in the 1981-82 season, he took control, and during his twelve full seasons, with little fanfare and, sometimes, little respect, he broke all the Petes' coaching records for wins in regular-season and playoff play. The Petes' former education consultant and current Buffalo Sabres scout, Don Barrie, says Todd "had the ability to listen and learn. He would listen to everyone and take it all in. He wasn't afraid to ask. He had no pretence of ever being a player and used all his contacts for advice. He was very intelligent. I'd go scouting with him and he'd see things I never thought of. He'd use a kid, find what his talent was, and put [him] in that niche. He wasn't encumbered with what you couldn't do or shouldn't do, but what you could do. He surrounded himself with good support people and was never intimidated . . . Neilson was innovative. Dick used everyone for information."

"Nobody appreciates what Dick did with the Petes," says Jeff Twohey, who came to the Petes as another inexperienced trainer when Todd was the coach. Twohey went on to become the team's general manager in the 1990s. "He understood the game. He could hardly skate but he understood players and he loved it. He had no ego, wasn't doing it for the money. He loved to coach. He'd call Roger for advice. He and Roger kept everything simple. I used to think hockey was so complicated but they simplified everything.

"The Petes have had such great success with coaches from Scotty to Roger, then Gary and Dick. Dick's daughter used to see him fall asleep watching videos of the games, right on the couch. If he had not left, he would have had far more than 1,000 wins." The significance of the 1,000 wins as a benchmark is that when the great Ottawa 67's coach Brian Kilrea passed the 1,000-win mark in 2003, he was inducted into the Hockey Hall of Fame.

Dick gives credit to Roger Neilson for his success, but it may have been his own attitude that really made the difference. "I think the kids know I treated them equally," he says. "I was responsible for all of them and had respect for all of them. The hardest thing to do was to cut them, let them go."

His success also owes something to the long, hard hours he put in. Dick was a working machine, much as his mentor had been. He continued scouting while coaching and managing, and at the same time was always looking for ways to fill the arena. He took seriously the team's tradition and commitment to making sure the kids were doing well in school and had good landparents.

He witnessed many changes over the years. When he started as a trainer, the players didn't come with agents – they would arrive accompanied only by their parents, and some even arrived alone. There were no lawyers, no multimillion-dollar futures to look at, and many of the players stayed in junior hockey until they were twenty. When Dick left the Petes in 1993, there were hockey agents every-where, looking for better deals, and even more ice time, and the best players were usually leaving by the time they were eighteen. There was also big money in the NHL for coaches – and there came a time when Dick Todd was ready to try the next level.

In 1993, when Roger Neilson was coaching the Florida Panthers, he promised Dick a job with the team, but GM Bob Clarke vetoed it. Clarke had several reasons for overruling the offer, but Dick thinks the biggest reason is that he had testified against the Flyers a few years before when former Petes player Glen Seabrooke sued a team doctor for malpractice and won the suit. Neilson then asked Mike Keenan to give Dick a chance with the Rangers, and Keenan, remembering his father's admonition that he was indebted to Dick for all his advice, guidance, and tolerance, hired him along with the other assistant coach, former Petes player Colin Campbell. In Dick's first year with the Rangers, they won the Stanley Cup. He coached with the team from 1993 to 1999, and then became a scout for the team.

Although Dick Todd's name is not usually at the top of the list when people talk about the great coaches who worked with the Petes, his record shows it should be. He won a Memorial Cup ring as a trainer, two World Junior Championship rings as a coach, and a Stanley Cup ring as an assistant coach. He put more than thirty teenagers into the NHL while coaching the Petes. His Petes teams won 477 games, lost 239, and tied 53 for a .655 winning percentage, which is still a record for OHL coaches. His team won the OHL championship twice, won its division four times, and made Memorial Cup appearances twice, in 1989 and 1993. As a coach he never had a losing season. He was with the Petes for twenty-one years as a trainer, business manager, then coach and general manager.

The lack of respect and notice by some critics and fans doesn't bother Dick because, as many of his former players and associates say, "He has no ego." You don't need one when you have the evidence to back you up.

Dick Todd was rehired as the Petes' coach in 2004.

The General Manager

After Dick Todd the Petes took on several coaches. Former Petes training-camp cut Dave MacQueen was the first to be hired by the new general manager, Jeff Twohey. Eventually they would win the OHL championship and play for the Memorial Cup. MacQueen would leave to be an assistant coach in the NHL for Florida before coming back to coach junior in Erie. Twohey had become the first Petes general manager not to also be the coach.

General manager Twohey knows running the Peterborough Petes is a heavy responsibility. He not only has to make sure the Petes continue their winning ways, but also has to honour the tradition of graduating players into the NHL. On the one hand, the Petes exist to put players into the NHL – they develop them for that purpose, and that's why kids join junior teams. On the other hand, the fans want a winning team – that's why they spend their hard-earned money on tickets. Of course, there's also a connection between the two. If the team doesn't have a winning record, the good players may be overlooked. It is Jeff's job to find players who will do both, attract coaches who will do both, and hope the fans and the Petes' executive approve.

Unlike most junior teams, which are privately owned, the Petes don't exist to make money, or at least not a profit. It's true, the team can't survive if it loses money, and in today's junior leagues, money is beginning to matter more than in the past. Players are seeking

The Peterborough Examiner

Jeff Twohey (centre) at Roger Neilson's funeral. OHL's Dave Branch on his right.

better education deals as part of the agreement to move to a particular OHL city. The Petes were the first team in the OHL to offer an
education package, which now amounts to $3,000 for every year a
player plays as a Pete if he doesn't turn pro. But now all junior teams
are offering education deals, American universities have also come
calling on more Canadians to join their teams, and Canadian universities are offering some packages they couldn't before. The biggest
change is that the wealthier teams in the junior leagues, though not
publicly, are offering players better financial deals through their
agents or parents, and the players tell teams that may draft them they
won't report it if they do. They may tell them they are going to university, only to turn around and play for a wealthier team when it
drafts them.

A volunteer executive runs the Petes' non-profit corporation, and
has done so since the Montreal Canadiens left the team to the community in 1966, but the general manager, coaches, trainers, market-
ing people, and scouts are paid out of ticket and advertising revenue
and money the NHL teams send their way if they draft their players
in the first two rounds. A first-rounder can mean as much as $75,000
to a team, and players drafted in lower rounds also get the team
money from the pro teams that take them. It's all based on a point

system, and general managers like Twohey are intimately familiar with it.

Twohey hired former Pete and Oshawa native Brian Drumm to coach the team after MacQueen left. Drumm was let go and Twohey tried coaching a few games himself but it was soon apparent to him his future was in management, and in that role he has added to the history and continued the tradition of the team. In 2003, his top player, eighteen-year-old Eric Staal, was picked second overall in the NHL draft and made the Carolina Hurricanes. The Petes had five players selected in the draft, more than any other OHL squad.

Carrying on the Petes' tradition is far more difficult today, when the junior league has twenty teams, than it was in the six-team Bowman era, twelve-team Neilson era, or even the sixteen-team (or fewer) Todd era. As general manager, Twohey has had to face the effects of a growing league – there are fewer chances to find players because there is more competition – more teams, more scouts, and more teams involved in the draft.

Twohey had been a mediocre minor-hockey player with a love for the game who dreamed of working for the Petes. In 1981, when he was a twenty-three-year-old Laurentian University sports-administration student from Lindsay, Ontario, Twohey approached the Petes about becoming a volunteer scout. Dave Dryden, the coach and general manager at the time, obviously liked the kid's nerve and took him on. Jeff took on the role as if he were being paid.

Dick Todd took over Dryden's job the next year and asked Jeff if he wanted to be the trainer. The fact that Jeff didn't know a thing about being a trainer didn't stop him from jumping at the chance. Todd also brought in Jacques Martin, a former college goalie, as the new assistant coach.

"The trainer's job was a world of underwear, washing clothes, selling ads, and doing a bit of scouting," says Jeff. "I knew nothing about sharpening skates. Nothing. I was living with Jacques Martin out at Roger Neilson's cottage, and training camp was at the Kinsmen Arena, which wasn't the Petes' arena. This arena had no skate-sharpening [facilities], no laundry room. It was sink or swim. I could only go to Dick and ask how to wrap a groin; the players didn't know I didn't know what I was doing."

When he joined, the club had only four water bottles and no towels. "I quickly learned things like building up an inventory from 'borrowing' at hockey schools. We were using rubber bands on practice socks, and during warm-ups I used to take back the tape that players were stealing." That was a trick Dick had learned in Roger Neilson's day, when players used to sneak out sticks, tape, and other equipment. Neilson or Todd would go into the players' cars during practice and take it all back into the rink.

Jeff also sold program ads, just as Bowman, Neilson, Green, and Todd had done before him. He would even be suspended for getting involved in some of the Petes' brawls. "It's phenomenal how everything goes in Peterborough," says former player Doug Evans as he looks back on Jeff's and Dick's rise up the hierarchy. "Jeff came in as a scout, then a trainer, then assistant coach, and worked hard. He got his foot in the door and loves hockey. He has maroon and white in his blood. He's the hardest worker they'd ever find."

When Jacques Martin left to become coach of the Guelph junior team, Jeff was asked to join Todd as an assistant coach. He would also be scouting with Todd and learning as he went along. When Todd took the team to the Memorial Cup in the 1992-93 season Jeff was the assistant general manager. And when Todd left to become assistant coach with the New York Rangers, the Petes hired Jeff as the general manager, ten years after he had started as trainer.

Brent Tully played on his team and said Twohey has "a passionate commitment for the game. He loves to sit and talk about hockey. In this town he gets criticized – especially when the team is losing, people saying he's not drafting the right players, doesn't have hockey experience, all the things any manager gets when they are losing – but I'd like to know what the Petes would be without him. Nobody works as hard as he does." But criticism comes with the job, as every manager from minor-league hockey to the NHL knows all too well.

When Twohey hired Dave MacQueen as the first new coach, the team included Jamie Langenbrunner, Steve Webb, Cameron Mann, and Zac Bierk, but that year it had the third-worst record in club history. During the season the criticism mounted and doubts about Twohey's appointment strengthened. But the Petes turned it around and went to the Memorial Cup in 1996, the first year Peterborough hosted it. The Petes didn't get into the final through the back door, either. The host team competes in the tournament anyway, but the Petes won their division and the OHL championship, earning them the right to play. The city was transfixed by the cup games for a week, and the Memorial Centre was jammed for every one. The Petes made it to the final game but lost 4-0 to Quebec's Granby Prédateurs.

Since that time they have had Drumm and another former Petes training-camp cut, Rick Allain, coaching them. Allain was fired near the end of the 2003-04 season after it became obvious the team wasn't going to make the playoffs for the first time in twenty-eight straight seasons, a junior record. The last time the Petes hadn't made the playoffs was Roger Neilson's last year. While the executive fired Allain, they have told Twohey and the public that his job is safe. In 2004, there were at least five Petes who were sure NHL draft picks, they have some fine sophomore players, and rookie Liam Reddox is already being labelled as a high draft pick, leading the team in scoring in the 2003-04 season. (The last rookie to do that was Rick MacLeish.) Reddox, from Whitby, led the under-eighteen Canadian team in the championships in Belarus in the spring of 2004.

Things are different in Peterborough. The rink is newly renovated (although the square corners that defencemen hate and forwards love are still there). The players have their own workout facilities. There is a brand-new alumni room and souvenir shop. The fans don't pack the place the way they do for junior games in many of the western provinces and Quebec, but they still treat the Petes as their own. The way things are done has also changed. While the team was sinking near the end of the season, Twohey went on a scouting mission to Newfoundland. He knew there would be some public argument about that, and there was. Former managers couldn't do that because they were the coaches – perhaps that's why some of the fans thought it was a strange thing to do at that time of the year. The fact that he told the public he went on the trip with one of their opponents' general managers (London Knights' Mark Hunter) didn't help the cause, especially for those who still believe hobnobbing with the enemy during the season is not the thing to do. Red Sullivan remembers in the 1940s, 1950s, and 1960s when the players would never shake hands after a game and wouldn't socialize even in the off-season.

In a very surprising move, almost magical for Petes fans, the board of directors hired their new coach, who turned out to be their old coach: Dick Todd. He has given up his Florida winters for the bus rides on cold Canadian nights after a ten-year absence. He said he was looking for something to do and wanted to get the Petes back on track. Now his former trainer, Twohey, is his boss. That's something Twohey and Todd both say they are comfortable with. Todd says Peterborough is known as the "hockey training capital of the world" and he wants to continue that tradition.

Peterborough and the area around it, and the kids growing up there in the minor-hockey systems, not just the Petes, are known for what they bring to the game. Several of the kids raised in Peterborough are among the OHL's top stars – like Corey Perry, who played in London in 2004, Nick Lees who played in Saginaw, and Sean Stefanski who played in Sudbury. (Both Lees and Stefanski are in the running for top over-age players.) "The scouts in the OHL are always amazed at the size of Peterborough and the number of kids that have been drafted out of here," says Twohey. "I don't know the reason for it, but maybe it is [because] so many ex-Petes [are] involved in minor hockey here, giving back what they got when they were growing up." Twohey is referring to people such as former Petes Bill Plager, Joe Johnston, Jim Johnston, Terry Bovair, Mike Posavad, Mike Fryia, Greg Millen, Steve Larmer, Steve Self, Steve Peters, Doug Gibson, Brent Tully, Doug Evans, Todd Gregory, Mark Wainman, Joe Hawley, and Dave Reid. They have all helped coach and many come out to help at practices.

Twohey has seen many things that concern him as he watches minor hockey while scouting. "What I see in Toronto concerns me. You go to a midget game and parents are basically hanging on to every move. The coaches are acting like pros. Scouts and agents are at the games. Parents want their kids to be pros. You start to wonder why the kids are playing. They're playing with their whole goal to get to the NHL, [and] so are the coaches and the parents. I'm concerned they're playing for the wrong reason – the goal is coming before the passion."

There is still a lot of passion for the game in smaller centres, says Twohey, and he should know – Jeff has travelled more than a million miles looking for kids who have what it takes to make it on a junior team. He works seven days a week during hockey season, travelling all over Ontario and even as far as Newfoundland looking for new players eligible to play in the OHL. He also has to make sure that the players have trustworthy landparents, that they don't get into trouble, that their education continues, that the business of the Petes runs smoothly, and that the team is doing well in the standings. It's a big job with no six-figure salary, but it's one he loves. Nothing makes Twohey happier (besides winning) than seeing a kid who comes to the Petes with questionable ability and makes it to the pros.

He cites Dallas Eakins as an example. Dallas was born in Florida and moved to Peterborough as a young boy when his mother married a Peterborough native. He played minor hockey in Peterborough, making the hometown Petes in 1984. His determination and work ethic eventually took him to the team captaincy in 1987.

In his twenty-three years with the Petes, Twohey picks Eakins as their best captain. "This isn't demeaning any of the others in any way. Dallas was special. He was a great leader. He was a hard worker, loyal, tough, and never afraid to confront people. He knew how to keep players in line.

"When he was joining us at seventeen or eighteen, he was already a man. With the ability he came to us with he shouldn't have had a career in the pros, but he worked at it. He would listen, he would practise. If Dick told him he needed work in a certain area, he would focus on it and work on that area. He wasn't a guy who would say one thing and do another."

Dallas Eakins has had a sixteen-year pro career, up and down between the minors and the NHL, playing in Baltimore, Moncton, Winnipeg, Florida, Cincinnati, Worcester, St. Louis, Springfield, Phoenix, Binghamton, New York, New Haven, Toronto, St. John's, Chicago, and Calgary during those years. In 2003, he was captain of the Manitoba Moose in the AHL. Eakins refused to quit. And that's something Twohey admires, something he can understand and respect.

In 2003, Twohey himself was trying a new thing for a general manager – he was billeting a Petes player. Maybe that change will become a Petes tradition, too.

The Players (III)

DOUG EVANS
Born in Peterborough, June 2, 1963
Peterborough Petes 1980-84
NHL career with St. Louis, Winnipeg, Philadelphia

Doug Evans and his brothers honed their hockey skills on the outdoor ice in Turner Park, in an older residential part of Peterborough. Doug had no fewer than four older brothers: Brian, older by fourteen years; Paul, by twelve years; David, by three years; Mark, by two years; as well as Kevin, younger by two years. Some or all of them were usually either at the park or playing in the street in front of their house. Their parents worked shift work, the mother, Barb, at the nearby General Electric plant, and the father, Paul, in Oshawa, at the General Motors plant. The Evans boys also had two sisters, Anne and Diane, both older than Doug, and the girls attempted to take charge of the younger kids.

"I remember the first time I had ever been to their house," says former Petes goalie Mike Kasmetis, who played junior hockey with Paul Jr. "I couldn't believe the place. The father was on the couch sleeping, the kids were playing on the floor by the couch, just drilling a tennis ball with mini-sticks, and their mother was walking over them with a bowl full of potatoes. The ball whipped right by her head and she didn't even twitch."

The Peterborough Examiner

From left: Kevin, Doug, Mark, Dave, and Paul Evans – five of the six Evans boys.

The boys had one bedroom, where they shared a bunk bed and one double bed. "You never knew which bed you were sleeping in on any night," Doug says, laughing, adding he wouldn't change his upbringing for anything.

"We didn't have much, but our parents always made do, they always had good clothes on our backs and plenty of food. We'd go to Loblaw's every week and get the biggest bag of potatoes you could get your arms around. We had the same meals, like clockwork, every day of the week."

Doug remembers either his father or grandmother (his mother never drove a car) taking the boys to power skating at the local rink at about five on Saturday mornings, to get lessons from a woman who never allowed them on the ice with sticks. "We'd get dressed along the way, half asleep, then we'd take this lesson with all the other kids and later play a game of house-league hockey to test out our new skills."

The Evans kids learned early to be independent, but they also looked out for one another. Even as young as eight, if they didn't have a ride they'd walk the half-mile to the rink, carrying their equipment over their shoulders. If their skates needed sharpening, they'd hop on a city bus and go get them sharpened.

Doug was a quick learner and a good listener and easily learned to skate. He quickly became a goal scorer, playing on two teams in

1970 when he was only seven. In the summer, the Evans boys played lacrosse, and all of them were top players in their age groups; all of them later played and starred in junior and senior lacrosse, winning provincial and national championships. They were the boys every team loved having with them but hated playing against. They were like cats, clawing, slashing, digging, pushing, fighting, swearing, cheating, and using their immense talents to get their team a victory. By 1970, Doug was so good in lacrosse that he once scored thirty-eight goals in five games, but that accomplishment is dwarfed by the feat he performed when he was eight: he was the team's goalie as well as its leading scorer!

Doug would go to any Peterborough Petes game he could, always looking for a way to sneak in. "I'd sit and watch those Petes games and learn how they played, where they played, where the puck went. I was always fascinated by the game." Then he'd go back to his games and try out some of the things he had learned.

As Doug matured, he became more successful, but although his talent grew, his body didn't. He was small, the smallest on every team, but he played big. "I learned I could do things to bring bigger people to my height. Sure, I'd fight them, but I'd also fight them with words – I won some of my fights with my mouth."

By the time he was in bantam in 1978, Doug was using his mouth to get the other team's players off their game, using it to get the edge on another player, or even to stick it in front of a puck – anything to win. "I hated to lose at anything, it didn't matter what. Whether it was against my brothers or anything, I hated to lose. I still hate to lose." He kept dreaming about being in the NHL, and firmly believed he could make it even though most hockey people didn't think he had a chance because of his small size. Bigger brother Paul had gone to play in the Central Hockey League and was called up to the Toronto Maple Leafs for a few games. Every member of the Evans family took great pride in that – there was Paul on *Hockey Night in Canada*, featured in newspapers for everyone to see and read about. That's what Doug wanted.

He had a couple of problems, though. One was that he wasn't drafted by any OHL team, and the other was that he was only 147 pounds and five-foot-eight. Those problems are related, of course, and when you're trying out for the Petes and your coach is former NHL player Dave Dryden, a big man used to big players, you're likely to be cut. And that's what happened.

"I got cut by the Petes, but I don't think it hurt as much because I just had success in lacrosse," he says. His lacrosse team that summer had won the national junior championship and Doug was a scoring star on the team, one of the best junior lacrosse players of his time. "So I went and played for the Junior B hockey team but always kept knocking at the Petes' door." That's why he always tells kids to never give up. Persistence and belief in yourself can pay off, as was proven by subsequent events – he played with the B team until after Christmas, when the Petes called him up, and he never went back.

Jeff Twohey was an assistant trainer with the Petes and remembers Evans from those days. "He was this scrawny little kid with great instinct who was never drafted but had such passion and was such a great agitator."

Doug soon became a fan favourite. Mike Brophy, now with *The Hockey News*, but a hockey writer with *The Peterborough Examiner* when Doug arrived on the scene, labelled him "The Brat." Doug started brawls that barroom brawlers would flee. During his Petes seasons, Oshawa was always the dreaded enemy. When Doug was a forward on the Petes, brother Mark was the team's goalie, the third brother to play for the Petes. (Youngest brother Kevin would join the team later, making him the fourth.)

Fighting remained a feature of the Evans brothers' play. One night in Oshawa a fight broke out before the game even started. Police had to come on the ice to grab Doug Evans, one of the main participants. Goalie Mark once got into two fights in one game in Oshawa, while also getting an assist and stopping more than fifty shots in the same game. He was selected the Petes' star of the game.

Former Petes executive Ed Rowe has seen decades of Petes hockey and said the Evans boys "were a different breed. I never saw anyone as competitive as Doug Evans." He was also one of the Petes' top players and scorers. He came second in scoring in 1981-82 with more points than teammate and future NHL great Steve Yzerman. He had 66 points in 55 games with 176 minutes in penalties. The next year he had 86 points in 55 games and led the team with 165 minutes in penalties.

But when it came to the NHL draft of 1983, once again Doug Evans was ignored. At least in games of pickup down at Turner Park you always got picked. Nobody in the NHL even chose him.

Evans played another year with the Petes, 1983-84, and this time led the team in scoring with 124 points in 61 games and actually brought his penalty total down below the 100-minute mark at 98 playing on a line with future NHLer and two-time Stanley Cup winner, Dave Reid. He was the leading goal scorer in the OHL that year and seventh in league points with 45 goals and 79 assists, but still no pro team was interested. But that didn't stop Doug Evans. He was determined to play in the NHL, whether the league liked it or not. In 1984, when he was twenty-one, he went to Peoria of the IHL and starred there, getting 97 points in each of his two full seasons there, as well as close to two hundred penalty minutes each year. He even got called up for a few NHL games, although he didn't play much. He was on a two-way contract and was always being sent back down to Peoria. He scratched his way through the IHL and then came what he calls the best memory of his pro life.

"I was trying to make the St. Louis Blues. I knew most of the other players were on a one-way contract, so they weren't being sent down. It was between only a few guys which one was going to stay up. I saw the coach, Brian Sutter, looking at me on the ice and thought, 'Oh-oh.'

"He skated over to me and said, 'I want you to find a place to live.'

"Those were the best words I've ever heard."

"Find a place to live" means you're staying with the team, you're going to get one-way money, and you're going to be playing regularly in the NHL where the players are much bigger, stronger, and more talented. "You've been accepted. You're going to get some respect," Doug says. It also meant he'd be on that TV screen back at the Evans house.

While he was in the NHL, he'd look at the other players, some of whom were not as good as he was. They weren't as gritty or talented, and he wished he had their size. His NHL career was plodding along in that first regular season of 1986-87 when something happened that gave him the most publicity he'd ever received in the NHL, but it wasn't for his scoring abilities. He became the only person Wayne Gretzky ever fought in the NHL.

"We were playing Edmonton in St. Louis," remembers Doug. "I wasn't getting on the ice much, and of course Gretzky was never off the ice. They were beating us pretty bad and I got a chance to go on. Gretzky was on, too, so I did my thing. I was tying him up, hooking him up, doing my job, I thought. He speared me and, not thinking, I reacted normally for me and we went at it. I found out quickly you don't fight Wayne Gretzky. There were three other guys jumping me."

He had no idea what a furor the fight would cause. "You would have thought I'd scored a hat trick." The media jumped all over it. "I was overwhelmed by what happened. Here I was a rookie, and didn't know what to think. It was funny: we got beat but you would have thought we won." Anyone who knew him back in Peterborough wasn't surprised. What was the big deal? The brothers used to fight each other. Gretzky was a player, Evans was a player: aren't you allowed to touch other players? Not that one.

During his pro career Doug played 355 NHL games with St. Louis, Winnipeg, and Philadelphia from 1984 to his retirement in 1999. His last six seasons were spent with Peoria, where his Peterborough wife and their two children wanted to settle because of the stability living in one place brought to their lives and because of the support Doug got from the community. As usual, he was the fan favourite in Peoria and became team captain. He was the Pest, for sure, the Brat, but he was also the little guy with the big heart and still a talented player. He was so well regarded there that after his retirement they retired his sweater.

The rest of the Evans brothers shone in the sports world, as well. Brian played senior lacrosse, progressing to national championships on several occasions. Paul played for junior and senior lacrosse championship teams; he was also a hockey player and played for the Petes, and for the Leafs in the NHL. Mark played for the Petes and junior and senior lacrosse championship teams. David played all-star hockey and on senior and junior lacrosse championship teams. Youngest brother Kevin played for the Minnesota North Stars in 1990 and the San Jose Sharks in 1992. He also played many seasons in the minors. With the Kalamazoo Wings of the IHL in 1987, he set the all-time record for penalty minutes in one season, 648 – that's more than ten full games spent in the box. He also scored 19 goals and 31 assists in those 73 games that year.

Doug Evans was better than all of them. As former *Examiner* writer Brophy said of him, "He was 147 pounds and 140 pounds of that was heart."

Doug Evans lives with his wife and two children in Peterborough, where he sells cars and coaches minor sports.

STEVE YZERMAN
Born in Cranbrook, B.C., May 9, 1965
Raised in Cranbrook and Kamloops, B.C., Ottawa, Ontario
Peterborough Petes 1981-83
NHL career with Detroit

It's funny how life works. If Ron Yzerman hadn't been transferred to Cranbrook, British Columbia, from his job as a social worker on Vancouver Island, who knows what Steve Yzerman would be doing today? By the time Ron Yzerman moved to Cranbrook, he had completed university with a degree in social work, had married Jean, who had studied to be a nurse, and was the father of two children, a daughter, Roni Jean, and a son, Michael. Another son, Stephen, was born in Cranbrook in 1965, just thirteen months after Michael.

Life for the Yzerman couple was busy. Jean, whose father came to Canada at the turn of the century as a young bachelor from Czechoslovakia and worked in the B.C. mines, was spending most of her time looking after the three children. Ron, whose father came from Holland in the early part of the century to Canada, where he was a lumber-camp cook, was busy with his career, which eventually took him to a top federal-government job in the field of children's

Steve Yzerman (middle row, third from right) and the Kamloops team.

social work. But in their early days in Cranbrook, they were struggling to make ends meet, and sports was certainly not part of Ron's
life, nor had it played any significant role in his upbringing.

When he moved to Cranbrook, however, that began to change.
"When Stephen and Michael were five and six, Cranbrook was probably the same as all little towns in Canada," he remembers. "There
was a minor-hockey association in the East Kootenay area that
needed volunteers. Winters were long and cold. There was plenty
of natural ice around.

"Nine of the ten youth hockey teams were run by RCMP
members. We had a sergeant in our neighbourhood with kids on a
team [and he] wanted to know if our kids wanted to play. Of course,"
Ron says, laughing, "he had an ulterior motive. If my kids wanted to
play, even though they had more than a one-year age difference, they
could play on the same team if I would coach."

The three Yzerman "boys" – Steve, Michael, and their dad – had
never been on skates. Undaunted, Steve and Michael both wanted
to try it, and Ron agreed. Skates he describes as "not much more than

pressed cardboard" were purchased, as was the equipment they needed: shin pads, socks, pants, elbow pads, and gloves.

"To call me a coach would be a joke. Coaches were really baby-sitters – this was all about learning to skate and having fun," says Ron.

The arena was only a few blocks from their home, so it was easy to get the boys there every Saturday morning. The ice surface was divided by boards into thirds, and the kids, about twenty-four at a time in each section, played for about fifty minutes, most of that just skating around, with the last fifteen minutes playing a game of shinny.

"They were just like water bugs," says Ron. "Every kid was falling, crawling around on their hands and knees, chasing after the puck. Wherever the puck went, they all went."

Michael was almost immediately a good skater, with a good stride, and he could glide. His brother had a different technique. "Steven learned to skate by running. He must have figured it out that if you ran fast you wouldn't fall down, so he just ran. His skating style was not much to behold. He fell a lot. There was not much the coach could do to teach him because he was still walking around the ice discovering how to skate himself." This introduction was all the boys needed. They loved it. The Saturday-morning ritual was established.

Somehow, although Ron's work meant that the family had to make two moves in the space of a few years, first to Kamloops, B.C., then in 1974 to Ottawa, the boys remained involved in minor hockey. Steve, in particular, rapidly showed that he had a special aptitude for the game, and the desire to win that is the difference between those who make it in the NHL and those who don't.

In fact, when Ron first went to Ottawa, the rest of the family, now numbering five kids (four boys and a girl), stayed put in Kamloops until the end of the school year. Jean would have the responsibility of bringing up the five kids for the next few months, getting them to school, after-school events, and the boys' hockey games.

They got through the winter while Ron looked at different residential neighbourhoods. A fellow worker suggested that he look in the growing city of Nepean, with a population of 70,000 then, near Ottawa. They stopped by Nepean's Woodruff Street rink (never dreaming that same rink would later bear Steve's name). "It had a double sheet of ice; I couldn't believe the place. It was the summer, and kids were playing hockey. It was then I learned hockey was being played year-round."

The Yzermans moved in August to a small three-bedroom home in Nepean. Since the boys would have to share a bedroom, the couple went shopping for some bunk beds. While they were at the furniture store, they got talking about minor hockey with the salesperson and quickly discovered that things would be different in Nepean. The Yzermans had learned something about the competition levels: Nepean had them all. They had house league, then a higher level called Nepean Indians, and the highest level, the Nepean Raiders. Once again, Steve and Michael would have to play on different teams because of their ages. Steve was still in atom, Michael still in peewee.

"By the time we got to Nepean, Steve was good, but we never thought he was that good. He was determined, and when playing soccer in the summers he was even more determined and more competitive, if that was possible," observes his mother, Jean. "He'd get angry with himself," she remembers. "He'd take that ball all the way down the field if he got angry with himself. He'd go through a brick wall to score."

The Yzermans once again took their kids out to house league, but this time the Yzerman brothers were the only two kids who could skate, says Ron. A league official and manager of a Raiders team told Ron to take them out to a better level. The boys went to the tryouts with about a hundred other kids. They had never seen or heard anything like it. Steve's first tryout featured one-on-one drills. Forwards would come down the ice on a defenceman who was standing still at the blue line.

"Quite frankly, *I* could have beaten the defenceman," remembers Ron.

Steve not only beat him each time, he made him look foolish. "It was obvious he belonged at the top level," Ron says, not with arrogance, but simply stating a fact. To be picked as one of the fifteen or so players when you're new to the area is quite an accomplishment – ask any hockey parent who has come in new and faced the often political tryouts of minor hockey. But Steve was too good to pass over and was selected by the Raiders. Michael, however, was cut by the Raiders, but made the Indians. The Yzermans had conflicting feelings: happy for Steve, disappointed for Michael.

"Michael's tryouts hadn't gone as smoothly. It was our first experience with reality, and it was real tough," says Ron.

The Raiders would be doing extensive travelling, and there were costs. Parents would have to pay for practice ice time, travel expenses, tournament fees, even team jackets. The Yzermans were unaware they were responsible for this outlay – it all had to be explained to them. "We didn't know anything about this. The coaches had to have credentials, and be interviewed for the positions, just like it was a job. It was obviously the end of my involvement," laughs Ron.

Whatever level he played, Steve continued to excel. "He was driven," says Jean Yzerman, who remembers one conversation in the family station wagon when her then ten-year-old son assured her that one day he'd play in the NHL. "I just said wait and see. It was everything I could do to stop laughing, but he was really serious."

Steve's atom team was very good, but it lost to a Toronto team in the provincial championships. The next year, in minor peewee, they outdid themselves, winning the Ontario championship by beating a Toronto team. That season they played 100 games, had two practices a week, and went to tournaments in Winnipeg, Boston, Quebec, and Hartford. Steve won the scoring championship both years. (Two other players from those teams, Jeff Brown and Dave Lowry, made it to the NHL, which is a high percentage from one area in one age group, but it reinforces the evidence that the vast majority of young hockey players never get to play a game in the NHL.)

In his last peewee season before bantam, Steve scored 90 goals and 100 assists in 100 games. The team won a Montreal tournament, and Steve was the MVP and leading scorer. In a peewee tournament in Oshawa, he was again the MVP and leading scorer. In the Quebec Winter Carnival tournament, his team won the gold medal. That's when he started playing summer hockey, taking power skating, and going to hockey schools in August, just before tryout time.

After the next season, in bantam, his parents started thinking there was a possibility Steve could get a hockey scholarship to an

American university. Although Steve wasn't thinking education, his parents certainly now hoped hockey might be a way to pay for one. Pro hockey wasn't on their minds at the time. His bantam year was another success story for Steve. He scored 90 goals and was rated the top fifteen-year-old in Ontario. After the bantam season ended, the Tier II Junior A team, also called the Nepean Raiders, put the fifteen-year-old on their protected list, meaning he'd have to play for them rather than any other junior team if he played junior that year. Meanwhile, a senior team, the Bridlewood Cougars, asked him to play in the Hardy Cup in Quebec, playing with men whose average age was twenty-three.

"The manager of the Raiders, Alf May, had told us not to let him go, saying, 'He'll get killed,'" says Ron. "The adults said they'd look after him. The reports came back with rave reviews on his play." The other players went to the bars after the games; Steve had to stay in his hotel room.

That summer Steve decided to skip midget hockey and play for the hometown Nepean Raiders juniors, in a league of players as old as twenty who travelled the region for league games. It was the end of his minor-hockey career. Ron could stop paying for ice, registration, tape, gloves, and helmets for Steve's hockey.

The five-foot-nine, 150-pound centre was a success. He was rookie of the year, midget-aged player of the year, and first-all-star centre. Nevertheless, there was concern he was too small and fragile to make it as a player, says Ron. "The first real time we thought he could make it as a player was when Charlie Henry, a bird dog for hockey agent Gus Badali, set up a meeting with us.

"An agent? Neither Stephen nor I thought we'd need an agent, but it wouldn't cost anything, so we met and were introduced to professionalism." Nothing was signed, but Badali agreed to represent them.

The OHL draft was held in Belleville that year, 1981, but Steve had already proclaimed publicly he wouldn't play for any team but his hometown Ottawa 67's. If some other team drafted him, he said, he would stay with the Nepean Raiders.

It was unlikely Steve would last in the draft until Ottawa picked, because they were choosing thirteenth out of the fourteen teams. And he didn't. Both Ron and Steve were at the draft when the Peterborough Petes took him as their first pick, fourth overall. Dan Quinn, Brian Bradley, and Pat Verbeek, all future NHLers, went ahead of him. His size was a concern to some teams, but not the Petes.

The Petes' coach and general manager, Dave Dryden, met with the Yzermans in their home. "He outlined the Petes' philosophy of staying in school. He was a real gentleman. He told us Peterborough was centrally located, so there wouldn't be many long road trips where kids would have to miss school." The Yzermans were impressed. So the fifteen-year-old Steve went to Peterborough.

Ron Yzerman remembers coming to a Petes game to see Steve play and barely recognizing him on the ice. "He had a longer stride, no longer that choppy running style." The Petes also had a new coach in Dick Todd, whom teammate Doug Evans said "always started the rookies on the fourth line and had them work their way up. It didn't take Dick long to move Steve up."

Steve's parents went to the home games, then to the home of Steve's first landparents – the Garveys – for a lunch, and would get home at three in the morning to rise for work at seven. "Every Thursday and Saturday for two years," say the Yzermans, who never let the weather stop them. They also went to as many other games as they could.

"Stephen would call home three times a week and I think at first he was homesick, but got over it," says his mother. "As parents, we really weren't apprehensive about the move to Peterborough. We knew he'd be close, knew he was in a good home, and knew Peterborough made sure he'd get educated. It certainly wasn't as bad as when he got drafted to the NHL and moved to Detroit. He was only eighteen and moving to Detroit on his own. That made us worry far more."

Steve never won the scoring championship in Peterborough, but got 91 points – 42 goals and 49 assists – in 56 games in his second year and was selected to the under-eighteen team that went to the

U.S.S.R. and won a bronze medal. His statistics in junior were deceptive, though. Many of the Petes are taught to play defence and a team game more than individual play. Todd also played four lines, unlike many of the other teams that played their top two lines more often. Defence has always been a strength of Yzerman's. Some critics have written that he became a good defensive player later in the NHL, but those who have seen him play through the years said he always understood the game and was always good defensively.

Former Petes executive Herb Warr says Yzerman was the best forward he had ever seen. "He had the ability to pass the puck off and move to an opening and pick the puck up again. He played so well without the puck he knew exactly where to be."

Don Barrie, former Petes education consultant, a retired teacher, and now a scout with the Buffalo Sabres, says Steve was a "great kid. Shy, not withdrawn, not cocky, but the opposite." He had a quiet confidence, Barrie says, and didn't seem to understand how good he really was. He says, "The day before he left Peterborough for the [1983] NHL draft, I was excited, because it was my first draft as an NHL scout. He was actually afraid he wouldn't get drafted or with all the hype about him being one of the top five he thought he wouldn't go too high.

"After he was picked [fourth by Detroit behind Brian Lawton, Sylvain Turgeon, and Pat LaFontaine], I went over to the Detroit table and he was all smiles. He was so thrilled, so relaxed. He was such a talent, without understanding his own ability, but nobody expected him to stay in the NHL that year."

He did, scoring 39 goals, the most ever by a Detroit rookie, and 87 points, finishing second to goalie Tom Barrasso for rookie-of-the-year honours.

Ron remembers after the draft walking with Steve and some other people, who were talking about the price of hockey sticks and equipment. Detroit owner Mike Ilitch turned to Ron and said, "Don't worry, I'll be buying his sticks from now on." Twenty-one years later, he was still buying those sticks for Yzerman.

Let's look at some of Steve Yzerman's hockey accomplishments: He was made captain of the Red Wings at the age of twenty-one, the youngest captain in their history. He scored 50 goals or more five times; scored 100 points or more six straight seasons; set all-time scoring marks for Detroit; played for Canada in international tournaments, including the Olympic win of 2002; in 1997 he was the first member of the Red Wings to hold up a Stanley Cup since 1955; the next year they won it again and he was the Conn Smythe Trophy winner for the MVP in those playoffs. They have won the Cup again since then, in 2002. That's not too shabby for a kid who was crawling, chasing pucks on the ice in Cranbrook, B.C., while his coach, a father who couldn't skate, looked on.

There aren't many pictures of the Yzerman kids playing hockey in the early years. "If I had known he was going to be in the NHL, I would have taken more," Jean says. But maybe she should have known. The memories are still clear from those early days. You don't need a photograph to bring back that moment when he was ten years old and declared he was going to play in the NHL someday. That was when Jean could hardly hold back the laughter, especially when he added after his declaration, "Mom, when I play in the NHL and in the summer go to university, what will I do in my off time, drive a truck or [go] deep-sea diving?"

In the 2004 playoffs, Steve Yzerman was struck in the face with a puck and suffered serious injury, but Team Canada still put him on the list for their team that fall. He intended to play another NHL season. He, his wife, and three children live in the Detroit area.

STEVE CHIASSON
Born in Barrie, Ontario, April 14, 1967
Raised in Peterborough
NHL career with Detroit, Calgary, Hartford, Carolina

In 1947, Joe Chiasson was only a teenager and had already spent two years working down in the coal mines of his hometown in Cape Breton, Nova Scotia. The experience convinced him he couldn't do that for the rest of his life. He moved to Toronto to join his brother,

but by the time he was twenty-one he yearned for something else, so in 1950 he volunteered for the army and eventually served in the Korean War. After being stationed in Germany and Cyprus, he returned to Canada in 1965, to Camp Borden, near Barrie, Ontario. There he met and fell in love with a woman who came with an instant family – Betty had five children: four girls and a boy. Joe left the army, and he and his new family moved to a small village near Barrie. That same year he and Betty had another child, Steve.

When Steve was about four years old, the family moved to a rural area just outside Peterborough, Betty's hometown. After a winter or two in the country, the family moved into the city to a neighbour-hood full of young boys who loved nothing better than to play sports, day and night if their parents allowed it (and most of them did). In this neighbourhood full of athletes, Steve Chiasson was one of the better ones.

Joe had played a bit of hockey in Nova Scotia, but Steve's mother was the real hockey fan and Steve was "her little baby." "Mom would do anything for Steve," says Sue, Steve's eldest sister. "Having been a single mom for years, trying to get by with all the kids, she finally had time to spend time with one [of us] and put a lot into Steve. Steve was her life."

And what a life it was. He played soccer, baseball, track, and, his first love, hockey. In 1975 his parents enrolled him in a novice church-league team for kids between the ages of seven and nine. These were just kids learning to play, with fun on their minds. Even though it wasn't competitive, it was clear Steve was the best player. He was a forward in novice and loved scoring goals. His novice coach, Joe Corrigan, was so impressed with the kid at eight that he was already predicting he'd play in the NHL one day.

As Steve got stronger and taller, he was dominating the play in his church league, so he was moved to the local AAA teams, the local all-star teams. These were very strong teams: in one minor tournament, his team scored thirty-two goals in five games, allowing only one goal against.

The teams he grew up with in the 1970s and early 1980s featured other future NHLers – Herb Raglan, Glen Seabrooke, Dallas Eakins, and Kerry Huffman. The number of kids who play hockey as youngsters and make it to the NHL is extremely small, so to have five kids from one small city, all within the same age range, reach their dreams is virtually unheard of.

Although Steve started his minor hockey as a forward, by the age of ten he was moved to defence, where the coaches thought his great shot, height, and skills could be used better. He was captain of his atom AAA hockey team, and in several hockey tournaments he won MVP or the top-rearguard award. By the time he reached peewee, when he was twelve, he was six feet tall, just like his father had been. That, and having so many talented teammates, helped him get to the prestigious Quebec peewee hockey tournament, where his team went to the finals, only to lose in overtime to a team with future NHL star and Peterborough alumnus Pete Ron Tugnutt playing in the net for the winners.

By 1979 Steve's peewee coach, Pete "Bubbs" McCarthy, says Steve was "head and shoulders above everyone else. His backward skating was weak, but he could shoot the puck as hard in peewee as any midget [four years older] player. You had to stay on him to keep him working or the lazy side would come out of him. He was the type of kid you'd pat on the back when he did well and give him hell when he didn't."

It might be expected that there would be great rivalry among the parents with so many talented hockey players on the team, but

McCarthy says they were a great bunch who never gave him any trouble, and he has coached enough teams where parents were a problem to know the difference.

During the peewee years, the Chiassons put Steve into power-skating classes, usually a week before the hockey season began. It was tough finding the time for hockey during the summer, as Steve was involved in soccer, baseball, swimming, and fishing. His peewee baseball team went to the all-Ontario championships, winning twenty-eight straight games. Steve had a batting average over .500. In addition, his track-and-field achievements were incredible for a twelve-year-old. He won the 1,500-metre run in 5:04.9. He threw the shot put 9.51 metres, the farthest anyone had thrown it in the entire intermediate Peterborough Catholic school system.

When he wasn't busy with one sport or another, he struggled with his schoolwork. "He wasn't a genius, but his marks were okay, average," say Joe, who also notes he was as stubborn as a bull, a family trait, but thinks that helped him improve in sports. It turned into determination. Steve would also take his mistakes to heart. "If he thought something was his fault, he'd be so angry [at himself]. He was stubborn like the rest of us," says his sister Sue.

The determination – or stubbornness – was evident in his single-minded ambition to play in the big leagues. "Ever since he was a little kid, it was his dream to play in the NHL," says his father. "When he was eight years old, watching the NHL on *Hockey Night in Canada*, he looked up from his special seat, the floor, and said, 'One day I'm going to be there.'" At twelve, the dream was still there. When an NHL player, in Peterborough doing some charity work, rushed away before signing autographs for all his adoring fans, Steve looked at his dad and said, "I'm not going to do that."

The tall, dark-haired, rugged Chiasson had a booming slapshot and played tough and without fear, so it was no surprise there were scouts looking at him by the time he was in bantam. When his bantam years ended in 1982, he decided to forgo midget hockey and end his minor hockey in favour of the local Junior B club where parents no longer have to pay and teams are usually privately owned. During that season, his junior draft year, scouts from the OHL Guelph Platers came to the Chiasson house to talk with Steve and his parents.

"They asked Steve if he would go there if they selected him in the draft," remembers his father. "He jumped at it."

Guelph did choose him in the 1983 draft and he couldn't wait to get there. Joe didn't worry about him moving but his mother was quite worried about her little boy leaving home and how much she'd miss him. Joe drove Steve to Guelph and dropped the big 190-pounder off with his landparents. If he was homesick, nobody could tell. Besides, there were lots of familiar faces to banish any yearning for home. Former Peterborough player Kerry Huffman was there. Their coach was former Petes assistant coach and future NHL head coach Jacques Martin. The Platers won the Memorial Cup in 1986, beating the Hull Olympiques in Portland, Oregon. Steve – now known as "Tank" – Chiasson was named the tournament MVP.

In 1985 the Detroit Red Wings selected him in the third round, fiftieth overall. Betty and Steve's dreams had come true. Betty and her daughter Sue went to see Steve play in an NHL exhibition game that October at Maple Leaf Gardens. "We saw him in that Detroit jersey and we cried," says Sue. "You don't often see your dreams come true, but there it was."

Besides playing NHL hockey, Steve had other dreams when he was a kid. He had always dreamed of owning a Corvette and bought one that first year in pro. He also remembered a promise the peewee players had made to their coach, Bubbs McCarthy. They had told him they would buy him a car if they ever played in the NHL. Of the five players who played in the NHL, only one fulfilled that promise – Steve Chiasson bought his old coach a Dinky toy car.

Steve continued to return to Peterborough during the summers, but he seldom talked about hockey. What he liked to do was fish, although he did also find time to marry Susan Turner. While he loved hockey, sister Sue says, he just didn't want to talk about it in the summer.

Steve spent thirteen years in the NHL, playing in 751 regular-season games, scoring 93 goals and 305 assists and getting 1,107 penalty minutes. He played in an All-Star Game and won a gold medal with Team Canada at the 1997 World Championships. He was with Detroit for eight years and was described by general manager

Ken Holland as a person the other players "would go to war for." He played three years in Calgary, with Gary Roberts, then spent a year with Hartford and two years with the Carolina Hurricanes, again with Roberts.

In February 1999, Steve had a shoulder injury and came home to Peterborough while he was healing. It was the first time he had been home for that long in the winter since 1983, the year he went to Guelph. He took his nephews outside for a little road hockey and went to their Cubs meeting that night so they could "show him off."

Three months later on Sunday, May 2, Chiasson and the Carolina Hurricanes lost to Boston and were eliminated from the playoffs. Steve played thirty minutes of that game. After the flight back to Raleigh, North Carolina, the team went to Gary Roberts's home to have a few beers and chase away the sour taste of losing. It was close to four in the morning, Monday, May 3, when Steve said to nobody in particular, "I'm ready to go home and see the kids."

He refused to wait for a taxi. The other players took away the keys to his pickup truck, intending to keep him from driving home, but he found the keys and drove away, intoxicated and without his seat belt fastened. Minutes later, his truck rolled off the highway. He was dead when teammates who had rushed after him arrived at the scene. His funeral in Peterborough was attended by all his teammates and many others he had played with and against from atom to the NHL. The NHL brass was there, as well as an honour guard of young Peterborough hockey players, wearing the minor Petes sweaters, the sweater Steve had worn growing up in Peterborough. Those players raised their sticks in a salute to him as his casket made its way into the church.

In an interview with *The Peterborough Examiner* in 1999 after the funeral that he attended, Wayne Gretzky said, "He was always tough for me to play against. He played with a tremendous amount of grit and always played hard and always played fair. He was a true NHL competitor and played the game the way it should be."

Steve's wife, Susan, told a packed cathedral, "He wasn't a hockey player, he was my best friend. . . . All of you go home and hug your significant others and kiss your children." We can remember Steve Chiasson not only as a good hockey player, but as someone with a good memory who never forgot what it was like to be a kid and never refused to sign autographs for them.

Susan Chiasson lives in Las Vegas with their three children. Shortly after Steve's death, his mother also died.

HERB RAGLAN
Born in Peterborough, August 5, 1967
NHL career with St. Louis, Quebec, Tampa Bay, Ottawa

Herb Raglan was the son of journeyman player Clare Raglan. Herb recalls his father's laconic presence when he was growing up in Peterborough. "In the summer, Dad would take us fishing at the Trent Canal. The first time, he took about eight of my buddies there in his car. He sat at a picnic table and read a newspaper while we fished. We didn't even know what we were doing. We'd get a fish on the line and ask him what to do. He'd sit reading his newspaper and say, 'It would be a good idea to reel it in.' When we got it in we'd ask, 'Now what?' and he'd say, 'It'd be best to take the hook out,' and turn a page of the newspaper."

Most of Herb's time was spent playing sports: baseball all summer and hockey when winter arrived. Money was tight. Herb's dad made it tighter with his philosophy of making do with what they had. Herb didn't have his own pair of new skates until he was playing with a junior team, when they were purchased for him by the team. "Dad didn't believe in spoiling the kids. My shoulder pads were from the Red Wings when *he* played. They were Litmanns from Detroit. I wore those for four years. The suspenders were right on my pants and they didn't give any protection. I wore them until they disintegrated." He played his first organized hockey in the church league. "I couldn't skate well but scored a lot – everyone did in house league," he says. "I remember the first game I had no garter belt so we put laces around my socks."

There were no power-skating or hockey camps for Herb, even though some of the other kids were getting that kind of help. Skating remained something of a weakness throughout his career. The senior Raglan coached Herb and some of his friends when they were about twelve. It was summer hockey, which was played from about May to July. "We went to a tournament," remembers Herb, "and we all went fishing and waterskiing and boating. We stayed on the lake all day. Dad was really pissed because we weren't ready to play hockey."

The next summer the senior Raglan found Herb a job as a brick-layer's helper. Herb says his father "was perceived to be a real hard-ass, and in hindsight, while I didn't like his criticism, and he was always critical, he was setting me up, preparing me for what was to come. He knew once you signed [a pro hockey contract] that you're a pony. If you don't run, they whip you harder or get rid of you.

"Dad and I had a lot fun," Herb continues. "He'd drive his '73 Dodge all over, lugging six kids and the luggage around to tourna-ments. He always had a full car. He'd take us all over, not just hockey but fishing and hunting."

Herb grew up to be big-muscled, thick-boned, and tough. He became known for his goal-scoring abilities, his skill in creating open ice, and his habit of hitting anyone who got in his way. At thirteen he had already played in front of 15,000 people at the Quebec peewee tournament, where his team lost in overtime in the finals to a Toronto team backed by goalie Ron Tugnutt (a future Peterborough Pete, who was with the Dallas Stars in 2004). Pete McCarthy, his peewee coach, says Herb "couldn't skate backwards well. But he was so pugnacious. He'd go through the boards to get the puck. He was big, strong as a bull, and did anything to win." McCarthy also says of Herb that he was "eager to learn. . . . Rags was on him about how to do things. I told Herb that things had changed since his father played in the NHL. Herb listened and was easy to coach."

For his part Herb says McCarthy "was a great coach, one of the best, if not the best, I ever had."

McCarthy has a few fond memories. Once in a playoff game he was dishing it out to his players between periods for a poor effort and told Herb to "get the brick out of your ass. I told him to start coming early to the games and sit in the can and let that brick out," he recalls. "From then on he would come early, right up to [when he was in] the NHL."

During the summer, Herb and his father helped build their family-owned resort in nearby Haliburton. Herb spent many of his summer days there working and playing. He'd fish in the summer and hunt deer in the winter while still going to school. Three days after his sixteenth birthday, he got his driver's licence and was picking up his friends for practices. "I was the parents' dream because the practices were at 6:30 a.m.," he says.

By the time he was seventeen, he was six feet tall, with 200 pounds of muscle, bigger than his dad was in his prime, and his ice presence was obvious to scouts. In one midget tournament, with blood dripping from a big gash on his chin, his white and maroon sweater was blood-soaked by the end of the game, but he never quit. The cut would break open again; he'd refuse stitches and go back out, bleeding again. The scouts and fans loved it.

He seemed to be taking his father's advice to heart. "I always told Herb if you don't want to play hockey, don't play," the senior Raglan told *The Peterborough Examiner* in an interview several years before his death. "Dad won't be mad if you don't play, but if you want to play, play hard, all the time."

The Peterborough Petes were watching Herb closely – Petes coach Dick Todd wanted him on his team. "We really were hoping to get Herb that year, but it wasn't to be." Herb was the Kingston Canadians' first pick, third overall in the 1984 draft. "I kind of knew Kingston would be taking me," he says, because they had expressed an interest during the winter and before the draft.

Herb remembers the day his father drove him to training camp. "Dad drove me right to the Kingston Memorial Centre. I got my stuff out of the trunk and dropped it on the parking lot. He said, 'Good luck,' and drove off. He left me in the parking lot. My stomach was churning. I was lost and I was hurling, I didn't know where I was going. But he was only gone a few minutes, swung around, and came back.

"I was homesick for the first week. It was all new to me, and I didn't know Kingston at all. The prison was at Kingston, and I had heard stories about it. My first night there, a chopper was in the sky with a spotlight. I heard the next day it was all about an escape at Collins Bay prison. I was scared, I didn't know what was going on.

"But when I got settled, I realized I was there to do something, something different." That something was to make a career out of hockey. He was Kingston's rookie of the year. Coach Fred O'Donnell said Herb "never took a day off." He always played the same: hard, with a mean streak that was evident in a playoff game against the Peterborough Petes, when he gave a vicious elbow to his long-time friend and former teammate Glen Seabrooke, knocking him out.

That summer he came home to a job for a bread company, driving a truck on a rural route and covering a few hundred miles each day. His training program was riding his bicycle about eight miles to pick up the truck. "Kingston didn't have a training program, so I'd ride my bike," he says.

At eighteen he was selected thirty-seventh in the 1985 NHL draft by St. Louis and made the team that September. His dad had delayed his own NHL career many years before, thinking he wasn't ready, but Herb had no such reluctance. However, he was still young and an inexperienced traveller. He remembers going to St. Louis: "It was the first time I had ever been on an airplane. My mom gave me rolls of

American coins, that's all we had. Security stopped me going through at the airport to check the rolls out. . . . I didn't even know the Blues gave you meal money."

In hindsight, it may have been a mistake to go to the NHL that early. His toughness was a bonus, but his poor skating and inexperience were evident. After a few short months, he was sent back to Kingston. St. Louis called him back up for the playoffs, where his hard hitting paid off for coach Jacques Demers's Blues. Herb scored his first NHL goal in the division final against the Leafs, whom the Blues defeated, with former Pete Greg Millen in the net.

St. Louis kept Herb for four years, and then he became a travelling man, just like his father. He had scored 26 goals and 39 assists and recorded 571 penalty minutes in 235 games with the Blues before being dealt to Quebec. At only twenty-three, he had already played in three of the cities (St. Louis, Kingston, and now Quebec) his father had played in. Herb stayed with Quebec for a year. He was hampered, just as his father had been, by injuries. He was also honest and forthright, making no attempt to soften his views or hold back on their expression.

He is just as honest now as he recalls the bitter taste of life as a fringe player. It was never more galling than after he was taken to hospital during a game in Quebec with a suspected broken jaw. Nobody, except teammates, checked to see if he was okay. Even after two days, a team representative hadn't called, visited, or talked with him.

As a marginal player, he had to go hard all the time, but you can't do that if you are injured. In 1992 he went to the minors at the start of the season, then back to the NHL with Tampa Bay for two games. Next he was sent to Atlanta in the old International Hockey League (IHL), then to Kalamazoo, and in 1993 he signed with the Ottawa Senators, playing twenty-nine games before going back to the IHL. That was followed by the Central Texas Stampede of the Western Professional Hockey League, then Brantford's senior team. He retired in 1998. In 343 NHL games, Herb Raglan scored 33 times, assisted on 56 goals, and had 775 minutes in penalties.

Herb had married a Peterborough woman when he was twenty-one, and they had spent their summers in Peterborough. After he retired, they moved back permanently. He's a softer father to their three daughters than his dad was to him. He's not as critical and not afraid to show emotion with his children. He doesn't play hockey any more and is not involved in it in any way – he still is bitter about his NHL experience.

Nevertheless, those years of playing hockey gave Herb many memories. There is one he describes as his "best night in hockey." It wasn't his first junior game. It wasn't being named rookie of the year in Kingston. It wasn't his first NHL game or any NHL game or goal. It was a bantam game he'll never forget.

The bantam Petes were playing their bitter rivals from Oshawa – "We hated that team," he says – and Oshawa was beating them in the final game of a best-of-seven playoff series. The score was 3-1 and there were five minutes left. Steve Chiasson, playing defence for the Petes, had the puck. Herb broke down the left wing in the neutral zone, skating toward the net. Steve passed to him. Herb took the puck, deked the goalie, and scored. Steve and Herb performed the same feat two more times for Herb's natural hat trick and a win.

"It was great, hilarious. I loved it!" he crows, relishing the sweet memory of a time when hockey was still full of fun.

Herb Raglan lives in Peterborough with his wife and three daughters.

GLEN SEABROOKE
Born in Peterborough, September 11, 1967
Peterborough Petes 1984-87
NHL career with Philadelphia

"He could stickhandle in a phone booth." Former peewee coach Pete "Bubbs" McCarthy is talking about Glen Seabrooke. "He was the most talented hockey player I ever saw."

Those are big words coming from a coach who handled dozens of players, watched thousands of games, and coached some other Peterborough kids like Steve Chiasson, Herb Raglan, and Dallas Eakins, who all made it in the NHL.

Glen Seabrooke grew up with these boys, had a passion and talent for the game of hockey, and shared many similar minor-hockey experiences, but his dream of one day playing in the NHL became a nightmare.

McCarthy figured Glen would be a great NHL player. "He was a nice kid – you couldn't meet a nicer kid. He never swore around us and was brought up well, easy to coach. You never had to tell him when he made a mistake; he always knew."

Glen Seabrooke, a natural skater, playmaker, and goal scorer, grew up in Peterborough. He was a big kid – by the time he got to the OHL junior draft when he was sixteen, he was six-foot-two and 190 pounds – and the Peterborough Petes took him as their first choice for the 1984-85 season. In that first year, he played on a team with Randy Burridge, Kris King, Terry Carkner, John Druce, Bruce Shoebottom, Dallas Eakins, Ron Tugnutt, and Kay Whitmore, Petes who would all go on to the NHL. He was ninth in team scoring, with 21 goals and 13 assists in 45 games. By the second year he was drafted by the Philadelphia Flyers in the first round, twenty-first overall.

That fall of 1985 the eighteen-year-old travelled to the Philadelphia training camp but was struck with a sudden illness that was diagnosed as a tumour in his pelvis. The tumour was removed, and after Glen underwent treatment in Peterborough, he worked his way back to play for the Petes that winter. He had missed the first forty-seven games of the Petes' season, but in the nineteen games he did play in, he scored 8 goals and got 12 assists. He returned to the Flyers' training camp the following season, 1986-87, but was sent back to the Petes to play with people like newcomers Tie Domi, Luke Richardson, and Billy Huard, more future NHLers.

A now-healthy Glen was named to the OHL all-star team that season. He played in 48 games for the Petes that year, scoring 30 goals and 39 assists, and was called up to play in ten games with the Philadelphia Flyers, scoring his first NHL goal and getting four assists. Everything seemed to be going his way.

In the 1987-88 hockey season, he went to the Flyers' training camp once again. This time he was truly finished with junior hockey, and he played most of the year with an AHL team, the Hershey Bears, scoring 32 goals and getting 40 assists in 73 games. It was a great year for the rookie.

The next fall he was back with Hershey. In an early-season game in November 1988, he was performing a manoeuvre he'd done many times – skating after a puck. However, he collided with the goalie, who had come out to beat him to it. He tripped, fell to the ice on his left shoulder, and hit the goalpost. It's the kind of fall a hockey player takes all the time.

He knew he was injured as he left the ice holding his shoulder, but it seemed like just another injury. Team doctor John Gregg looked at it after the game, and over the next few days the doctor diagnosed torn cartilage, advised him to do some physiotherapy, and assured Glen he would be back on the ice in no time.

As advised, Glen undertook the physiotherapy, but the more he did, the more the shoulder hurt. He tried going back to hockey and finished the season, but his arm still wasn't working properly. Something was terribly wrong. Glen couldn't lift anything with his left arm. His shoulder movement was restricted. He couldn't hold things upright. He couldn't even play golf – and hockey was out of the question. His doctor recommended an operation. He had three. The operations, the diagnosis, and the resulting wrong treatment all made the injury worse. He had a shoulder injury but it had been wrongly diagnosed and treated. He sued the team doctor for malpractice.

"Not only was hockey my livelihood, but it has been my life," he told the Canadian Press at the time. "That in itself has been difficult to deal with, but it went beyond hockey. It is everything else that goes along with it. Athletics were a big part of my life, but they were taken away."

In 1995, Seabrooke won the lawsuit, and a Philadelphia jury awarded him US $5.5 million, the least amount they considered he would have made as a pro hockey player had he been healthy. The jury recognized Glen Seabrooke would have been a player in the NHL. He still has shoulder restriction and hasn't played any sports since then.

Glen Seabrooke lives with his family in Peterborough and owns a business there.

TIE DOMI
Born in Windsor, Ontario, November 1, 1969
Raised in Belle River, Ontario
Peterborough Petes 1986-89
NHL career in New York, Winnipeg, Toronto

When Tie Domi was a kid, he had more energy than a dog let loose after being stuck in a house all day. He had so much energy his family and teachers were worried about his aggressiveness. What to do?

His parents thought hockey might help him work off some of that energy. He already played soccer in the summer and that kept him busy, but no one in his family had ever played hockey. From what they'd seen, it looked aggressive enough.

Domi's father, John, had arrived in Canada after escaping to Yugoslavia from Albania, meeting his wife, Maiyem, there, and deciding to make a new life in Canada. By the 1950s they had landed in Windsor, Ontario, to build their lives together. Two children, Dash and Trish, were born in the 1960s, and a second son, Tahir, was born on November 1, 1969. They settled in the little town of Belle River, near Windsor. Belle River, a population of 4,000, is a place where, as its slogan goes, "everybody loves everybody." Tahir just had a strange way of showing that love with all his energy.

Tie has said, "I was hyper as a child. If somebody upset me, I'd get really, really mad. I was a bully at school, and I was always getting in fights at the playground."

His big brother, Dash, and two cousins introduced him to hockey by registering him and taking him to house-league games in Belle River. When he first stepped on ice in 1978, he had never been on skates before and had had no interest in hockey. He kept falling down, but he also kept getting back up, and soon, even though he had trouble standing up on that Belle River arena ice, he loved going to the rink. By the end of the season he was not only the most improved player but also the most valuable. Tie Domi had arrived with a bang, as he always does.

He was small and stocky, dark-haired with thick black eyebrows, just like his father. He didn't grow tall over the years, but his arms

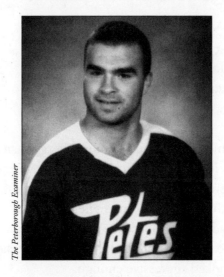

The Peterborough Examiner

and legs, chest and shoulders had turned from pebbles to boulders
by the time he was a teenager. He used his strong body to great advantage in three sports, continuing to star in soccer, and shining in high-
school football as well as hockey.

His reputation was one of toughness and it showed even in his
sports heroes: the Leafs' Tiger Williams and the Flyers' Bobby
Clarke, two tenacious players who would go through a river of acid
if it meant the team could get to the other side. In hockey Tie was
the team's tough guy by the time he was fourteen and playing for the
Belle River Junior C team. In the 1983-84 season, only five years after
his introduction to hockey, he was playing with teammates already
more than twenty years old.

Domi feared nobody. He could score, fight, and hit. The older,
bigger players mistook his short stature for weakness and tried to push
him around. Mistake number one. They also thought they could get
away with cheap shots because of his age and size. Mistake number
two. He says, "That got me mad. That's when I started fighting."

The people in Belle River loved him during his two seasons of
Junior C there. Scouts also began to take notice of him, but they
weren't sure about his talent or size – he was only five-foot-seven then.

Peterborough's then trainer and part-time scout, Jeff Twohey, was
one of those who had an eye on Domi in 1986. The Petes had been
beaten out the year before by a rugged Belleville team and were on

the lookout for someone to add that toughness to their team. "We had to get someone and had watched Tie. His Junior C coach was former NHLer Marcel Pronovost and we asked him about Tie. 'That kid has balls,'" was all he told them. Based on that recommendation, coach and general manager Dick Todd decided to try to get him in the draft.

The Petes knew the Hamilton Steelhawks were also interested in Domi, but Hamilton had picked a goalie before the Petes because, as Twohey says, "they didn't think Peterborough would take a guy like Tie."

Peterborough drafted Tie and he made the move away from home. He was homesick at first, missed his mother's great meals, and wasn't getting the attention or ice time he was used to back home in Belle River and Windsor. Here, it was different. He was treated like everyone else and wasn't looked upon as a starter. In fact, Todd told him at training camp he was going to have him split the year between the Petes and their Junior B squad in Peterborough.

"The first year he was borderline," remembers then assistant coach and former Pete Terry Bovair. "His problems probably outweighed his value. We didn't have any idea how he was going to be our enforcer. He was so small, we didn't know what he could do."

He was a problem in other ways. He'd show up late for practice, kept complaining about being hurt, and about his equipment. The Petes always had their players go for a run in the morning and Tie would straggle in near the end. "Tie didn't think he could run," says Todd. "He blamed his short legs. I told Tie it's not in your legs, it's in your heart."

Bovair says Tie knew he had to fight if he was going to get anywhere in hockey, but his aggressive nature seemed to have been sidetracked somehow. Team executive Herb Warr remembers one of the year's first exhibition games when opponent Mathieu Schneider, normally not a fighter, put Tie down with little response, and Schneider later asked, "He's supposed to be the tough guy?" Warr wondered the same thing.

According to Todd, Tie, then turning seventeen, almost quit and went home just before the regular season started. "Tie was packing it in," he says. "He broke a knuckle and I sat him out one game, and he quit, he was going home. I told him he shouldn't be happy about being a big fish in a little pond. He wanted a trade and I told him I'd never trade his rights."

Twohey adds that Tie was demanding more ice time and told Dick he was going to quit if he didn't get it. "Dick just said, 'Okay, bye.'" Tie quit. Twohey sat Domi down in the dressing room and said, "You're making a big mistake."

It all fell on deaf ears. Tie went to his landparent at the time, Lou Ellis, and told him he was quitting. Both Ellis and team leader Dallas Eakins tried to talk him out of it. Tie headed off to the bus station, but he had some time for reflection while he waited for the bus. He thought of his future and how it would be affected if he left. He knew hockey was his only way of getting ahead, and became quite fearful of the consequences of quitting. He had never quit before and decided not to start now. He returned to the team and his attitude began to change. Todd welcomed him back and told him he had confidence in him. They knew he could fight, but did anyone else? He would have to prove himself to his teammates and the rest of the league.

His first big fight came early in the season, at the team's second game at the end of September. They were playing in Kingston, against the Kingston Canadians, a team that boasted the league's tough guy, Marc Laforge, six-foot-three, 215 pounds, and with 248 minutes in penalties in the previous season. The Petes players were talking about Laforge in the dressing room before the game. Tie asked what they were talking about and they told him how tough Laforge was.

Twohey says Tie boasted, "Don't worry, I'll take care of him." The players, who had never seen Tie scrap, just shook their heads.

Twohey continues, "I told Dick what he had said and that the players had laughed, thinking it was a big joke." Halfway through the game, Dick sent Tie on the ice with Laforge. Tie knew exactly why. The two went at it, and Tie dropped Laforge. It was a case of David defeating Goliath in a one-on-one battle, and it not only boosted the morale of the Petes, but spread Tie's tough-guy reputation around the league. It gave the Petes a much-needed team ingredient . . . intimidation.

The Petes had been losing the game 7-5 when the fight broke out at 18:09 of the third period. Laforge was "reputed to be the OHL's best pugilist," Mike Brophy wrote in the *Examiner* when he reported on Tie's first OHL fight: "Laforge landed a couple of quick lefts but they didn't faze Domi. Domi wrestled Laforge to the ice and then landed a couple of lefts of his own. As Tie made his way to the dressing room he received congratulations from his teammates and coach."

Twohey says that first year all Tie wanted to do was fight. He spent most of the season playing for the Bs and played only 18 games with the Petes (1 goal, 1 assist, 79 minutes in penalties). Todd wanted him to become more than a fighter, more than a goon. "He had to learn to be a player, and by the second year," says Twohey, "he had figured it out. I credit Dick for working with him." He also moved up to be in the top five finishers in the morning jogs.

Bovair says Tie went to teammates Kris King and Dallas Eakins, who knew their way around the fight game, and got pointers not only on how to be tougher, but how to get the upper hand to win the fights. What amazed observers, besides the way he was winning the battles against players five to eight inches taller and much heavier, was his ability to take punches to the head. The combatants would usually get their helmets off to do battle. Tie would actually laugh as the opposition's punches struck his head (one junior opponent, Bryan Marchment, a Leafs teammate in 2003-04, said it was the hardest head he had ever hit).

"He watched, he listened, he learned, and by the second year he was much better with his attitude, fighting, and even his play," says Bovair.

Another attention catcher and confirmation of Tie's toughness that year was when he fought the Belleville Bulls' tough guy, Troy Crowder, seven inches taller, forty pounds heavier. Tie put him down. "That was the turning point," says Bovair. "He learned from older guys and started spending a lot of time with Dick."

One more learning experience occurred off the ice. After a summer working for his uncle at a Toronto food market, carrying watermelons, Domi came back, says Todd, firmly convinced he didn't want to do that all his life.

On the ice, the home fans loved the fearless kid who protected Petes star players as fiercely as a lion protects its young. They would throw ties on the ice after his fight victories. Fans in the other rinks would throw other things. Todd remembers that at one game a fan tossed a banana at Tie and called him a monkey. "Tie went over, picked up the banana, peeled it and ate it coming off the ice."

Twohey recalls a game in Windsor where the fans were really getting on Tie. A commotion broke out in the crowd, and Twohey looked up to see Tie's father fighting in the stands. He pointed this out to Tie, who looked up and shrugged his shoulders. Later, on the bus ride home, Twohey asked Tie how he could be so calm about it. Tie replied, "He escaped from Albania, dodging machine-gun bullets. I think he could handle that guy."

Tie's family moved to Toronto while he was with the Petes, so it was easy for them to get to most of the Petes' games. Tie's landparent, Debbie Ralph, says the senior Domi would come to their house and spend the whole time thanking them for taking in his son. His mother would bring a Greek pasta to the house, complete with silverware. Mrs. Domi would go to the games, but spend the entire time pacing in the lobby. She never once watched a game when Tie was with the Petes. Twohey remembers seeing her sitting on a bench outside the Petes' dressing room for the whole game, so he asked Tie about it. Tie said she didn't want to see him get hurt. Years later, she finally went to an NHL game in Toronto.

"Tie knew hockey was all he had. He knew he had nothing to fall back on – he wasn't strong academically, so he put everything into hockey," says Debbie. "He was so good to all the organizations in town, groups who would ask him to go see kids or speak to them. It was unbelievable how many calls we got here. We kidded him once that he should run for mayor.

"When he was in a room full of people he was the show, but when he was alone he was quiet."

Tie liked being the show, and although he was known for having a cement head, he wasn't a cementhead. He knew the value of publicity, getting his name in print and his face over the airwaves, and it made for a lot of interest when his 1989 draft year came up. Todd says that "teams were calling me about Tie. I'd tell them another team, higher up in the draft selection, was also interested, so it kept moving him up in draft. It went so high he went in the second round, twenty-seventh overall.

"Imagine, twenty-seventh-best player in the world." Todd shakes his head, smiling at the thought.

The Leafs signed him and sent him to their farm team in the AHL, the Newmarket Saints, where he scored 14 goals and 11 assists and piled up 285 minutes in penalties, most of them for fighting. He was called up for two games, and although he didn't register a point, he got 42 minutes in penalties. It was clear he knew his future in the NHL was with fighting.

In 1990 he was traded to the New York Rangers. He started the season with the Binghamton Rangers in the AHL, where he scored 11 goals and 6 assists but had an amazing 219 minutes in the penalty box in 25 games. The Rangers called him up to bring not only some toughness to the team but also excitement for the New York fans. He didn't disappoint, getting 246 penalty minutes in 42 games, again the vast majority of these for fighting (and winning). It was in New York he "rode his stick" when he scored, putting it between his legs and gliding down the New York ice for the home crowd to cheer.

The fan favourite spent two seasons with the Rangers before being traded to the Winnipeg Jets, where he spent two-and-a-half seasons before going back to Toronto in 1994, the team that originally drafted him from the Petes. He could look back with satisfaction at the time he had spent with the Petes. The team had been successful during Tie's years there. They had gone to the Memorial Cup in 1989 in Saskatoon, where, in addition to scoring two goals, he fought Kevin Kaminski of the Saskatoon Blades and Gino Odjick of Laval Titan, both of them more than six feet tall and 200 pounds.

As of 2004, after 943 NHL games in sixteen seasons, Tie has served more than 3,400 minutes in the penalty box, making him one of the four most penalized players in league history (the leader is his childhood hockey hero, Dave "Tiger" Williams), scored 99 goals in regular-season play and 130 assists. This was the same kid who as a fifteen-year-old in Belle River scored 7 goals and 5 assists and had 96 penalty minutes in 28 games of Junior C. In recognition of his NHL success and minor hockey career, the Belle River Canadians junior C team retired Tie's number 9 on January 22, 1999.

Tie Domi was still playing and fighting for the Toronto Maple Leafs in 2004. He lives in Toronto with his wife and three children.

MIKE RICCI

Born in Scarborough, Ontario, October 27, 1971
Peterborough Petes 1987-90
NHL *career with Philadelphia, Quebec, Colorado, San Jose*

Mike Ricci was only a bantam – fifteen years old – in the 1986-87 season when he caught the eye of Petes scout Norm Bryan at a game in Toronto. The Italian kid had plenty of talent, and Bryan was afraid the Petes wouldn't be able to hide him. For some reason, probably because he was still a bantam, he was rated only two-hundredth in the OHL draft. "We looked at him," says then coach Dick Todd. "He didn't seem to be really quick but he was strong along the boards. . . . He wasn't getting much ice time, but every time he did he would score."

The Petes took Peterborough boy Joe Hawley in the first round, then took the unusual step of choosing Ricci in the second round. They had never drafted a bantam before, and in those days bantams usually weren't drafted. It turns out the Petes had been the only OHA junior team to even talk to him.

Mike "Ratdawg" Ricci was now a Peterborough Pete. The day one of his two older brother's coaches had seen the two-year-old handling a stick in a Scarborough arena must have seemed a long time ago to the sixteen-year-old. The coach was so impressed that day he told Ricci's parents he should start walking around on skates in the house to get better balance. Mike did. He walked on his skates

Marlow Banks

everywhere in the house, and maybe that's why, when he was three and hit the ice for his first skate, he could do it better than anyone his age, which meant simply that he could skate and not fall down.

He was so good at street hockey that the other neighbourhood teams demanded, "If you get Mike, we get two goals before the game starts." Ricci grew up in Scarborough as an arena player, the start of a generation that learned most of its ice hockey indoors rather than on outside rinks. He always tells people he didn't have any fear of playing against other players because he figured if he could play with and against his brothers he could play against anyone. "Nobody was tougher than my brothers," he says.

Ricci's two brothers were born in France and they got their toughness naturally. The Ricci boys' father, Mario, had been a soccer star in Italy, where both parents experienced the dropping of German bombs near the end of the war. Mrs. Ricci's hearing was affected by it for the rest of her life. Mario and Anna were married soon after they met, when Mario was twenty-five and Anna only sixteen. Mario dreamed of a soccer career and the couple moved to France, where Mario turned pro, but his temper got him into several fights and he soon decided to give up. The family moved to Canada in 1965 and Mario got work as a steelworker and Anna became a seamstress. Mike was born six years later.

The Riccis' youngest boy displayed talent for both soccer and hockey. The hockey Mike first played in Scarborough was house league, but his superior talents shone through and he was soon playing all-star and enjoying what has become one of his favourite hockey memories: "The coach worked for Christie's and would bring us cookies and milk after the games – I loved that."

As in hockey, Mike played all-star soccer. His parents had never pushed him to play or excel in sports – it was something he wanted to do. Even as a kid, he didn't just want to play the game, he wanted to be the best in whatever sport he played. The year he was drafted to the Petes he was on the under-seventeen soccer team playing for the national championship. The championship was held at the same time as the Petes' training camp, but he decided to go to Peterborough (his soccer team lost 1-0).

Mike was a skinny, wiry child, but when he arrived in Peterborough in 1987, he was six feet and 185 pounds, and some Petes officials were comparing him to Steve Yzerman and even Wayne Gretzky. Todd would only say what he had never said about anyone before: "He'll be the best player in the world." When Mike learned the Petes were interested in him and that he could be drafted coming out of bantam hockey, he did what was becoming quite common for junior players: he hired an agent, Anton Thun. Todd deplored agents. Agents had no role, no reason for being in junior hockey, he thought. The Petes' kids were treated fine. Todd just ignored the agent, as he did all of them at that time.

At his first Petes home game, Mike scored a goal and added three assists. He never looked back. A shoulder injury slowed him down in his first year. He was out for three months in 1987-88 but still got 24 goals and 37 assists in 41 games. The next year he broke the league's goal-scoring streak, held by Brian Dobbin, scoring goals in nineteen straight games. The Petes finished first in their division and Ricci was tenth in league scoring, with 54 goals and 52 assists.

Jeff Twohey, the Petes' assistant manager, remembers asking, "Kid, are you surprised you're scoring so much? Because we're amazed." He just looked up at Twohey and said with a quiet confidence, "No, I always score."

"Not once did I ever see him unhappy at the rink. He loved to play, loved being on the ice."

Petes fans saw Ricci's commitment to the game many times, in particular the year he played in the Memorial Cup with chicken pox. He fought a fever, the itching sores on his body, and the vomiting on the bench.

When Mike played in an all-star game in Montreal in 1989, he made sure his parents were there, especially his dad, because this was where his favourite team played. Mike's landparent, Walter DiClemente, remembers Mike's dad, who spoke broken English, walking around the Montreal Forum and seeing Habs star Bob Gainey. "He actually started talking loudly – 'Gainey, Gainey, Gainey.' Here he was with his son, who had just been named first star of the all-star game, one of the best junior players in the world, and he was doing that." Walter laughs at the precious memory.

Mike did more than play hockey when he was in Peterborough. He got involved in the community. He played in charity ball games, supported children's causes by attending events, went into schools and to the hospital to talk to children, and generally responded positively when asked to help.

In his second year, the eagle-nosed, good-looking Ricci played for the Canadian team in the World Junior Championship in Anchorage, Alaska, against future NHL stars Mike Modano, Jeremy Roenick, and Alex Mogilny.

By 1990, the teen with the neatly cropped black hair was playing in his second World Junior Championship and was the co-captain of the Canadian team that won the gold medal in Finland. It was the same year he was selected MVP in Canadian junior hockey and its most gentlemanly player. Many expected that he would go first in the draft, but in the end that honour went to Owen Nolan, now with the Leafs.

"As the picks went on, I could feel everyone staring at me," Ricci told *The Peterborough Examiner* many years later. "That's the only thing I remember – were people looking at me thinking, 'I wonder if he is angry'? I wasn't really overly angry. Once Philly picked me, I was pretty happy. You don't dream about going one, two, or three, you dream about being drafted . . . then you dream about making the team and then you dream about winning the Stanley Cup."

All these dreams came true.

In the end, he was selected fourth behind Nolan, Peter Nedved, and Keith Primeau. He was later traded to Quebec in the big Lindros squabble and moved with that team to Colorado, winning the Stanley Cup in 1996. Ricci was traded in 1997 to the San Jose Sharks, where he was still playing in the 2003-04 season. He has had six seasons with more than twenty goals, but the goal production he displayed through minor hockey and the Petes didn't continue. He has turned into a top checking forward known for his tenacity and as a quality centreman.

Something else has also changed. He went from a short-haired, innocent-looking kid in Peterborough to an adult with shoulder-length hair that drips out of his helmet, bounces as he plays, making him stand out in North American rinks and television broadcasts. The change in appearance is unusual for Mike, who has always been known for his shyness and humility. Petes executive member Ed Rowe says of Mike, "He had a mildness to him, you wouldn't think he'd be so competitive. He really stood out in junior – but I don't know about that long hair now," he adds with a laugh.

Mike's joking explanation for the long hair is that it's to "hide my big nose."

As of 2004, he has scored 233 goals and 355 assists in 1,014 regular-season games. The 1,000-game mark is a feat most NHL players never reach – by 2004 only about 180 players had reached this milestone. Ricci is now in a class of other stellar players with Peterborough connections – Dit Clapper, Jim Roberts, Craig Ramsay, Bob Gainey, Wayne Gretzky, Keith Acton, Larry Murphy, Steve Larmer, Steve Yzerman, and Luke Richardson – who accomplished it before him.

Mike Ricci lives in San Jose with his wife and two children. They have a cottage near Peterborough. In the summer of 2004 he signed with the Phoenix Coyotes.

BRENT TULLY
Born in Peterborough, March 26, 1974
Peterborough Petes 1990-94

Brent Tully might be a good example for Canadian minor-hockey parents who harbour dreams that their child will one day play in the NHL.

By the time he was sixteen he was six-foot-two, a big defence-man with a hard shot and Hollywood good looks. His hockey resumé in those teen years and into his early twenties predicted nothing but success and a long hockey career. He was chosen to play for Ontario's under-seventeen team in Prince Edward Island, where they won the gold medal in the national championship. A year later he was chosen for Canada's under-eighteen team that went to Japan and won the silver medal in the world championship. When he was eighteen, in 1992, he was selected by the Vancouver Canucks in the fourth round of the NHL draft. At nineteen, he played for Team Canada in Sweden for the World Junior Championship, and won the gold medal. The next year, he was captain of the Team Canada juniors who won the gold medal, and had played for his hometown OHL team, the Peterborough Petes, for which he was also the captain. When he was twenty-one, he was playing in the AHL, where he stayed for three years before moving to Europe for another three years. At twenty-seven he was out of professional hockey.

He wasn't a heavy drinker, never got into drugs, was always a decent, polite, well-mannered boy and man and a talented hockey player with good size and excellent credentials, but he hadn't played a single game in the NHL.

By the time he was five, Brent Tully was playing organized hockey on indoor rinks and attending city-sponsored youth skating lessons. "I can always remember the first time [I skated] because I was afraid to take the skate guards off my skates," he says.

Brent was born in the mid-1970s and was raised in the 1980s, a time when kids moved indoors to organized hockey, in which all-star teams played twice a week and got in two practices a week. They were in the rink four out of seven days, but for only fifty minutes at a time. Boys in the 1950s and 1960s spent that much time outside skating, sometimes before breakfast, on most winter days. However, some of the old ways hadn't died – Brent played some hockey in his basement, although with his only sibling a younger sister, he wasn't down there as much as some people who came from larger families. He also had a shooting board outside in the backyard, "but I wasn't out there all the time." He did play a lot of road hockey, almost every day in the fall and spring. "I think that's where I got my hand skills," he says.

Brent remembers only "bits and pieces" of his first organized hockey experiences, when he played for a local church-league mites team on a rink surface divided in half by a "big board" so four teams could play at the same time every Saturday morning.

"The coach used to make us all take turns playing goal. When it was my turn, I skated up the ice with goal pads and all [playing like a forward], and he never played me in goal again. I liked that," he says with a laugh. Although he was accepted by the local AAA novice team, his parents, Walter, a grocery-store employee, and Mary, a teacher, decided not to let him play.

"I was quite upset, but I suppose they had their reasons. I think they found out how much travelling there would be."

Two years later, when he was nine, he tried out for the minor atom AAA team as a centre. He made the team, but his coach put him back on defence, a position he played for the rest of his hockey career.

"My parents always pushed me to try my best and that's the philosophy I kept right up to the pros, and all the way they were always there telling me to try my best. My mother was a yeller at the games, cheering us all on. They were typical hockey parents, supporting me all the way."

His father was also a tall man, had played hockey growing up in Peterborough and was good enough to be selected to many of the all-star teams. Hockey players were in the family. Cousin Joe Hawley would play and star for the Petes; another cousin, Colin Beardsmore, also played OHL hockey. Both went on to play semi-pro and to Europe.

As Tully was growing up, he didn't think of playing junior hockey or going to the OHL. He'd go watch the Petes play but never imagined one day he'd put on the maroon-and-white sweater and play at the "big rink." Brent's dreams were bigger.

"I always dreamed, like other kids, of playing in the NHL. Even in road-hockey games or warm-ups to our kids' games, even on the lake, that's what motivates us, what makes you better. You dreamed you were in the NHL.

"If you don't have any dreams, there's no hope of moving on to other levels. You want to have ambitions to improve or do better. You always have to have the dream; that's what drives you."

By the time he was minor-bantam age, he had grown to a man's size and wanted to play major bantam, a group a year older, but the local hockey council had a rule against kids playing up an age group. However, after a controversy, the council relented and he was allowed to play.

Later that year, he heard teammates talking about the OHL draft and saw some of the older kids talking with scouts. Some of them were later drafted. Because he was younger than his teammates, he couldn't be approached for another year, but he was intrigued. The idea of being drafted drove him to improve. He began skating harder, playing high-school hockey as well as all-star, practising his shooting until he had one of the hardest shots on the point of any bantam player in Ontario. His bantam team went to the all-Ontario championships in 1990.

In his draft year, Petes coach Dick Todd and trainer Jeff Twohey talked to Brent, telling him they would draft him if it was possible. Brent says, "I grew up watching the Petes. They were the be-all and end-all. Before the draft, Dick once took me on a tour of the dressing room. He said there are three things you can think about when you're a teenager and you have to decide which two you're going to do: 1. School; 2. Hockey; 3. Girls. I'll never forget that."

Brent went to the junior draft in 1990 but "it wasn't something I had really put anything into. I was sixteen and didn't really get that excited about something like a draft. But I was ecstatic to be picked by the Petes."

He was also chosen to play on Ontario's under-seventeen team, a team with an even bigger kid than Brent, a tall, lanky kid by the name of Chris Pronger. The team went to the Canadian championships being held in P.E.I. and won the gold medal.

That year, when he was sixteen, Brent was playing for both the Junior B and Junior A Peterborough teams and getting plenty of ice time with both. One day, when he was seventeen, he got a letter in the mail that he thought was an invitation to try out for the Team Canada under-eighteen team to go to the world championships. "But it wasn't an invitation [for a tryout]. The letter was telling me I had made it, there would be no tryouts. It stated, 'You've been chosen to play for Team Canada, to play in Japan. . . .' It was halfway around the world, across the ocean. I couldn't believe it."

Those games were held in August, and the heat was unbearable in Japan. Nevertheless, the Canadians came home with the silver medal; the Soviet Union took the gold. That year Brent became a regular with the Peterborough Petes alongside a familiar face, Chris Pronger. The following year both made the team that would represent Canada at the World Junior Championship in Sweden.

Brent says, "Being on that team [Team Canada] didn't really hit me at the time; you don't realize how big a deal it is. You don't realize how much pressure is on you. We were in Sweden, so we really didn't know the kind of media coverage it got back in Canada. Kids are under such pressure at that age to produce. I remember Peter Forsberg was playing for Sweden and predicted his team would win." Forsberg was wrong. Canada brought back the gold, and Brent was selected to the tournament all-star team.

By now, Brent's name was being tossed around professional-hockey circles. His NHL draft year was 1992 and he was rated by that league's central scouting to go in the second or even first round.

"I didn't have exceptional numbers so I was a bit surprised at how high I was being talked about," he says. "When I was predicted for the first round, I was surprised. By the end of the year I had dropped to the second round with only two defencemen ahead of me. I couldn't believe it. All the people were telling me how high I was rated, but Dick bluntly put it to me: 'I don't know why you're being rated so highly. I'd say third round – don't forget it's the first year for the Russians to be drafted.'"

But Brent was taken over by the hype. He attended the draft, only to be heartbroken. Boston had told him they'd probably take him, but when he saw they took a thirty-four-year-old forward before him, "that's when I was exposed to the corruption of what people tell you. . . . Up to this point I had good, upfront people like Jeff and Dick who would tell me the way it really was, but now I had people telling me other things." He's not angry or bitter as he recounts this experience; he just sees it is the way of hockey.

Brent sat through three rounds of the draft without being picked. "I had been pumped up with all the ratings and the hype in my head. I went expecting to be drafted high and was disappointed. It was a letdown, but the sad thing is it shouldn't have been. It should have been a big moment; after all, Vancouver drafted me in the fourth round. I had been drafted by an NHL team – thousands of kids would have been excited." He signed a three-year $1.25-million contract with a quarter-million-dollar signing bonus.

He played all of 1992-93 and the fall of 1993 for the Petes and was again invited to the junior Team Canada camp. He remembers the tryouts, which were held in Kitchener; his confidence obviously wasn't the greatest. The team had been told the last cuts would be made that day and players would get a phone call to see the coach if they were being cut. He was rooming with Chris Pronger, still a fellow Pete.

"I had no doubt Chris would play, so if the phone rang, it would be for me," Brent says.

Instead of a six a.m. phone call, they got a pounding on their door at four a.m. "One of the equipment guys was standing there saying I'd been cut, but [then] they laughed and told us they had to pack our luggage – we had made the team."

He was surprised, honoured, and proud when he not only made the team again but was voted its captain by teammates. "It meant so much to me. It was my best experience ever. Those Canadian junior coaches were amazing. It was amazing how coaches had to be so talented and creative to put a team together so quickly. I don't think Canadians realize this."

This time they were going to Switzerland. Team Canada had Pronger, Jason Smith, Alexandre Daigle, Chris Gratton, Martin Lapointe, Jason Dawe (another Pete), and goalie Manny Legace, who together brought home the gold medal.

Brent says, "I had never sat down and watched the video [until 2003]. It was amazing how much media coverage it got. I watched the junior team [in 2003] and felt for the guys when they lost . . . playing in Halifax. When we won, we were so far away we didn't even know how important it was in this country."

Tully had gained so much confidence, learned so much, worked so hard, dreamed so much, and now his time in junior hockey was over. Teammate Pronger had already quickly gone through the junior league and moved on to the NHL, signing for more than a million dollars Canadian with the Hartford Whalers. Brent went to the Vancouver Canucks' camp but was disappointed when he was sent to its farm team in Syracuse, New York, to what he calls his worst hockey experiences.

"We had six rookies on defence, the youngest team in the league. I never played on any power plays or short-handed units as I had all through my years. They wanted me to play defensive hockey. I led the team in scoring at training camp and then they didn't use me. The coach [Jack McIlhargey] didn't like me – there was no doubt that was the case – and I had him for three years. He was old-school; his way or no way. The flip side of that is that I should have been able to deal with it; that's what professionals have to do. I even asked to be moved to the International Hockey League, their Manitoba team, and they wouldn't let me. Asking for that didn't help my cause – I was left off the playoff roster. That certainly didn't help me the next year at the Vancouver camp.

"My third year in Syracuse I started off half decent, was getting some ice time, then I had a concussion, which created some problems."

That marked the end of his North American pro career.

Tully says he is not bitter at the North American pro-hockey experience, but does think if he had been with another team, another coach, things might have been different. "At the end of the day I can't really complain. I got eight years of professional hockey out of it."

He takes the way things have turned out in his stride and still has a few chuckles about the past. "Chris Pronger and I used to go to Trent University, and between classes we used to play the NHL hockey video games. Now I laugh when I see them because last year Chris was on the cover of the game."

Why didn't he make the NHL? Some former coaches say he made too many untimely mistakes on the ice. Scouts say he just didn't have the heart: "You have to be willing to knock out a guy's teeth if it means winning." Others say playing with Pronger in junior made him look better than he really was. They don't mean he wasn't good, just that maybe these are some of the reasons for his not getting into the NHL. Many of these reasons are hard to accept, considering the number of teams today in the NHL and how watered down it is.

Jeff Twohey doesn't understand it. "I've never been able to figure it out. Maybe it was just an uncomfortable situation for him."

Tully lives in Peterborough with his wife and son, still playing some pickup hockey, helping a bantam AAA team with the defence, and getting ready for the day when his young son plays hockey in Peterborough and grows up dreaming of playing in the NHL. He certainly won't discourage him, because, he says, "you have to have your dreams."

Brent Tully works as an investment dealer.

CHRIS PRONGER
Born in Dryden, Ontario, October 10, 1974
Peterborough Petes 1991-93
NHL career with Hartford, St. Louis

When Chris Pronger was four years old, his parents asked him if he wanted to play hockey like his brother Sean, who was two years older and his only sibling. He said no, and sat in a rink every Saturday for an entire season of 1978-79 watching Sean's games. It wasn't until the season ended in the spring that he finally told his parents he wanted to play.

First, his parents insisted, he would have to learn to skate better, so his father, who had built a rink in the backyard, taught him the basics of skating that winter, giving him the opportunity to learn by doing, before playing organized hockey. "Learning how to skate first probably helped my game," Chris says.

The Pronger family had strong roots in Dryden, a small town of 6,500 people in Ontario, 355 kilometres northwest of Thunder Bay. Chris's great-great-grandfather had been a judge and Crown land agent known as Thirty Days or Thirty Dollars Pronger. Subsequent generations of Prongers stayed in Dryden and were well-known business people, right up to his father, Jim, who was an accountant. Jim had also played some hockey when he was attending Lakehead University in Thunder Bay. He married Eila, a Finnish woman, who had been in the Finnish army and was a skier and long-distance runner. Jim says Chris gets his height – he's six-foot-six – from his mother. He adds with a laugh that he gets his temper from his mother as well.

"The two boys were passionate about sports," Jim says. "Chris was especially intense. Even playing T-ball he'd turn any kind of hit into a home run. He was more advanced than most kids were. When he was two he was trying to control things. As he grew older he didn't like losing, didn't matter what it was he played: baseball – a catcher with an arm so strong he could have been a pitcher – basketball, volleyball, or hockey."

Once Chris got his skating skills honed, he began to play organized hockey on an outdoor rink – the arena that Sean had played in had burned down in 1978. His father says that right away it was clear Chris was the best in his five-year-old age group. Because of that, he was moved up two or three age groups, but he still dominated. Even though a new rink was built, there was a lot of competition for it – it was the only rink in Dryden at the time – so many of Chris's games were played outside.

He was a forward when he first started to play and scored 130 goals one season when he was only about eight. Most of the coaches, he says, were parents who "didn't have to shorten the benches. We usually only had three D and two forward lines. I think that's why I finally chose to play defence: you could get to play every second shift or even stay on for several shifts – and I loved to play." Because Dryden had a small player base to choose from, the travelling teams were made up of combined age groups. Chris says, "I enjoyed the competition, always playing with, and against, older kids and my older brother, so I learned more and had to play at their levels."

He was playing all-star hockey every year, but at ten he was playing against fifteen-year-olds, skating better than most of them, and already starting to grow. His skating skills had definitely improved from when he was five. Every year, the local Lions Club had skating contests, and when Chris was nine he won the nine-, ten-, eleven-, twelve-, and thirteen-year-old divisions. He failed to win the fourteen-year-old division when he missed a corner.

He also quite often showed what his family jokingly called his "mother's temper." He would shout at the other kids on the ice, telling them how and where to play. He caused so much chaos it became his nickname at home: "Chaos" Pronger. He'd scream so loudly at other kids, his own teammates were afraid of him. Even when he was only seven years old, the kids didn't want to go near him because he'd yell at them for making mistakes. Another intimidating factor was his size – he was big even then, always the tallest kid on the ice, even in the older age groups.

Jim remembers some of his tantrums. "I was coaching one year. Chris was eleven. He was obviously the best player and was an atom playing against peewees. Chris wanted to play that whole game. I wouldn't let him." Chris shouted that the team would lose if he wasn't played more often or even all the time. But his father wouldn't allow it.

"He got mad and walked home on his skates, about four or five blocks away, so we had a meeting and I agreed I would not coach him again if he agreed to change his attitude." He did manage to mute his outbursts somewhat, but many of his teammates – even in junior and the NHL – will always remember being yelled at by Chris. He knew the game so well, wanted to win so much, and wanted everyone to play at his level, but he didn't seem to realize it wasn't that they *wouldn't* play like him; they *couldn't*. "We didn't really know at that time that he would do what he did. We could see he was special, but we really had nothing to compare him with," says Jim.

In peewee hockey, Chris played AAA (the highest form of all-star youth hockey in Dryden and many other parts of Ontario) for two seasons with Kenora, another northern Ontario town, advancing to the all-Ontario championships. "That's when we got to see him play against that high level of peewees," says his father. It was then they knew he could compete with and against the best.

When Chris was fifteen, he took the unusual step of quitting all-star to play high-school hockey. Although it was believed that better hockey was played on all-star teams, and that if you played on one of these teams you had a better chance of being seen by hockey scouts, Chris looked at the travelling his all-star midget team would have to do, going to such places as Sioux Lookout, Kenora, Fort Frances, and Red Lake, and decided it wasn't for him. Besides, he wanted to play with his Dryden friends.

"All through hockey I had always played on winning teams, I loved to win. Nobody who plays likes to lose. The high-school team had a good chance of winning." He was right about that. The team went to the all-Ontario high-school championships and Chris, now six-foot-one and still growing, stood out at the games.

It was a smart move for another reason. Scouts for junior hockey teams were seldom in Dryden at games, but they were there for those high-school championship games played in southern Ontario. His Dryden team made the quarter-finals, and Chris was selected to the all-star team. Dryden's best-kept secret was out.

But Chris knew very little about the scouts or even about the world of junior hockey. He says, "We [lived] in the middle of nowhere and knew nothing about Peterborough or the Petes. We were secluded, [and] I didn't know anything about junior hockey." But in the next year he was going to find out. At the age of sixteen he was going to move to Stratford, Ontario, to play Tier II hockey. His brother had done the same thing when he moved to Thunder Bay to advance to the U.S. college level, a step below the OHL, but more competitive than what he had been used to. Also, by playing in this league, he kept his college eligibility open. Players who played in the OHL at that time or stayed in an OHL training camp for more than forty-eight hours or played a game lost their eligibility to attend U.S. colleges on scholarships.

Before he went to Stratford, Chris was invited to try out for the Ontario under-seventeen team in Thunder Bay which would compete in the national championship, but for the first time in his life, he was cut. He was not among the seven players the coaches picked to go to the next tryout in Waterloo. "He was upset about that," says Jim, "and so were we."

Chris's high-school coaches were also surprised at his not making the team, so they approached the Ontario under-seventeen team manager, Sam McMaster, and got Chris a wild-card opening. At the tryout in Waterloo, he made the team, but the seven kids who'd been chosen over him from the regional camp didn't. The team that was put together from those tryouts went on to win the gold medal at the Canadian junior hockey championships held in Prince Edward Island in 1990.

Chris's brother, Sean, had left home at sixteen to play hockey in Thunder Bay and subsequently got a hockey scholarship to Bowling Green, Ohio. Chris planned to follow in his footsteps.

"The first time Chris was away from home [to go to Stratford to play] it was tough on us and tough to be empty-nesters," says Jim. "He was sixteen. He probably struggled with [being away from home] for a couple of months. We were always worried about what he was going to get tangled up with and if you're doing the right thing. . . . We knew he had to do something to develop his talent. While he was [in Stratford] he picked up so fast. The level was much higher, but a couple of games into it [it] was just like his whole life had been planned for this."

He played well that first season and also completed grade eleven. "I felt comfortable in Stratford," says Chris. "It was competitive." He was playing against twenty-one-year-olds. But he adds, "It was my first time away from home and I loved it, although my parents had lost both kids to hockey." He still planned to go to college, where U.S. schools were duelling over him, and his parents had decided to get an agent to help them.

All the OHL junior teams knew about Chris's plan to go the U.S., so many of them weren't going to waste their time drafting him. On draft day, Peterborough Petes coach Dick Todd was asking his scouts around their table whom they should take in the sixth round and they couldn't decide. According to current Petes general manager, Jeff Twohey, Todd "got frustrated, slammed the table, and went up to the mike and chose Pronger." The Prongers, who weren't at the draft and had no intention of sending their son to the OHL, were as surprised as anyone.

Twohey explains it this way: "The stability of the team allowed us to take chances. Coaches were secure in making decisions." Todd had decided to waste a draft choice and risk that he could talk the kid into moving to Peterborough. But before Chris could do anything, it was time for another hockey team, this time the under-eighteen team that would represent Canada in Japan at the world championships in 1991. Chris, along with Canadian teammate and future NHL star Paul Kariya, was picked for the tournament all-star team and came home with a silver medal. "I think that kind of clued him in that he might be pretty good, and he decided to give the Peterborough camp a try," says his father.

That spring the Petes flew the family to Peterborough. "On the way there, Chris was still thinking college," says Jim, "but then he got there and talked to people. My wife is a special-ed teacher and convinced me that if you're exceptional, you should challenge yourself." It helped that Brent Tully, also on the under-seventeen and -eighteen teams that Chris had played for, was a member of the Petes.

"I was still thinking college," says Chris, "but Dick talked me out of it. I had no intentions to play junior, but he kept after me. He said, 'Just come up to Peterborough, see the team play, see where you might stay and where you'll play.'"

Chris agreed to stay for forty-eight hours at training camp. Todd says that, for the first time in his hockey career, he sat down with an agent to negotiate a deal. Todd knew he and the Petes executive were taking a big chance, because they'd be offering Pronger the richest education deal the team had ever offered. If Pronger didn't do what Todd suspected – star in the NHL – and went the education route, the team would have to shell out more than $100,000 for his education. But at Pronger's first practice, everyone there knew he was going to be a star. He was a vicious guy with his stick, smart with the puck, and the best defenceman they had ever seen at any of their camps.

Chris was placed with landparents who eased the transition to living away from home. He also was finding the Petes a good team to be with. He says, "At the Petes' training camp I got comfortable. I knew I could play and kept finding I could play with them, be competitive and tough. I knew if I was playing and practising with them all the time I would get better."

The Petes had offered Chris the richest education deal they could, but as Todd saw it, the kid was going to be in the NHL and make millions, so the Petes weren't likely to lose. Meanwhile, he was treated like the rest of the players. He was paid $70 a week, and the Petes paid his room and board. They put his pay in a savings account for the end of the season and gave him $20 a week – almost the same deal Scotty Bowman gave players in the 1950s.

As the season progressed, Pronger was the team's best plus-minus player and the best defenceman on the team and in the league. Director Herb Warr says, "He could read the ice beautifully, pass, move offensively to take a pass when the wing was blocked out."

Brent Tully, his Petes defence partner most of the time, describes Chris as the most intelligent player he has ever seen. "He was too smart for the OHL. He could control the game and did what he wanted. We'd almost laugh at him when he'd carve [yell at] us. The guys knew he could do what he wanted and we knew he wanted us to do it too. He could have coached the team and would probably make a good hockey commissioner.

"He's one of these guys you knew was going to be successful. His personality and talent were way ahead of his time in all areas. *He* knew he was going to be a success. You don't come across people like that very often."

In 1993, when he was eighteen, Chris was drafted by the Hartford Whalers as their number-one pick and second overall, behind Ottawa's choice, Quebec star Alexandre Daigle. He was traded to the St. Louis Blues in 1995.

Seven years after joining the NHL, in 2000, he was team captain for the Blues and had accomplished what no NHL player other than Bobby Orr has done: receive the Norris Trophy as the league's top defenceman and the Hart Trophy as the league's most valuable player in the same season.

Chris had promised the Petes that when he signed a pro deal, he would replace the terrible stereo and sound system in the Petes' dressing room. The summer he signed onto the NHL he kept his word and bought them the best system he could find. In 2003 he became one of the co-owners of the OHL Mississauga Ice Dogs, saying he wanted to model the team on the Petes.

Not bad for a kid who once refused to play the game and sat out an entire season at four years old.

Chris Pronger lives in St. Louis with his wife and two children.

JAMIE LANGENBRUNNER
Born in Duluth, Minnesota, July 25, 1975
Peterborough Petes 1993-95
NHL *career with Dallas, New Jersey*

The first time Jamie Langenbrunner tried to skate, he thought he'd just get on the ice and away he'd go. After his mother tied up his skates at the rink in International Falls, Minnesota, he ran on the ice and fell flat on his face. His mother had taken Jamie, then aged three, to preschool figure skating, because "that was what all the other preschoolers were doing."

While his mother sat drinking coffee, talking to the other parents every week, Jamie was persevering and learning, climbing up through the various levels of figure skating.

Jamie's parents are both second-generation American – his father's family came from Germany, his mother's, from Finland. Both parents were involved in education. John was a special-education director and his mother, Patrice, was a preschool teacher when they met. They were living in Moose Lake, a village of "1,500 people on a busy day," near Duluth, where Jamie was born in 1975. When Jamie was three, the family moved to International Falls (near Fort Frances at the Ontario border), where he embarked on his figure-skating career. By the time he was four, he was appearing in local figure-skating shows, skating around in his dazzling costumes while his proud parents watched.

They took him to hockey just for the fun of it. "I was clueless," says Mrs. Langenbrunner. Her husband didn't know much, either, but the squirts (five- and six-year-olds) team needed a coach, so he volunteered. That was his first and only year coaching the kids. "It was just a whole bunch of kids like little lemmings playing in the indoor rink," he recalls.

Jamie stayed in figure skating until the family moved to Cloquet, Minnesota, also near Duluth, with a population of about 10,000. Jamie was in fourth grade by then and he was quick to check out the locations of the many outdoor rinks. One of the rinks was near the family's home, and the neighbourhood kids, including the

Langenbrunner boys, were there most of the time. "Hockey was more organized in Cloquet, not as laid-back," says Mrs. Langenbrunner. "If I had known what it was like here, I might not have got into it. It was so busy with the kids, games, and practices, playing against towns around here."

Although little Jamie was the tiniest kid on the team, he was pretty good at hockey and was usually the team's top scorer. "It was not a big deal though. He would score four or five goals a game. When they're kids, you don't really think about anything except it's a game," says his mother.

Jamie was playing plenty of other sports, starring in baseball, golf, soccer, wrestling, and football. But each summer, sports were forgotten for a while when the kids got to go to a week-long Bible camp. The town had no summer ice, so hockey usually didn't start until November and was over by February, a far cry from Canada's year-round rinks and a winter schedule of September until April. Cloquet doesn't start its select teams until the kids are twelve, or at peewee level, while Ontario starts the all-stars right at the age of seven.

Still, hockey was the most popular sport in the town, and as soon as Jamie was twelve, he joined the peewee selects (the local all-star team for that age group), playing in a six-team league with other towns on outdoor rinks.

Jamie was usually the top scorer and was becoming well known for his hockey ability. When he got to high school, the teams he

played on moved to the indoor rink, and he was on the school team. The games were so popular they attracted as many as 4,000 people, many of whom lined up outside the rink before it opened to be sure of getting in. It was a great team and was state champion twice, with Jamie the lead scorer. In his last year, he scored 89 points in 25 games. When he was only fifteen, he was picked to go to the United States' under-seventeen training camp. He didn't make the cut, though, and it hurt him, but it also helped him. He was motivated to work harder.

The next year he was invited to the training camp again, and this time he made the team, which went to Japan to represent the United States at the world junior hockey championships. The following year he was on the under-eighteen team and was picked Associated Press player of the year. Jamie was now one of the top high-school hockey players in America. He was so good that the Dallas Stars drafted him in the second round at the age of seventeen. (Today you can't go to the draft unless you're eighteen.)

When Jamie and his parents went to Quebec for the 1993 NHL draft, Stars coach and general manager Bob Gainey called them to the team's room and asked about a contract. Mrs. Langenbrunner says, "Contract? We didn't have any agent, didn't know a thing. We were overwhelmed." U.S. colleges were chasing after him with scholarships in their hands before and after the draft. "We talked, talked, and talked," says Mrs. Langenbrunner. Gainey suggested that Jamie play junior hockey in Canada, but the Langenbrunners didn't even know what junior was. His mother says, "We had to pick a junior league [to be drafted] and we said the OHL because Ontario was closer to us. There was pressure from U.S. colleges [who were] saying, 'Don't listen to the pros, play college.'

"It was unusual for kids from Minnesota not to go on to college," she added. Jamie was in grade eleven, a top student. Hockey, college, and media people in Minnesota were counting on him to play for Minnesota. If Jamie were to stay in the state for college hockey he'd have to stay another year at home in high school first, but that wasn't what the Dallas Stars wanted. "Bob [Gainey] didn't want him to stay in high school another year. We wanted him to stay [home]."

In 1993, Gainey went to their home to talk about Jamie's future with the Stars. Later that year, when Jamie was attending a U.S. hockey camp in San Antonio, a Dallas representative brought a contract to their room. The family still hesitated – they didn't sign. Meanwhile, the Peterborough Petes drafted him. He went in the later rounds partly because he hadn't proven himself to be any more than a high-school player, and partly because of his stated intention of playing U.S. college hockey.

Gainey wasn't giving up. He again suggested Peterborough would be a good place for the young lad rather than going back to high school. Gainey wanted him to get into better competition and a longer hockey season. The Dallas Stars flew the Langenbrunners to Peterborough in the summer of 1993 so they could see where Gainey wanted their son to go. Jamie was to be billeted with Chris Pronger's former landparents, Roger and Debbie White, and although the Whites weren't home, they got to see the house he would be staying at and were comforted by the surroundings.

The family also met with school officials, who answered their questions about the education system. When they got home, they once again started talking contract. They wanted Jamie's college expenses to be paid and all "the bases covered." But they hadn't signed yet. "Jamie was still hesitant, [and] so were we. We didn't want him to go. He was a real homebody. He probably wouldn't have gone to Minneapolis because it was too far away for college," says Mrs. Langenbrunner.

Finally, the Langenbrunners asked if the Stars would fly the family to Peterborough every month to see Jamie. Dallas agreed. After some further worried discussion within the family, they decided to sign. Jamie was persuaded: "I thought this would make me a better player than going back to high school."

Jamie and his family came in for criticism from the American media and college-hockey fans for not staying in Minnesota. It was a tough decision. But the Petes had made a good case. "The kid wanted to be here," says former Petes executive Ed Rowe. "He was willing to do anything to get here, his parents let our people know that, but we had to stay out of it. We're proud of him here – he gives everything he has and always did."

Jamie and his mother packed their Explorer and headed for Canada. Jamie, at six feet, 180 pounds, was heading to Hockey Town on a seventeen-hour trip with a stopover in Woodstock, Ontario. It was just when Peterborough was starting a new era with a new general manager, Jeff Twohey, and new coach, Dave MacQueen.

Mrs. Langenbrunner asked MacQueen if Jamie would have to fight. He laughed and said, "That's why we have Matt Johnson." Johnson was one of the toughest guys in the league then; he now plays in the NHL for the Minnesota Wild.

Jamie had a lot to deal with in those first weeks of the 1993-94 season. He was arriving late for training camp – the other players had hit the ice a week before and, the day before he arrived, seven prospects had already been cut. Twohey knew the fans had high expectations for the young teen who was just coming out of high-school hockey. He said at the time, "That's a tremendous jump for him. I hope people don't expect him to be Jason Dawe [the Petes' leading scorer and star]. He'll be a good rookie. That's all he is."

In that first season, the family flew to Peterborough every month as the Stars had promised. They took car trips to other games. His mother was worried that he wasn't getting to church on Sundays, but he assured her he was. (The story may be told now – in truth, he didn't get there very often.)

During the year, Jamie returned home to play for the U.S. team in the World Junior Championship, but while he was there, he starting missing Peterborough. The Whites had made the transition easier for Jamie. Jamie says, "It was like going home [when I returned to Peterborough]. I made some good friends there who made me feel welcome and hockey-wise it was just great. The Petes' team made the professional game easier and I wouldn't change the experience for anything."

That first year he was the team's rookie of the year and broke a twenty-year-old rookie scoring record set by Gainey's friend and Dallas Stars scout J.J. Johnston. And despite Twohey's cautious warning to the fans, Langenbrunner led the team in scoring in his first year with 33 goals, 58 assists for 91 points in 62 games.

Former teammate and Petes captain Brent Tully points to Jamie's great work ethic as a basis for his success. "He came to play, determined. It was his first time away from home and he flourished. It wasn't as evident as Chris Pronger, but there were a lot of good indications that he'd be an NHL player."

Twohey says, "I remember the night we were going into Ottawa for a seventh and deciding game of a playoff. The bus was tense, and when we piled off the bus you could see the players were nervous and tense, but Jamie was happy, he really wanted to play. He wanted to compete in this game and he carried the team that night." Nevertheless, they lost in overtime 5-4.

The Petes lost more games than they won that year, but Jamie's father wasn't as downhearted as one might expect. He confided in Twohey that he believed losing had been good for Jamie. He had never lost before.

In Jamie's second season, he scored an amazing 42 goals and 57 assists for 99 points in 62 games, and the team had a much better year. Right after the Petes' season ended, Jamie had to leave Peterborough and head to Kalamazoo, Michigan, to play for the Stars' farm team. He was nineteen and his junior days were over.

"He came into the house to tell me about it," says Debbie White. "I cried. He tried to comfort me, but I kept sobbing." In his two-year stay, he had become part of the family.

Jamie spent his first season after the Petes, 1995-96, in Kalamazoo of the IHL, and played in twelve NHL games. He started playing full-time for Dallas in 1996 and stuck with them until 2001, becoming a premier forechecker and penalty killer, and winning the Stanley Cup in 1999. He was traded in 2001 to the New Jersey Devils, who won the Stanley Cup in 2003, in which Jamie had the most points of any forward in the playoffs. Immediately after the final game, Jamie was interviewed on the ice as the team celebrated their big win around him. He did something most players have never done on national television after winning the Stanley Cup: he thanked his Peterborough landparents. The Whites couldn't believe it. "What a thrill," said Debbie. And that summer he took the Stanley Cup home to his parents.

"When he brought the Cup home," says Mrs. Langenbrunner, "we had an autograph session in Cloquet. It was great. There was one sad moment when one parent didn't let his son touch the Cup because, he said, he'd touch it when he won it someday."

But there was one great moment, one they will never forget.

"One of the parents said his four-year-old son was going to grow up to be the next Jamie Langenbrunner."

Maybe Cloquet, Minnesota, has another star shining in its rink.

Jamie Langenbrunner and his wife, Elizabeth, have two children. They live in New Jersey during the season and have a summer home in Minnesota near Cloquet.

ZAC BIERK
Born in Peterborough, September 17, 1976
Peterborough Petes 1993-96
NHL career with Tampa Bay, Minnesota Wild, Phoenix

Nothing about Zac Bierk's background suggested he would ever be a hockey player. His family's interests have nothing to do with sports, let alone hockey. But Zac grew up in a family where dreams were allowed, and the efforts to reach them were supported.

David Bierk was a California artist who came to Canada – Peterborough, to be precise – to teach art in the early 1970s. Once

The Peterborough Examiner

settled, he started an artists' co-operative called Artspace and began changing Peterborough from strictly Jock City to a more diverse artistic community. At least he tried to. The 1970s downtown co-operative attracted people many in Peterborough weren't used to seeing in the small conservative city – men wearing earrings and girls with purple hair. And the clothes! What in the world was the Bierk guy doing to our downtown?

Bierk was being creative, giving others the freedom to be free and a place to do it all. He hooked up with poet Dennis Tourbin, and they grew creatively. Eventually Bierk left the co-operative and dedicated his time to his art, which was gaining recognition across North America. He had shows in major North American centres and in Paris.

One of his sons, Sebastian, wanted to be a rock star. He attended the private Lakefield College where he performed for the students. He left the city in his teen years and eventually became the lead singer for Skid Row. He also starred in *Jesus Christ Superstar* and *Jekyll and Hyde* on Broadway. His sister had a modelling career and moved to Australia, where she starred in a television series.

But big Zac wanted to play hockey.

Frank Quinn, a retired OPP sergeant who had played junior and senior hockey, was the house-league coach of the novice team. He remembers the first time eight-year-old Zac came to play at the Peterborough rink: "He came out to the game with this orange motorcycle helmet with Woody Woodpecker painted on the side of it. He had a man's full-length stick, a pair of gloves, his mom's garter belt to hold up his socks, no shin pads, and no idea what he was doing," says Frank, laughing at the recollection.

Frank didn't let the kid play, but he met with Zac's father to let him know what equipment Zac would need for the next week's game.

"Funny, when he stepped on that ice, he was a natural. He was quite a goal scorer. By Christmas I was trying to hide him after he scored seven goals in one game. I put him in net. He loved it and wanted to play more. [But] I didn't think that was right at that age to stick a guy in the net permanently. I wanted the kids to learn to skate properly first." But Zac had the bug. It's something about the feel of being shot at by a rubber disc, something about the glory of being the last guy back, or the guy responsible for stopping the goals. There is something about being the guy shouting directions, clearing the puck, and wearing all that equipment. There was something about Zac that made him want to be a goalie.

Quinn didn't let him play goal regularly until his second year. "He loved it. He asked, if he got the goal pads, could he play goal all the time, and I said yes. He was a natural. He'd angle the puck, he'd listen, he'd learn."

Quinn was set to be his coach in the third year but cut him. "He was too good," says Quinn. "I didn't want him wasting his time with me. He was so competitive, so good. I told him to go play AAA. He did and won the MVP at the Golden Horseshoe tournament." As Zac grew and became more experienced, Quinn became even more impressed. He suggested to former NHL goalie Marv Edwards, who was helping the Peterborough Petes, that he go watch Bierk at one of his games. He pronounced Zac's name "Burke," in the local idiom. "Marv came back and said he didn't find that Burke kid, but there was this great goalie, a foreign kid by the name of 'Beer-uk.'"

Zac didn't play Junior B hockey; instead, he decided to attend the private Trinity College School in Port Hope and to play for their hockey team. That's where Petes general manager Jeff Twohey saw him. "He was this big [six-foot-two, 200 pounds] gangly kid, and so athletic. I invited him to camp as a walk-on." Twohey was in a minority, however. Only scout Shane Turner agreed with Twohey. The Petes' executive thought he was awful.

Twohey was in the driver's seat, though, and was willing to take a risk. "I don't know why I did it, but I signed him and he made the most of it. He joined us as a second- and, most of the time, third-string goalie that year. (He played only nine games, with a 5.22 goals-against average.) The next year at camp I told him it was [a choice] between him and another kid." Bierk won the starting-goalie role. Since he was eight, he had dreamed of this, and now that dream was coming true.

That year, 1996, nineteen-year-old Zac was one of the biggest reasons the Petes went to the Memorial Cup, when the junior championship was held in Peterborough for the first time. With him as the regular goalie, they reached the cup's final game. The tournament was a bit of a family affair. His brother, now known as Sebastian Bach, was invited to sing the national anthem at centre ice at the opening game, in which the Petes played. Sebastian kept his eyes glued to his brother in the net while he was singing; Zac was looking at the huge portrait of Queen Elizabeth on the south wall of the Memorial Centre painted by his father. It was a moment they and the hometown hockey fans have not forgotten. The Petes won that opening game 6-3 over Quebec's entry, the Granby Prédateurs, but lost in the final of the tournament to the same team 4-0.

The Tampa Bay Lightning drafted Zac in 1995, in the ninth round, 212th overall. He played with them for a while after leaving the Petes in 1996, then was stricken with an ear infection that caused balance problems. He worked at correcting this and made his way back into hockey. In 2003, he was the property of Wayne Gretzky's Phoenix Coyotes. In the first game he played for them, he got a shutout in a 0-0 game against the Chicago Blackhawks. It was a noteworthy game for several reasons. Not only was it the first NHL shutout for both goalies, but the Blackhawks' goalie, Michael Leighton, was playing in his first-ever NHL game. After the game,

Zac took the puck, gave it to forward Steve Sullivan, telling him to give it to Leighton and saying, "This will mean even more to him."

Zac Bierk lives in Phoenix, where he plays for the Coyotes. His father, David, who believed in dreams, died in 2002.

MIKE FISHER
Born in Peterborough, June 5, 1980
NHL career with Ottawa

Mike Fisher's case isn't quite one of familiarity breeding contempt, but it's a reminder that being a Peterborough kid, and one who has obvious hockey talent, is no guarantee you'll be taken on by the Petes. Mike Fisher grew up just outside Peterborough, in the village of Bridgenorth. His family has lived in Peterborough for several generations, and his father, Jim, works at the family business, started by Jim's uncle. The uncle, a toolmaker, kept fiddling around in his workshop until he developed ways to make parts for machines. This turned into Fishercast, a firm that now supplies parts for airplanes, automobiles, and other machinery, and the creativity and ingenuity exhibited by that uncle are still evident in the Fisher family. So is a competitive nature, although Mike may have inherited this from his mother, Karen, who played sports when she was growing up outside Peterborough. She admits she just "hated to lose." Jim, too, had had some involvement in sports, playing house-league hockey as a youngster.

Mike started figure-skating lessons when he was four. His father wanted Mike to learn how to skate before he put on hockey equipment. When he did get hockey gear, it was usually castoffs from older brother Rob, including his first skates, which had been bought for Rob at a garage sale for five dollars.

Mike joined the church league, where he quickly stood out as one of the better players. When Steve, the father of Mike's friend Tristan Senior, was taking his son for novice Petes tryouts, he suggested to Jim that the all-star system might be good for Mike too. Away they

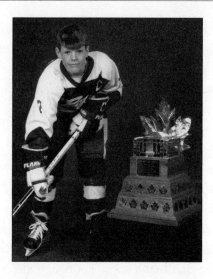

went. "We were surprised that first year that he made it," says Jim.
"The coach, Chris Mattucci, told us early that he'd made the team.
We really didn't know what it meant or what was going on. We
wanted to know the commitment it would mean and when they
would play."

When they learned it meant playing on Sundays, the family hesitated. Sunday was a day for church. The Fishers, devout Christians
for generations, had once forbidden sports on Sundays – not unusual
for many Canadian Christian families in the 1970s. After some discussion, the family decided they could accommodate the Sunday
games, which were scheduled to be at home at one in the afternoon.
Karen would pack a lunch, they'd go to the church around the corner
from the rink, then go to the arena, where Mike would eat his lunch
in the parking lot before going in to play.

"Mike had made a commitment to Christ at six, asking God into
his life, which is a growing process, and it helped Mike through the
hurdle he had," says Jim.

As Mike grew older, and his hockey skills improved even more –
his ability to "see" the ice was remarkable – he didn't talk about a
career in hockey but the sport was still his favourite. He played some
summer sports, but only at a house-league level, and when an opportunity to play summer hockey came, he took it, though "summer"
hockey was a bit of a misnomer – a more accurate description would

be "spring." Soon after the winter season ended, the summer team was formed to practise and play in tournaments until July, when school ended. Mike had fallen in love with hockey. "I don't know why, I just loved the competition and always wanted to get better," he says.

Jim and Karen tried not to interfere with their son's hockey decisions. They believed in letting the coaches do the coaching and they would do the parenting. There was one time, though, when Jim ventured an opinion to Mike's atom hockey coach, Bob Walsh, who laughs as he recounts the story. The team was on its way by bus to an out-of-town game, and Jim and Bob were sitting together. Bob had decided to play Mike on the wing instead of his usual centre position. Jim told him he thought Mike might be better used at centre. Bob felt Mike had been struggling there and the wing might help him find the ice and the net. Jim wasn't too happy with the move but accepted the coach's opinion. "I think Mike scored four goals that game. I never heard from Jim again. They were great parents, but we laugh at that one," says Bob, who later put Mike back at centre.

When Mike started playing as an under-ager with the Tier II team, the family began to take a bit more seriously the idea that hockey might be a career for Mike. He was midget age, but made the team coached by his former peewee coach, J.J. Johnston, who already knew Mike's ability. He had been the best player on that peewee team and got even better at bantam. He was small – too small, some felt – but he hadn't hit his growth spurt yet.

While Mike was playing for the Tier II team, some OHL teams began to take an interest in him, too. The local Petes were showing no interest, however. Mike had worn the Peterborough Petes' maroon and white and watched the team since he was in novice and had shown he was one of the best players in the city, but the local club didn't seem to have noticed. In fact, the dreaded enemy, the Oshawa Generals, did.

Representatives from the Oshawa team visited the Fishers in their home – the Oshawa visitors could scarcely have failed to notice the maroon-and-white jackets, sweaters, and hats that were hanging everywhere in the house. After the visit, the Fishers talked with coach Johnston and Doug Gibson, the former captain of the junior Petes. "J.J. said it would be best for him to play elsewhere. There may be less pressure and it was the best thing to do. We had no idea where he was going to go," said Jim.

Petes general manager Jeff Twohey admits that Mike is one of the players the Petes missed and regrets the decision not to go after him. The draft choice they made instead of Mike that year really never worked out. However, the family has no regrets. "In hindsight," says Jim, "it was best for Mike and was in God's plan."

In 1997, the Sudbury Wolves, not the Oshawa Generals, drafted the young centre, who had grown to five-foot-eleven, 175 pounds. Seventeen-year-old Mike was leaving home the same year his brother Rob, nineteen, was leaving for university. A younger sister and brother were still at home, so the parents weren't left completely alone.

That summer the nervous Fisher parents went to Sudbury to meet the team personnel and see where Mike would be staying. The whole family, all six of them, packed up and went on the trip. Everything seemed fine until they took Mike to training camp. There they discovered there had been a change of billets. Mike was going to be staying with a single male parent with two teenage sons. Mike's parents were full of trepidation, nervousness, and doubt. But there was no time to try to change the arrangement because they also had to drive Rob to Hamilton, where he would be attending McMaster University. When they later met the parent, Rob Barilli, all their fears were put to rest. Barilli says, "My kids learned a lot from Mikey. He would be right home after practices and games and seldom out with the boys from the team. We'd sit around and play cards."

Barilli is Catholic and was impressed with Mike's "Christian ways." "He didn't swear, drink, or smoke, and he went to church. I'd shake my head," he says with a laugh. "I'd sometimes swear but it didn't bother him. He'd shovel snow from the driveway, our back deck before I got home, and his room was spotless." Rob says with a grin, "I'd ask, 'Where did I go wrong with my kids?'"

"His mom told me at Christmas that she was really nervous because I was a single parent, but Mike was always in control. He was always in contact with his family, even his grandparents. It was great. He was so good, so determined, [I've] never seen anyone so focused.

"I had two sons when he came and three when he left."

Once Mike was settled into his new home and his family's life had returned to what was now going to be normal, the Fishers made a point of travelling to Mike's games to "see him for ten minutes after the games when he still had his 'game face' on. I'd want to get into the car and then I'd cry," says Karen. On the other hand, Mike says he was never homesick and was "ready to accept the challenge" of living away from home. Mike's "game face" came on before every game. He was a tenacious checker with a hunger for the puck. He did what it took to win and wasn't afraid to drop the gloves if he had to. The "game face" was different after the game, depending on the outcome.

The following year Mike was named captain of the Wolves. He was leading the team not only on the ice but off the ice too. He had formed a Christian group that had chapel meetings. Although some of the players teased him a few times, it was nothing serious.

He was never once invited to a junior-prospect game; these games supposedly highlighted the top junior players in the country. In fact, the night the junior-prospect game was underway, his team was playing elsewhere and he broke the Sudbury scoring record for one game with four goals and three assists. He was going virtually unnoticed, except by NHL scouts who knew better.

He had a year left in junior when he was drafted forty-fourth overall in the second round by the NHL's Ottawa Senators. The Senators liked his checking ability, which created turnovers, something he had done since novice hockey. They signed him to a three-year deal, but the expectation at training camp was that the nineteen-year-old would go back to Sudbury for his last year of junior – everyone knew that Ottawa coach Jacques Martin didn't like to keep juniors if they weren't going to get much ice time. However, Mike never went back to play for Sudbury, where in his last year he had 41 goals and 65 assists in 68 games, with 106 penalty minutes. He was now an Ottawa Senator. He didn't forget his Peterborough minor-hockey coaches. He rented a van and had them all come up for a Senators game. He didn't forget his billet, either; he has had the Barilli family to Ottawa for games and meals.

As for his parents, they were the glue that made him stick, he says. "My parents always gave me the choice of playing or not, and from a kid's perspective that was great. I can't remember once when my dad or mom criticized my play in hockey. They always gave me support and encouragement – they were my biggest fans."

As important as hockey is to Mike, his religious beliefs are even more important. In the summer of 2003, at the age of twenty-two, he was baptized in Peterborough, according to the beliefs of his Protestant church, which prefers that believers choose their own time for baptism, so they do it thoughtfully and with full commitment. Mike continues to live his life according to the words of his faith: "In God's eyes it's what you do for Him that counts."

Mike Fisher lives in Ottawa and plays for the Ottawa Senators. He is the honorary chairman of the Roger Neilson Foundation.

ERIC STAAL
Born in Thunder Bay, Ontario, October 29, 1984
Peterborough Petes 2000-03
NHL career with Carolina

Not many kids' parents build them a regulation-size backyard rink, as Eric Staal's father did, and it may have had more than a little to do with Eric's emergence as possibly the greatest hockey player ever to come out of Thunder Bay. (Of course, fans of the 1950s, 1960s, and 1970s Detroit Red Wings star Alex Delvecchio may argue this claim.) Time will tell. Staal still has plenty of time to grab his own star in the NHL.

Although Eric was on the ice most winter days, it didn't immediately make him the best player in Thunder Bay. In fact, for a long time he was barely recognized even as a good hockey player. In bantam, at the age of fourteen, no one involved in hockey in Thunder Bay could have predicted this little kid, no more than five-foot-seven,

Eric Staal at an NHL draft with his Peterborough landparents family,
the Reesons.

would ever become a first-round NHL draft pick or even star in
junior hockey with the Peterborough Petes. Nobody believed it
would happen, especially not Eric Staal or anyone in his family. In
fact, in the summer of 1999, Eric decided that instead of trying out
for the major-bantam all-star team, he would go camping and remain
with his minor-bantam team the next year. He loved camping, but
he also didn't think he could make the major-bantam team, so he
chose to stay with his age group.

That winter, however, things began to change. The biggest
change was his height. He sprouted to six-foot-one, and, because he
was taller than most on the ice and maturing as a player, he began,
as hockey scouts and coaches like to say, to "see" the ice better. His
skills improved and he got hockey-smart. It helped that he had a
passion to play, and that he and his brothers made good use of that
outdoor rink to practise their skills. It also helped that growing up
on the farm and doing his chores had instilled in him a proper work
ethic. He also learned to balance humility, an important concept in
the Christian family he was raised in, with competing between
himself and his two younger brothers. The next winter he joined the
major-bantam team and was one of the better hockey players in
Thunder Bay, a city with excellent minor-hockey systems, coaches,
volunteers, and players. Eric scored twelve goals in the provincial

bantam cup tournament that season, and yet, amazingly, maybe because he was so skinny, he still wasn't touted as a top player. He did, however, catch the eye of Peterborough Petes general manager, Jeff Twohey.

The Petes drafted Eric thirteenth overall in 1999 – twelve other teams had a chance at him but decided not to take him. Twohey thought Eric had something special, and he was right. His first two seasons, starting in 1999, were average, but there wasn't a hockey person in the crowd who couldn't see the kid possessed special abilities in skating, passing, shooting, and thinking, and his size was an advantage too. In his final year, 2002-03, he blossomed. He also filled out, growing another two inches to six-foot-three and gaining fifteen pounds on his now 170-pound frame (making him a solid 185 pounds). That year he scored 39 goals and 98 points, but was best known as the "total package": a kid who could skate, think, see the ice, had size, could score, and played both ways. His coach on the Petes, Rick Allain, made good use of him, playing him on special teams and regular units and using him as their number-one centre. He was the team's leading scorer and its 2003 MVP.

At the 2003 NHL draft, Staal became only the second Peterborough Pete, Chris Pronger being the first, to be selected second overall.

Apart from his now-obvious hockey skills, Staal has another thing going for him: good clean living and a Christian upbringing with that Bobby Orr type of humble demeanour. (In fact, Bobby Orr was his agent.) His mother, Linda, couldn't believe "all the fuss" being made about him. To her he was still the kid coming home for the summer in Thunder Bay doing his chores. The best thing about Eric Staal is that he still enjoys those chores.

Eric may not even be the best player to come off that rink of dreams. His younger brother, Marc, was picked in the 2003 junior draft by the Sudbury Wolves in the OHL and made the all-star team. In the spring of 2004 the Peterborough Petes drafted another younger brother Jordan. He was the Petes' first selection and third overall in the league. He was to join the tradition in the fall of 2004 at the age of sixteen.

Epilogue:

A Tie That Binds

Eric Staal's world is so different from Red Sullivan's Depression era and war era of the 1930s and 1940s; so different from the Plagers', who left home at fourteen to try out for a junior team; and different even from Bob Gainey's pre-electronic era, in which homes had one television, one telephone, families sat down together for meals, and kids were outside playing because they didn't want to be inside.

Players of Staal's era grew up in a world of Internet, televisions, satellite dishes, videos, CDs, cellphones, Nintendo games, e-mail, hockey agents, lawyers, and salaries that have exploded from the $9,000 Red Sullivan received annually to the $10 million some of today's players earn every year. Staal is on his way to that kind of money – he was paid a million dollars, at only eighteen, to join the Carolina Hurricanes in 2003.

He also grew up in an era when many outdoor community rinks have melted into our memories. Peterborough had more outdoor rinks in just one part of the city in the 1970s than it has in the entire city now, although there are still nineteen outdoor rinks operated by volunteers each winter. Street hockey is not as popular as it once was; there are few reasons for children to want, or need, to go outside now, with electronic hockey games and all the indoor comforts of home and the protective parents who have made games organized, structured, and built for the comfort of adults. Some adults complain now about the kids being on the ice as frequently as four days a week. Those four days usually consist of two fifty-minute practices and two sixty-minute games. The players growing up in the decades from the 1940s to the 1970s got this much ice time on the outdoor rinks after school in one day, or in a Saturday of road hockey, where they learned their skills playing with ten to twenty kids of all ages on the pavement. Staal, with his outdoor rink, is an exception to the new reality.

Jeff Twohey tells about telephoning the Staals one night after Eric's final season with the Petes was over, when he was being rated one of the top young hockey players in the world. "I was talking with [his father] Henry and I heard this scream in the background. I thought someone must have scored on a game they were watching on the television set or something, and asked Henry this, but Henry tells me, no, the boys are playing mini-sticks and Eric just scored. Now that's a kid who loves to play the game."

The kids who came through Peterborough had that kind of passion, an obsession that propelled them into the NHL. They loved to play or coach the game, twenty-four hours a day if they could. They would also do anything it took to score a goal or win a game. They hated to lose. They didn't play the game because their parents wanted them to or only when someone took them to a rink. They didn't play the game with the goal of improving their skills or making it into the NHL. Making it to the NHL was a dream, not a goal. They didn't play in those outdoor rinks, streets, parks, and parking lots thinking it would be good to *practise*. They never wanted to practise, they just wanted to play games.

They played hockey because they loved to compete, loved to win, and loved to beat the other guy.

Why were these players so successful? Size, natural talent, competitive spirit, thousands of hours playing the game, genes, lack of injury, a fearless ability to punish and be punished, timing, parental support, coming to Peterborough – all these ingredients went into the mix.

But when you stir all the ingredients, the one elusive but necessary part of the recipe for them to rise to the top is passion, that desire to play hockey more than do anything else in the world.

And one thing they will always have in common: it's like a fraternity, an old-boys' club, a tie that binds . . . Hockey Town.

Appendix:

Players, Coaches, and Others Who Made Peterborough Hockey Town

(Names in **boldface** are profiled in *Hockey Town*)

Players who played in Peterborough before founding of the Petes in 1956:

Jack Adams: Detroit
Bob Armstrong: Boston
Ace Bailey: Toronto
Hank Blade: Chicago
Norm Calladine: Boston
George "Red" Sullivan: Chicago, Boston, New York

Players from 1956 who did not play for the Petes, but played in Peterborough's minor-hockey system or the Peterborough Junior Tier II team:

Steve Chiasson (born in Barrie, Ont., played minor hockey in Peterborough, junior in Guelph, Ont.): Detroit, Calgary, Hartford, Carolina
Doug Crossman (born in Peterborough, raised in London, Ont.): Chicago, Philadelphia, Los Angeles, New York Islanders, Hartford, Detroit, Tampa Bay, St. Louis
Mike Fisher (born in Peterborough, played junior in Sudbury, Ont.): Ottawa
Aaron Gavey (born in Sudbury, Ont., played most of his minor hockey in Peterborough, played junior in Sault Ste. Marie, Ont.); Tampa Bay, Calgary, Dallas, Minnesota, Toronto

Kerry Huffman (born in Peterborough, played junior for Guelph, Ont.):
Philadelphia, Quebec, Ottawa

Jeff Larmer (born in Peterborough, played junior in Kitchener, Ont.):
Colorado, New Jersey, Chicago

Steve Larmer (born in Peterborough, played one year of junior with
the Petes, then drafted by Niagara Falls, Ont.): Chicago, New York
Rangers

Eric Manlow (born in Belleville, Ont., played minor hockey in
Peterborough, junior in Kitchener, Ont.): Boston, New York
Islanders

Darren McCarty (born in Burnaby, B.C., played for the Peterborough
Tier II team, major junior in Belleville, Ont.): Detroit

Dean Morton (born in Peterborough, played junior in Ottawa and
Oshawa, Ont.): Detroit

Herb Raglan (born in Peterborough, played junior in Kingston, Ont.):
St. Louis, Quebec, Tampa Bay, Ottawa

Brian Wesenberg (born in Peterborough, played junior in Guelph, Ont.):
Philadelphia

*Players who came to Peterborough to play Junior A hockey with the Peterborough
Petes and went on to the NHL. In brackets are their hometowns followed by the
NHL cities they played in:*

1950S

1956-59   Tom Thurlby (Kingston, Ont.): Oakland
1956-57   Keith McCreary (Sundridge, Ont.): Montreal, Pittsburgh,
           Atlanta
1956-58   Jim Mikol (Kitchener, Ont.): Toronto, NYR
1956-58   Irv Spencer (Kitchener, Ont.): NYR, Boston, Detroit
           (birthplace: Sudbury)
1956-59   Chuck Hamilton (Kirkland Lake, Ont.): Montreal, St. Louis
1956-60   **Wayne Connelly** (Rouyn, Que.): Montreal, Boston,
           Minnesota, Detroit, St. Louis, Vancouver
1957-58   Gerry Brisson (Winnipeg, Man.): Montreal (birthplace:
           St. Boniface, Man.)
1957-59   Jacques Caron (Noranda, Que.): L.A., St. Louis, Vancouver

1957-61   **Barclay Plager** (Kirkland Lake, Ont.): St. Louis

1958-59   Denis DeJordy (Sorel, Que.): Chicago, L.A., Montreal,
           Detroit (birthplace: St. Hyacinthe, Que.)

1958-60   Bob Rivard (Jonquière, Que.): Pittsburgh (birthplace:
           Sherbrooke, Que.)

1958-60   Jimmy Roberts (Port Hope, Ont.): Montreal, St. Louis
           (birthplace: Toronto, Ont.)

1959-62   Claude Larose (Hearst, Ont.): Montreal, Minnesota,
           St. Louis

1959-63   **Bryan Watson** (Bancroft, Ont.): Montreal, Detroit,
           Oakland, Pittsburgh, St. Louis, Washington

1960s

1960-64   Keith Wright (Newmarket, Ont.): Philadelphia (birthplace:
           Aurora)

1961-63   Danny O'Shea (Ajax, Ont.): Minnesota, Chicago, St. Louis
           (birthplace: Toronto, Ont.)

1962-66   **Danny Grant** (Fredericton, N.B.): Montreal, Minnesota,
           Detroit, L.A.

1962-66   **Bill Plager** (Kirkland Lake, Ont.): Minnesota, St. Louis,
           Atlanta

1963-64   Bob Berry (Montreal, Que.): Montreal, L.A.

1964-65   Leo Thiffault (Montreal, Que.): Minnesota

1963-67   **Mickey Redmond** (Kirkland Lake, Ont., minor hockey in
           Peterborough): Montreal, Detroit

1964-66   **André Lacroix** (Lauzon, Que.): Philadelphia, Chicago,
           Hartford

1964-67   Garry Monahan (Barrie, Ont.): Montreal, Detroit, L.A,
           Toronto, Vancouver

1964-67   **Joey Johnston** (Peterborough): Minnesota, California,
           Chicago

1963-67   Paul Curtis (Peterborough): Montreal, L.A., St. Louis

1965-66   Fern Rivard (Montreal, Que.): Minnesota (birthplace:
           Grand-Mère, Que.)

1966-67   John Schella (Port Arthur, Ont.): Vancouver

1966-67   Hugh Harris (Toronto, Ont.): Buffalo

1966-67   Dunc Wilson (Toronto, Ont.): Philadelphia, Vancouver,
           Toronto, NYR, Pittsburgh

1966-69	**Dick Redmond** (Kirkland Lake, , Ont., minor hockey in Peterborough): Minnesota, California, Chicago, St. Louis, Atlanta, Boston
1967-68	Bob Jones (unknown): NYR
1967-69	Tony Featherstone (Toronto, Ont.): Oakland, California, Minnesota
1967-69	Ron Stackhouse (Haliburton, Ont.): California, Detroit, Pittsburgh
1966-70	**Rick MacLeish** (Cannington, Ont.): Philadelphia, Hartford, Pittsburgh, Detroit (birthplace: Lindsay, Ont.)
1967-70	Ron Plumb (Kingston, Ont.): Hartford
1967-71	**Craig Ramsay** (Weston, Ont.): Buffalo
1968-69	Pete Sullivan (Toronto, Ont.): Winnipeg
1968-70	Dennis Patterson (Peterborough): Kansas City, Philadelphia
1968-71	Ken Richardson (North Bay, Ont.): St. Louis
1969-71	John Garrett (Trenton, Ont.): Hartford, Quebec, Vancouver
1969-72	Danny Gloor (Mitchell, Ont.): Vancouver (birthplace: Stratford, Ont.)

1970s

1971-72	Scott Garland (Sarnia, Ont.): Toronto, L.A. (birthplace: Regina, Sask.)
1970-72	Ron Lalonde (Toronto, Ont.): Pittsburgh, Washington
1970-73	Doug Gibson (Peterborough): Boston, Washington
1970-73	**Colin Campbell** (Tillsonburg, Ont.): Pittsburgh, Colorado, Edmonton, Vancouver, Detroit (birthplace: London, Ont.)
1970-73	**Bob Gainey** (Peterborough): Montreal
1970-73	Jimmy Jones (Woodbridge, Ont.): Toronto
1971-73	Bob Neely (Sarnia, Ont.): Toronto, Colorado
1971-72	Steve Lyon (Toronto, Ont.): Pittsburgh
1971-72	Mike Veisor (Toronto, Ont.): Chicago, Hartford, Winnipeg
1971-73	Rick Chinnick (Chatham, Ont.): Minnesota
1971-74	Paul McIntosh (Molesworth, Ont.): Buffalo (birthplace: Listowel, Ont.)
1972-75	Paul Evans (Peterborough): Toronto
1972-75	**Doug Jarvis** (Brantford, Ont.): Montreal, Washington, Hartford

1972-75   **Stan Jonathan** (Six Nations, Ont.): Boston, Pittsburgh (birthplace: Ohsweken, Ont.)

1973-74   Greg Redquest (Toronto, Ont.): Pittsburgh

1973-75   Doug Halward (Toronto, Ont.): Boston, L.A., Vancouver, Detroit, Edmonton

1973-75   Don Laurence (Hespeler, Ont.): Atlanta, St. Louis (birthplace: Galt, Ont.)

1973-75   Peter Scamurra (Buffalo, N.Y.): Washington

1973-76   Tony Cassolato (Guelph, Ont.): Washington

1974-76   Dave Shand (Toronto, Ont.): Atlanta, Toronto, Washington (birthplace: Cold Lake, Alta.)

1974-77   **Greg Millen** (Don Mills, Ont.): Pittsburgh, Hartford, St. Louis, Quebec, Chicago, Detroit (birthplace: Toronto, Ont.)

1975-76   Jeff Allan (Toronto, Ont.): Cleveland (birthplace: Hull, Que.)

1975-77   Rick Vasko (Toronto, Ont.): Detroit (birthplace: St. Catharines, Ont.)

1975-78   Keith Acton (Stouffville, Ont.): Montreal, Minnesota, Edmonton, Philadelphia, Washington, NYI

1975-78   Mark Kirton (Toronto, Ont.): Toronto, Detroit, Vancouver (birthplace: Regina, Sask.)

1975-78   Paul MacKinnon (Brantford, Ont.): Washington

1975-78   Randy Johnston (Toronto, Ont.): NYI (birthplace: Brampton, Ont.)

1976-77   Frank Nigro (Toronto, Ont.): Toronto (birthplace: Richmond Hill, Ont.)

1976-77   **Wayne Gretzky** (Brantford, Ont.): Edmonton, L.A., St. Louis, NYR

1976-77   Steve Peters (Peterborough): Colorado

1976-80   Bill Gardner (Toronto, Ont.): Chicago, Hartford

1976-79   Bob Attwell (Sundridge, Ont.): Colorado (birthplace: Spokane, WA)

1976-78   Jeff Brubaker (Hagerstown, Maryland): Hartford, Montreal, Calgary, Toronto, Edmonton, NYR, Detroit (birthplace: Frederick, MA)

1976-79   Keith Crowder (Essex, Ont.): Boston, L.A. (birthplace: Windsor, Ont.)

1976-79   **Greg Theberge** (Peterborough): Washington

1976-79   Tim Trimper (Brampton, Ont.): Chicago, Winnipeg,
           Minnesota (birthplace: Windsor, Ont.)

1977-78   **Steve Larmer** (Peterborough): Chicago, NYR

1977-78   Mike Meeker (Ottawa, Ont.): Pittsburgh (birthplace:
           Kingston, Ont.)

1977-79   Ken Ellacott (Hespeler, Ont.): Vancouver (birthplace: Paris,
           Ont.)

1977-80   Dave Fenyves (Dunnville, Ont.): Buffalo, Philadelphia

1977-80   Mark Reeds (Toronto, Ont.): St. Louis, Hartford
           (birthplace: Burlington, Ont.)

1977-80   Stu Smith (Toronto, Ont.): Hartford

1978-79   Annsi Melametsa (Helsinki, Finland): Winnipeg (birthplace:
           Jyvaskyla, Finland)

1978-79   Jim Pavese (New York, N.Y.): St. Louis, NYR, Detroit,
           Hartford

1978-80   **Larry Murphy** (Toronto, Ont.): L.A., Washington,
           Minnesota, Pittsburgh, Toronto, Detroit (birthplace:
           Scarborough, Ont.)

1978-81   Rick Laferriere (North Bay, Ont.): Colorado (birthplace:
           Hawkesbury, Ont.)

1978-82   Larry Floyd (Peterborough): New Jersey

1979-81   Tom Fergus (St. George, Ont.): Boston, Toronto, Vancouver
           (birthplace: Chicago, IL)

1979-81   Andre Hidi (Mississauga, Ont.): Washington (birthplace:
           Toronto, Ont.)

1979-82   Dave Morrison (Toronto, Ont.): L.A., Vancouver

1979-82   Andy Schliebener (Ottawa, Ont.): Vancouver

1978-81   Jim Wiemer (Sudbury, Ont.): Buffalo, NYR, Edmonton,
           L.A., Boston

1980s

1980-83   Bob Errey (Montreal, Que.): Pittsburgh, Buffalo, San Jose,
           Detroit, Dallas, NYR

1980-83   Ken Strong (Toronto, Ont.): Toronto

1980-84   Mike Posavad (Brantford, Ont.): St. Louis

1981-83   Scott McLellan (Toronto, Ont.): Boston

1981-83   **Steve Yzerman** (Nepean): Detroit (birthplace: Cranbrook,
           B.C.)

1980-84   **Doug Evans** (Peterborough): St. Louis, Winnipeg,
Philadelphia

1981-84   Dave Reid (Toronto, Ont.): Boston, Toronto, Dallas,
Colorado

1981-85   Bruce Shoebottom (Windsor, Ont.): Boston

1982-84   Steve Seguin (Cornwall, Ont.): L.A.

1982-84   Derrick Smith (Toronto, Ont.): Philadelphia, Minnesota,
Dallas (birthplace: Scarborough, Ont.)

1982-85   Shawn Evans (Kingston, Ont.): St. Louis, NYI

1983-84   Kevin Evans (Peterborough): Minnesota, San Jose

1983-86   Randy Burridge (Fort Erie, Ont.): Boston, Washington,
L.A., Buffalo

1983-86   Terry Carkner (Winchester, Ont.): NYR, Quebec,
Philadelphia, Detroit, Florida (birthplace: Smiths Falls,
Ont.)

1983-86   John Druce (Peterborough): Washington, Winnipeg, L.A.
Philadelphia

1983-87   Kris King (Bracebridge, Ont.): Detroit, NYR, Winnipeg,
Phoenix, Toronto, Chicago

1983-87   Kevin MacDonald (Prescott, Ont.): Ottawa

1983-87   Kay Whitmore (Sudbury, Ont.): Hartford, Vancouver,
Boston, Calgary

1984-86   Brad Aitken (London, Ont.): Pittsburgh, Edmonton

1984-87   Rob Murray (Toronto, Ont.): Washington, Winnipeg,
Phoenix

1984-87   **Glen Seabrooke** (Peterborough): Philadelphia

1984-87   Ron Tugnutt (Toronto, Ont.): Quebec, Edmonton,
Anaheim, Montreal, Ottawa, Pittsburgh, Columbus, Dallas
(birthplace: Scarborough, Ont.)

1984-88   Dallas Eakins (Florida, minor hockey in Peterborough):
Winnipeg, Florida, St. Louis, Phoenix, NYR, Toronto, NYI,
Calgary (birthplace: Dade City, FL)

1985-88   Mark Freer (Peterborough): Philadelphia, Ottawa, Calgary

1985-88   Jody Hull (Cambridge, Ont.): Hartford, NYR, Ottawa,
Florida, Tampa, Philadelphia (birthplace: Petrolia, Ont.)

1986-89   **Tie Domi** (Belle River, Ont.): Toronto, NYR, Winnipeg
(birthplace: Windsor, Ont.)

1986-89   Corey Foster (Ottawa, Ont.): New Jersey, Philadelphia,
Pittsburgh, NYI

1987-90   **Mike Ricci** (Toronto, Ont.): Philadelphia, Quebec,
           Colorado, San Jose (birthplace: Scarborough, Ont.)
1987-90   John Tanner (Cambridge, Ont.): Quebec
1988-92   Jassen Cullimore (Port Dover, Ont.): Vancouver, Montreal,
           Tampa (birthplace: Simcoe, Ont.)
1985-88   Bill Huard (Fort Erie, Ont.): Boston, Ottawa, Quebec,
           Dallas, Edmonton, L.A. (birthplace: Welland, Ont.)
1989-93   Jason Dawe (Toronto, Ont.): Buffalo, NYI, Montreal, NYR
           (birthplace: North York, Ont.)
1989-93   Dale McTavish (Eganville, Ont.): Calgary

1990s-2000s
1990-94   Brent Tully (Peterborough): Vancouver
1991-93   Shawn Heins (Eganville): San Jose
1991-93   **Chris Pronger** (Dryden, Ont.): Hartford, St. Louis
1991-94   Dave Roche (Peterborough): Pittsburgh, Calgary
1992-93   Cory Stillman (Peterborough): Calgary, St. Louis, Tampa
1992-95   Matt Johnson (Pelham, Ont.): L.A., Atlanta, Minnesota
           (birthplace: Welland, Ont.)
1993-97   **Zac Bierk** (Peterborough): Tampa, Minnesota, Phoenix
1993-95   **Jamie Langenbrunner** (Cloquet, Minnesota): Dallas,
           New Jersey (birthplace: Duluth, MN)
1993-97   Cameron Mann (Balmerton, Ont.): Boston, Nashville
           (birthplace: Thompson, Man.)
1993-95   Steve Webb (Peterborough): NYI, Pittsburgh
1994-97   Dave Duerden (Oshawa, Ont.): Florida
1995-99   Scott Barney (Oshawa, Ont.): L.A.
1995-97   Shawn Thornton (Oshawa, Ont.): Chicago
1995-98   Evgeny Korolev (Moscow, U.S.S.R.): NYI
1996-99   Pat Cavanagh (Ottawa, Ont.): Vancouver
1996-2000 Jason Williams (London, Ont.): Detroit
1999-2000 Steve Montador (Vancouver, B.C.): Calgary
2000-2003 Lukas Krajicek (Prostejov, Czechoslovakia): Florida
2000-2003 **Eric Staal** (Thunder Bay, Ont.): Carolina

Players, coaches, and managers with the Petes who became general managers in the NHL:

Scotty Bowman	**Mike Keenan**
Bob Gainey	**Sam Pollock**

Players and coaches with the Petes who became coaches in the NHL:

Keith Acton	Bill Mahoney
Jack Adams	Jacques Martin
Bob Berry	Dave MacQueen
Scotty Bowman	**Roger Neilson**
Colin Campbell	**Barclay Plager**
Jacques Caron	**Craig Ramsay**
Bob Gainey	Jimmy Roberts
Gary Green	**Dick Todd**
Doug Jarvis	**Bryan Watson**
Mike Keenan	

Players and coaches who came from the NHL to coach the Petes:

Dave Dryden	Garry Young
Ted Kennedy	

Players and coaches with the Petes who became NHL executives:

Jack Adams	**Wayne Gretzky**
Colin Campbell	Kris King
Aubrey "Dit" Clapper	**Steve Larmer** (NHLPA)
Gary Darling	**Barclay Plager**
Bill Evo	**Bob Plager**
Bob Gainey	**Craig Ramsay**

Players and coaches who went through Peterborough hockey who became Hockey Hall of Famers:

Jack Adams	**Wayne Gretzky**
Ace Bailey	**Ted Kennedy**
Scotty Bowman	**Roger Neilson**
Frank Buckham	Larry Murphy
Aubrey "Dit" Clapper	Fred Whitcroft
Bob Gainey	

Players who went through Peterborough hockey who became NHL captains or alternates:

Keith Acton	**Rick MacLeish**
Colin Campbell	**Larry Murphy**
Steve Chiasson	**Barclay Plager**
Aubrey "Dit" Clapper	**Bob Plager**
Bob Errey	**Chris Pronger**
Bob Gainey	**Craig Ramsay**
Danny Grant	**Mickey Redmond**
Wayne Gretzky	Dave Reid
Doug Jarvis	**Mike Ricci**
Joey Johnston	Luke Richardson
Stan Jonathan	Jim Roberts
Kris King	Cory Stillman
Jamie Langenbrunner	**George "Red" Sullivan**
Steve Larmer	Steve Webb
Claude Larose	**Steve Yzerman**

Players who went through Peterborough hockey who became NHL *broadcasters and media personalities:*

John Druce

Bob Errey

Bill Gardner

John Garrett

Greg Millen

Larry Murphy

Mickey Redmond

Dave Reid

Kay Whitmore

Players and coaches who went through Peterborough hockey or live there who became NHL *scouts:*

Don Barrie

Roger Bedard

Scotty Bowman

Gary Darling

Doug Gibson

J.J. Johnston

Paul MacIntosh

Frank Mario

Dave Morrison

Roger Neilson

Dennis Patterson

Darryl Porter

George "Red" Sullivan

Dick Todd

Jeff Twohey

ACKNOWLEDGEMENTS

Pulling together a book of this scope takes plenty of great references, good sources for material, and a lot of co-operative people who have not only allowed you into their homes, shared their memories, and opened their scrapbooks, but also shared their lives and experiences. For opening their doors, I thank all the players, coaches, friends, scouts, acquaintances, and most importantly the families of many of these people. We tend to forget that when junior players leave home, they are not men; they are only kids. Without the parents' support of their children and willingness to let them leave home, live with strangers, and grow up out of their sight, there would be no book. The parents are the true stars, the people who supported their boys as they pursued their dreams. I hope these stories will inspire and provide some insight into hockey players before the pros and the real secret of success in hockey: obsession with the game, not by the parents, but by the kids.

I would be remiss if I didn't acknowledge all the superb hockey books written over the years. In Peterborough, Don Barrie, Kevin Varrin, and Gary Baldwin produced a detailed statistical book of the Petes' first fifty years which proved invaluable for many reasons. *The Peterborough Examiner* archives was another important source of information, as were the stories of *Examiner* writers, past and present, especially Mike Brophy, Mike Davies, and Bob Feaver, and the many clippings from the daily newspapers of the centres the players and coaches were in during their NHL years.

Past members of the Petes' organizations were very helpful and I thank them for their time and memories. The family of Ray Tanner kept many important documents, as did Ken Self. And I thank all the people involved in the statistics included in various NHL stats books and posted on Internet sites, so many statistics it becomes almost mind-boggling, especially when there are so many conflicting pieces of information.

Roy MacGregor, a wonderful Canadian and excellent writer, encouraged me with this project. His encouragement meant a lot. Editor Wendy Thomas has been a jewel through this and I thank her for her patience, insightfulness, and invaluable contribution. Jonathan Webb, Elizabeth Kribs, Peter Buck, and the people at M&S believed enough in the project to let me loose on it and I thank them for that. But most of all, I thank the players for having this love for the best team sport in the world. These athletes not only do all that they do, but they do it on blades while skating on ice. Incredible.

INDEX